Outdoor Photography: **Portraits**

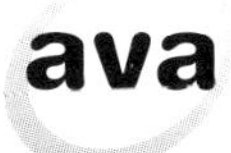

AVA Publishing SA
Switzerland

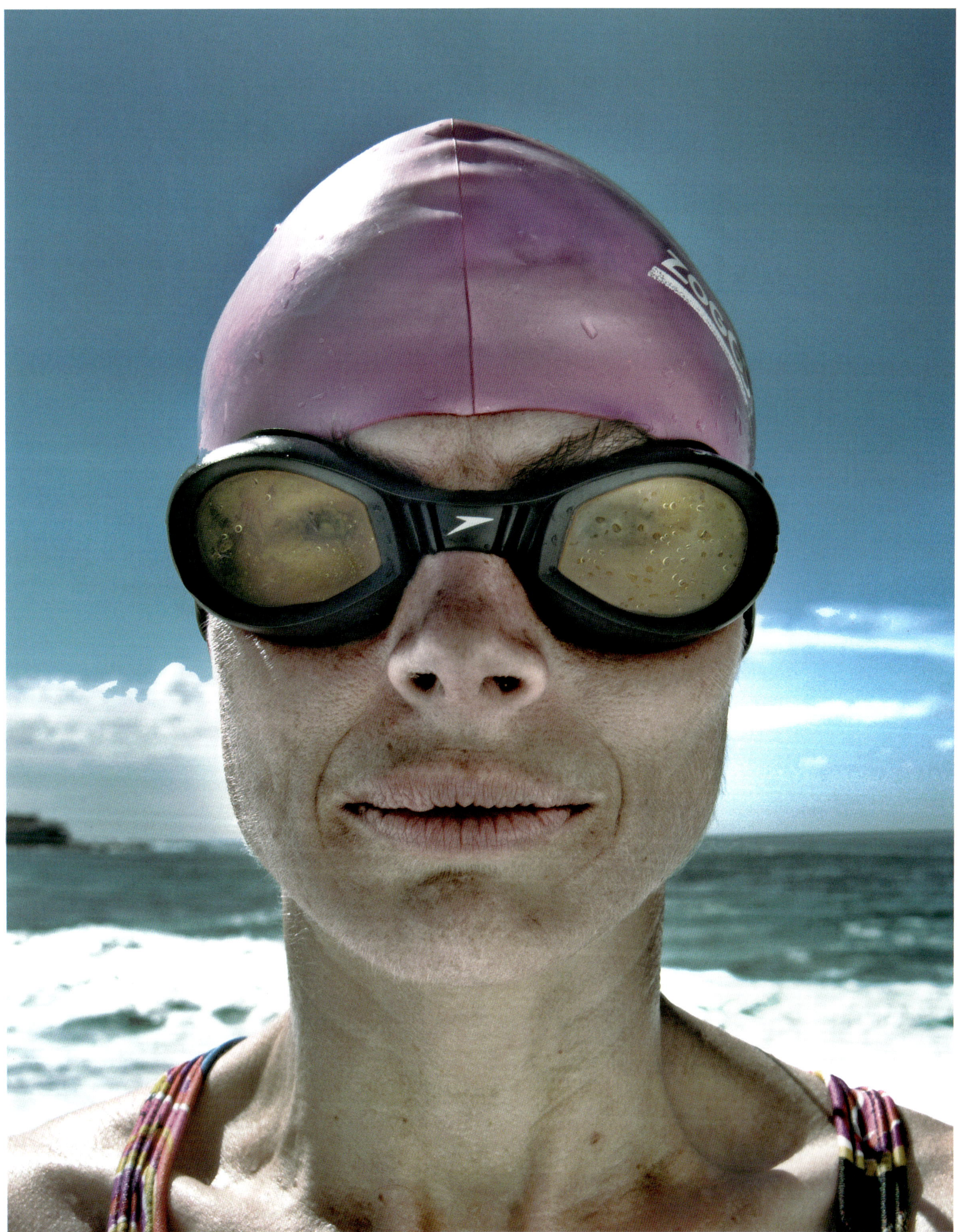

Matt Hoyle

Cathy Joseph

Outdoor Photography: **Portraits**

An AVA Book
Published by AVA Publishing SA
Chemin de la Joliette 2
Case postale 96
1000 Lausanne 6
Switzerland
Tel: +41 786 005 109
Email: enquiries@avabooks.ch

Distributed by Thames & Hudson (ex-North America)
181a High Holborn
London WC1V 7QX
United Kingdom
Tel: +44 20 7845 5000
Fax: +44 20 7845 5055
Email: sales@thameshudson.co.uk
www.thamesandhudson.com

Distributed by Sterling Publishing Co., Inc.
in the USA
387 Park Avenue South
New York, NY 10016-8810
Tel: +1 212 532 7160
Fax: +1 212 213 2495
www.sterlingpub.com

in Canada
Sterling Publishing
c/o Canadian Manda Group
One Atlantic Avenue, Suite 105
Toronto, Ontario M6K 3E7

English Language Support Office
AVA Publishing (UK) Ltd.
Tel: +44 1903 204 455
Email: enquiries@avabooks.co.uk

ISBN 2-88479-061-6

10 9 8 7 6 5 4 3 2 1

Design by Gavin Ambrose
Picture research by Sarah Jameson

Production and separations by AVA Book Production Pte. Ltd., Singapore
Tel: +65 6334 8173
Fax: +65 6334 0752
Email: production@avabooks.com.sg

Acknowledgements

This book would not have been possible without the wonderful contributions from all the photographers. Many thanks are due to them, not only for their photographs, but for their generosity in sharing their expertise and providing insights into their work. Thanks also for the team at AVA Publishing – Brian Morris and Natalia Price-Cabrera – Sarah Jameson for the picture research and Gavin Ambrose for the design.

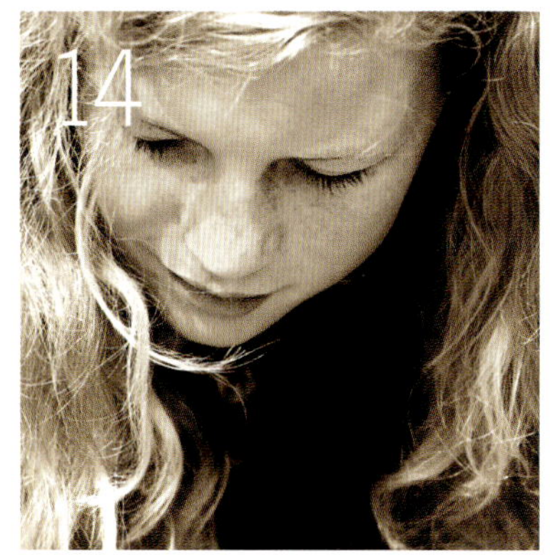
14

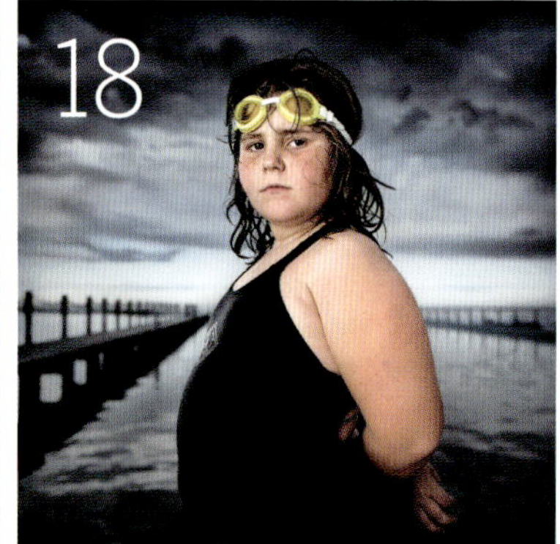
18

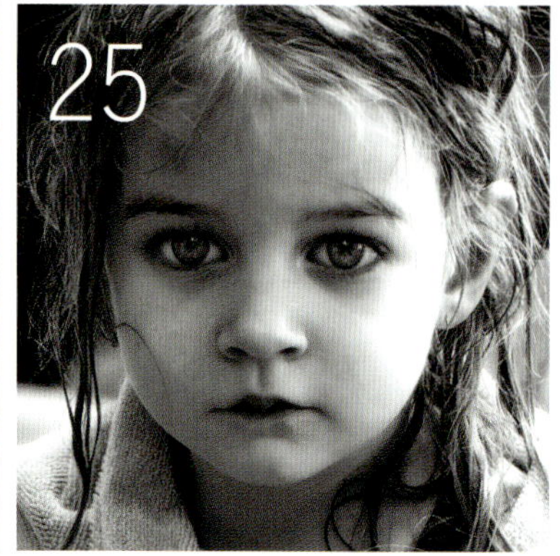
25

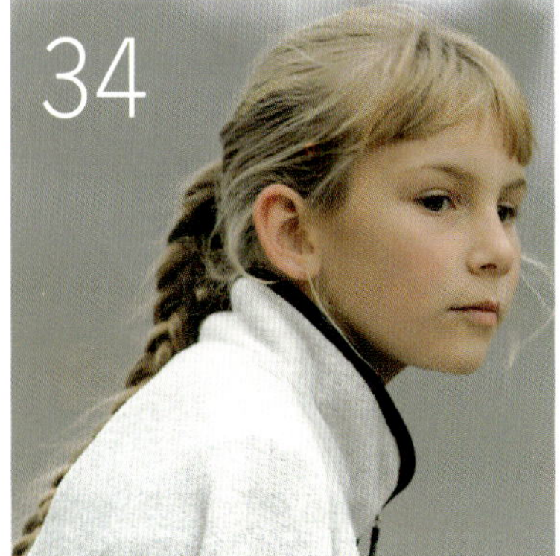
34

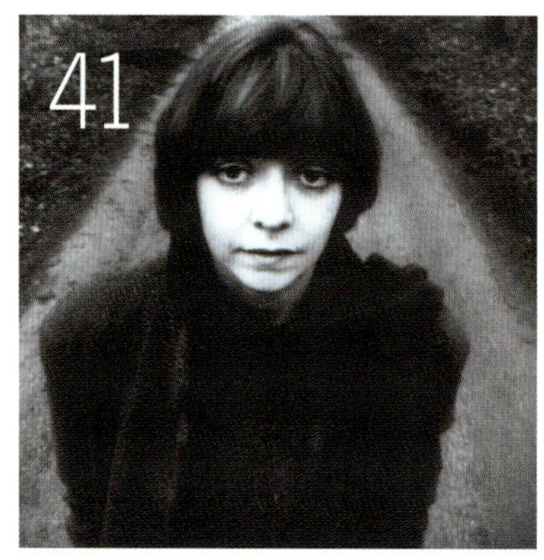
41

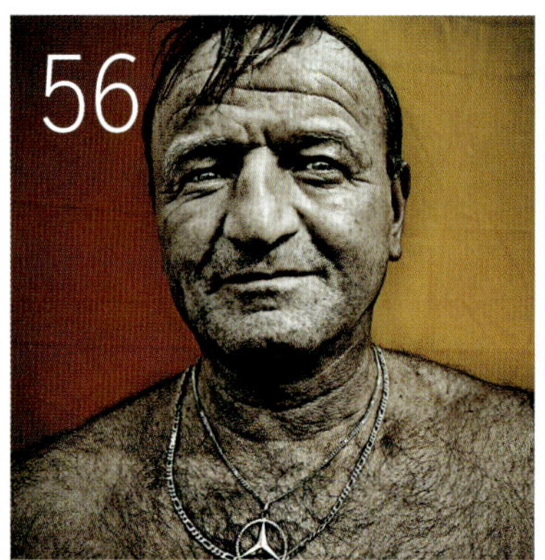
56

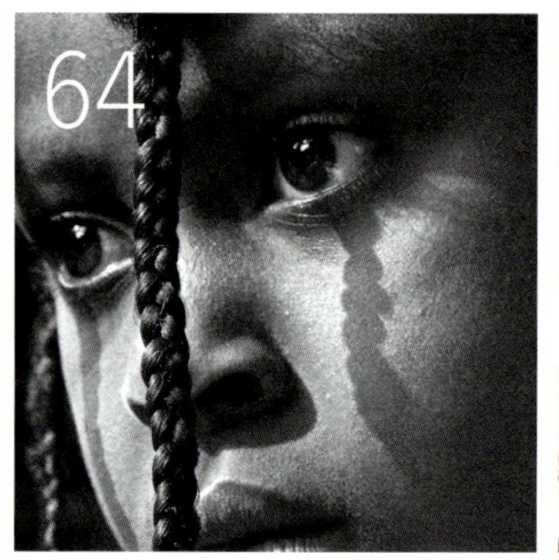
64

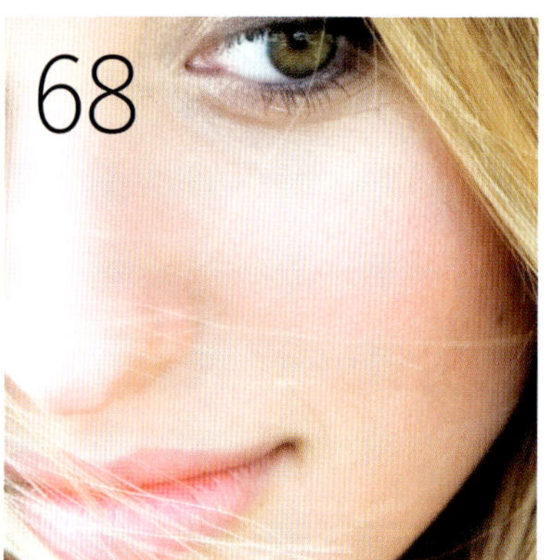
68

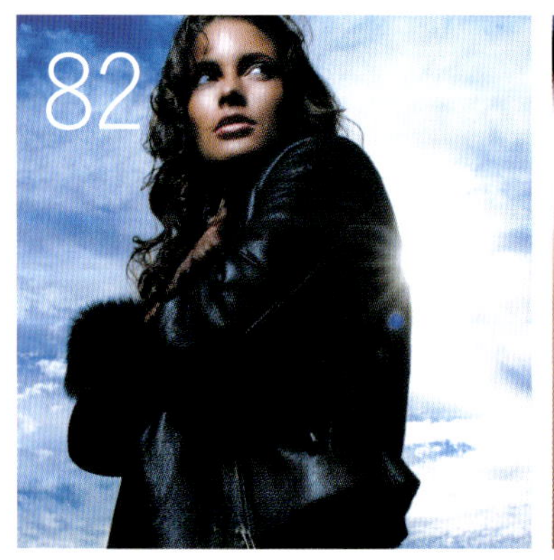
82

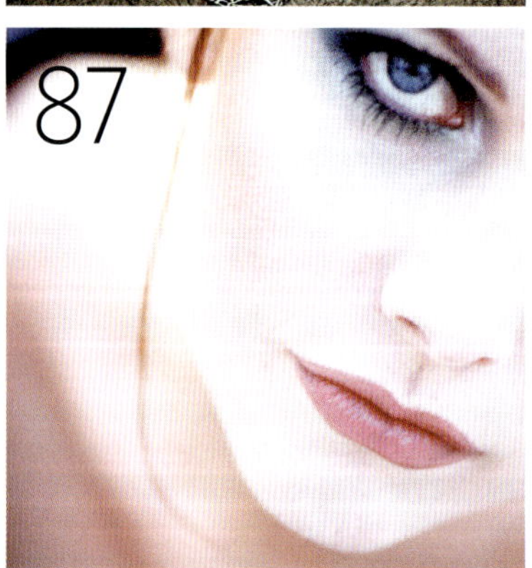
87

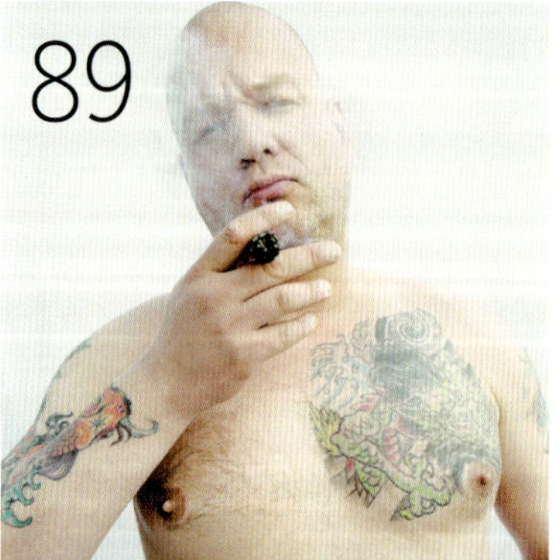
89

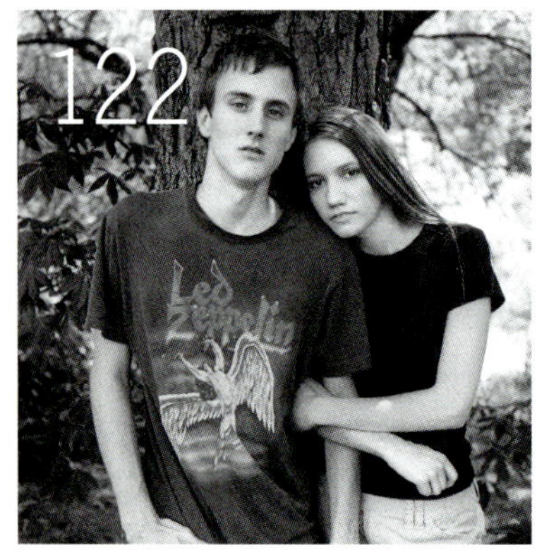
122
Led Zeppelin

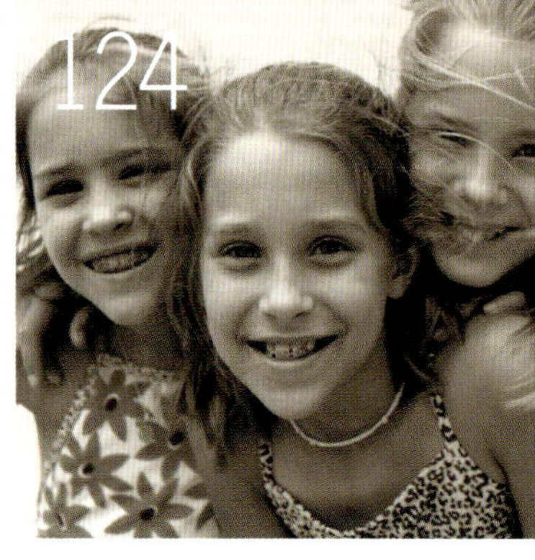
124

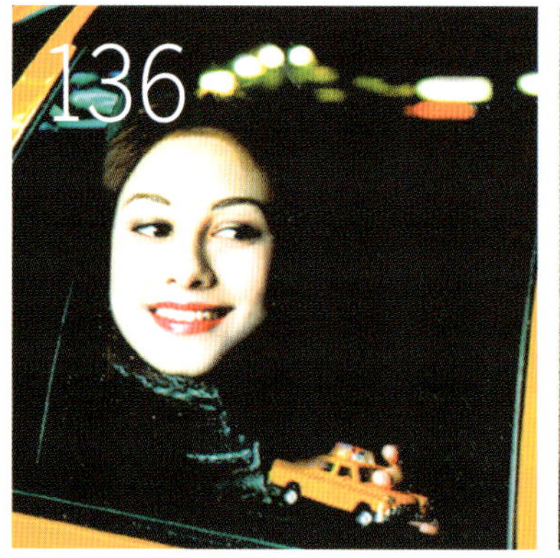
136

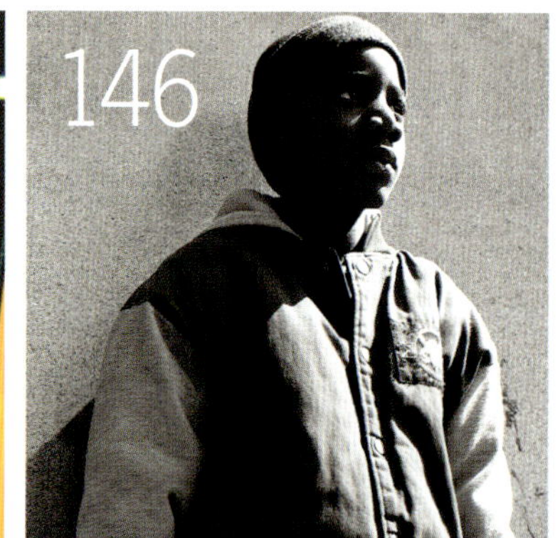
146

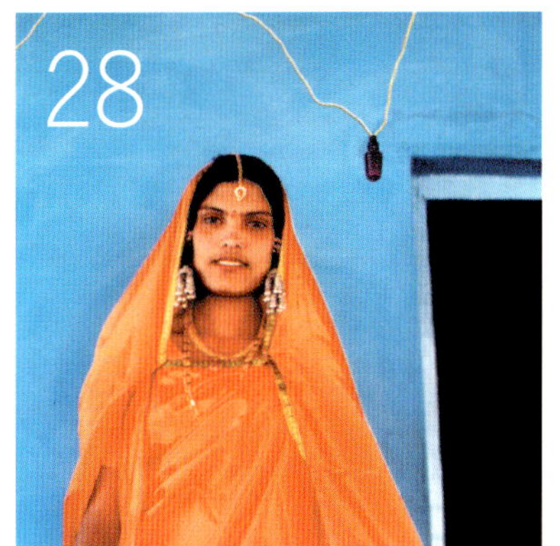

Contents

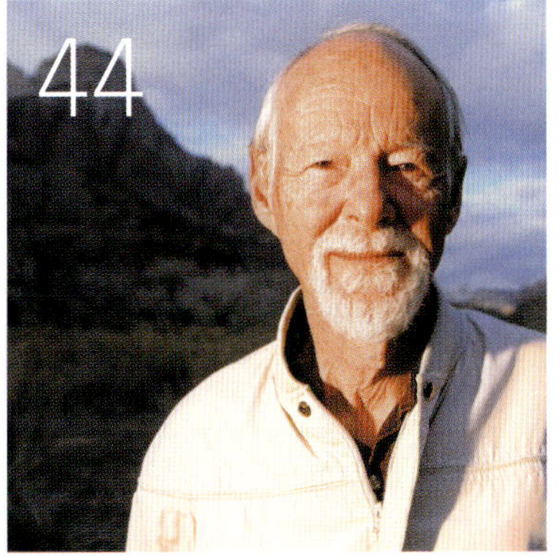

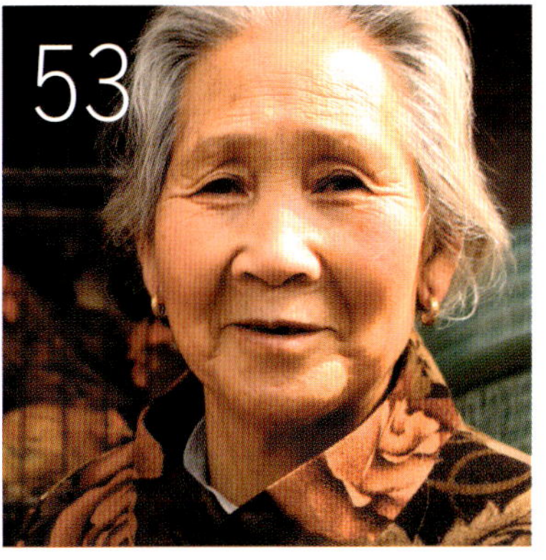

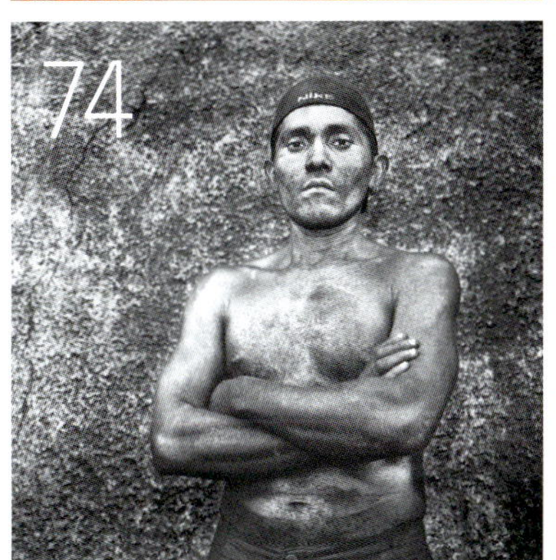

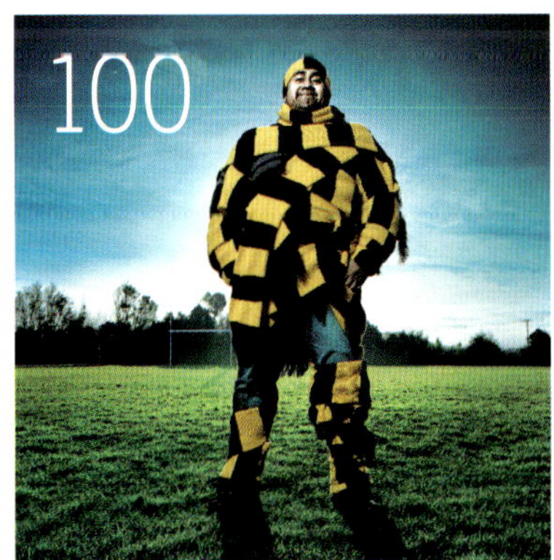

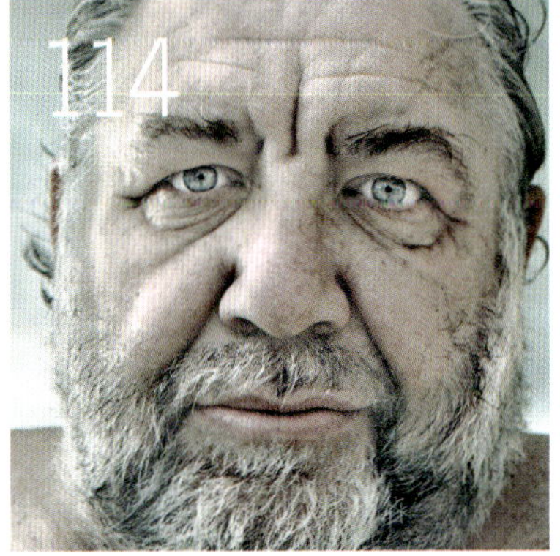

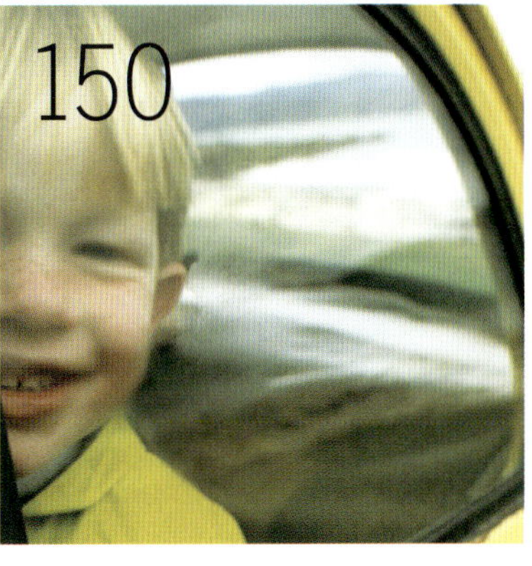

Introduction

Ever since cave dwellers learned to make pigments to decorate their walls, people have been representing themselves and others through portraiture. Now that the camera is practically as common to a household as a TV set, everyone can have a go at creating a portrait, regardless of their skills with a pencil, paintbrush or piece of stone or clay. While wildlife and landscape photography has, arguably, a more specialist band of followers, photos of family and friends are widely taken, displayed and enjoyed as an invaluable personal record.

To take portrait photography a few steps further, perhaps developing it as a career or at least a serious interest, involves a lot more thought than filling the viewfinder with a head and shoulders. Whether you are shooting your best friend at a wedding or candids in the street, you need to decide what you are trying to achieve before you press the shutter. This book concentrates on pictures taken outdoors where there is huge scope for using the different qualities of natural light, selecting the background and having freedom of movement for yourself and the subject. There are many choices to be made and all will affect the outcome of your final image.

Part of people's enduring fascination with looking at their own and others' images is the desire to look good to the outside world. Flattery certainly plays a strong part in some types of portraiture. If you are being commissioned by a client to take some shots of their family, for example, they are not going to thank you for a 'warts-and-all' approach, no matter how much store you set by honesty. Everyone likes to be seen to look their best – or, ideally, a little better than that.

There is much more to portraiture than satisfying vanity, though. One of the greatest challenges is trying to capture an essence of a person's character. It could be a momentary expression, a look in the eyes or a way they place their arms and hands. Even if the subject is someone close to you this is not easy to achieve – most people spontaneously stiffen up as soon as they see a lens pointing at them. It's harder still if you are trying to take a prearranged portrait of someone you have never met before. Some photographers have all the skills of a warm-up artist at a comedy club, enabling their subjects to feel relaxed and at ease. Others take more of a back seat, letting the subject appear to take charge of the session, with just a few nudges and suggestions about possible poses. The latter approach can be just as effective; sometimes the image people like to present to the camera reveals more about them than they think.

You don't have to be paid for your time to enjoy taking portraits, but you do have to be driven by an interest in people and the lives they lead. Photography can play a valuable part in spreading information about different cultures, it can speak volumes about social history and it can also entertain by poking gentle fun at people's behaviour and eccentricities.

The pictures in this book have been chosen because they represent a wide range of styles and approaches to outdoor portraiture. Some were commissioned and planned way in advance, others part of long-term projects and some purely spontaneous, often the chance result of having the camera to hand in one of those magical moments when the light complements the subject perfectly.

Luck cannot be relied on when taking pictures outdoors, however. A planned shoot can be ruined by the weather, with harsh sunlight as potentially troublesome as rain. While there may be no other option than to pack up and go home, other ways can often be found to make the best of the light, perhaps by changing the angle of the camera or position of the subject, finding shade or using flash and reflectors.

Since the quality of light is so vital to outdoor photography, diagrams to illustrate the position and strength of the sun accompany many of the pictures in the book. The background to the images is also explored, to show what the photographer was setting out to achieve, how he or she went about it, why the location was chosen as well as the strengths of the final composition. Technical notes describe the equipment and exposure used and, where digital techniques had a large part to play, these are explained.

The purpose of this information is to show some of the thought processes that go behind every successful picture. An armoury of knowledge combined with patience and practice is a great way of getting the best out of every subject as well as discovering new opportunities. Packed with high quality pictures, the aim of the following pages is to reveal some of the very many aspects of outdoor portraiture and to inspire you to make your own contribution to a most exciting and rewarding area of photography.

Michael Hall

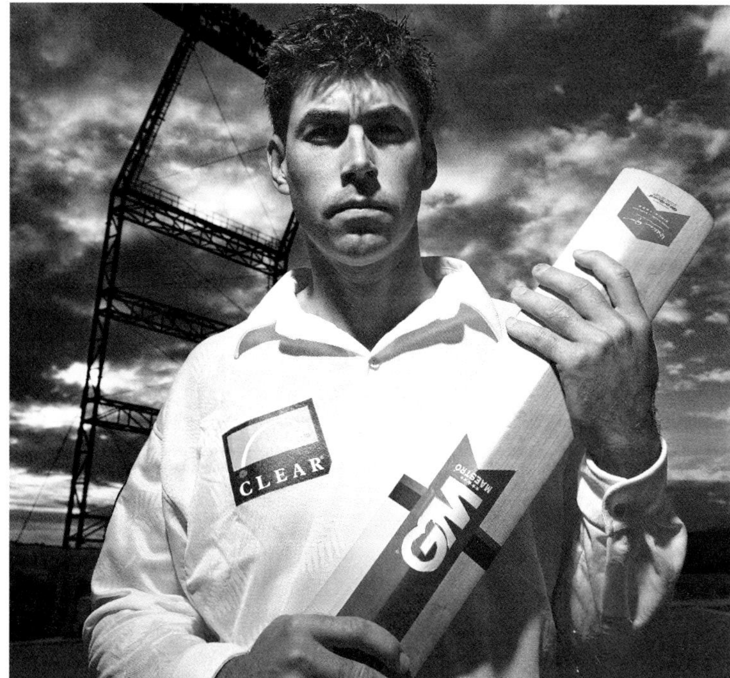

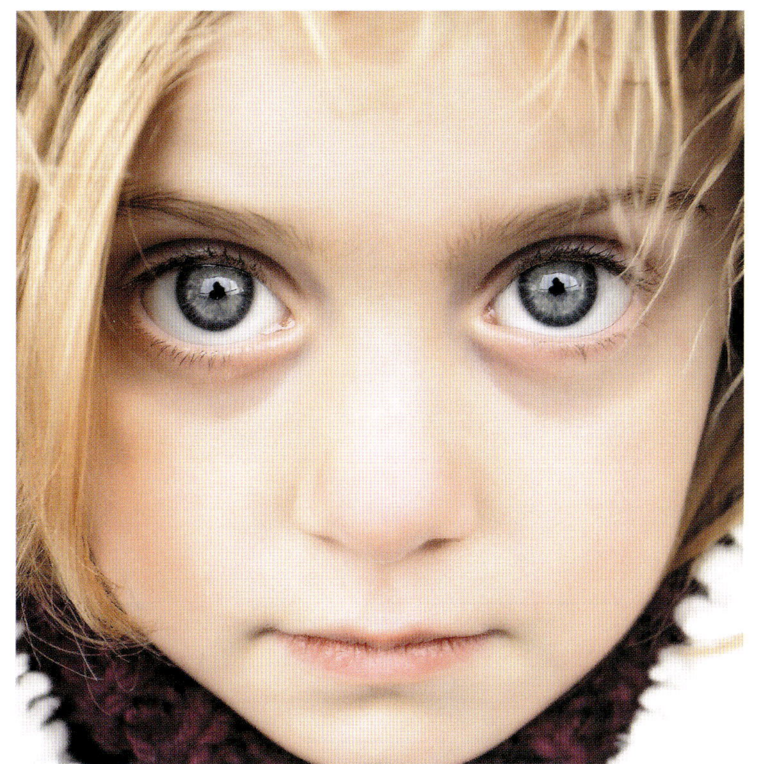

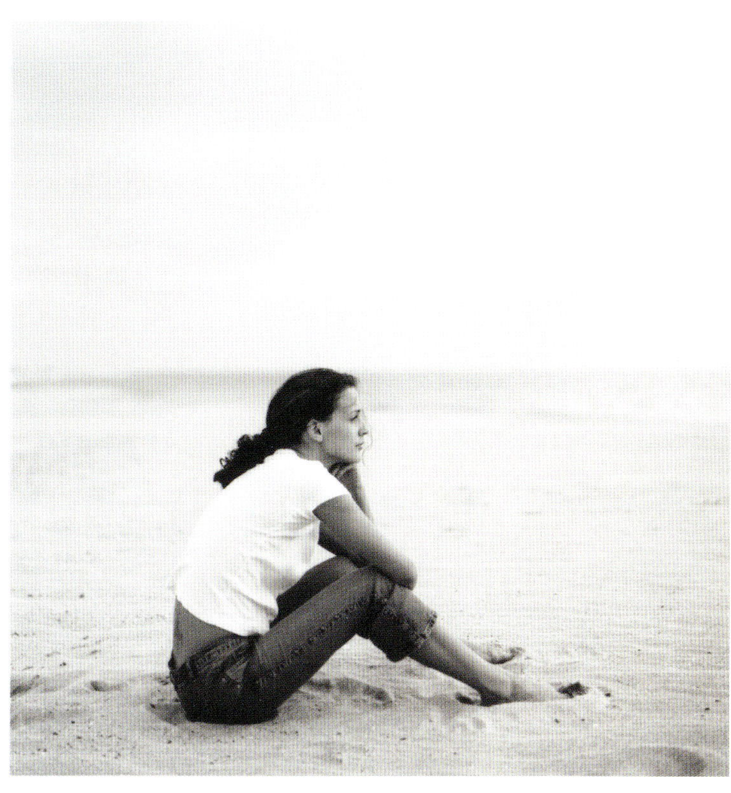

Rene de Haan

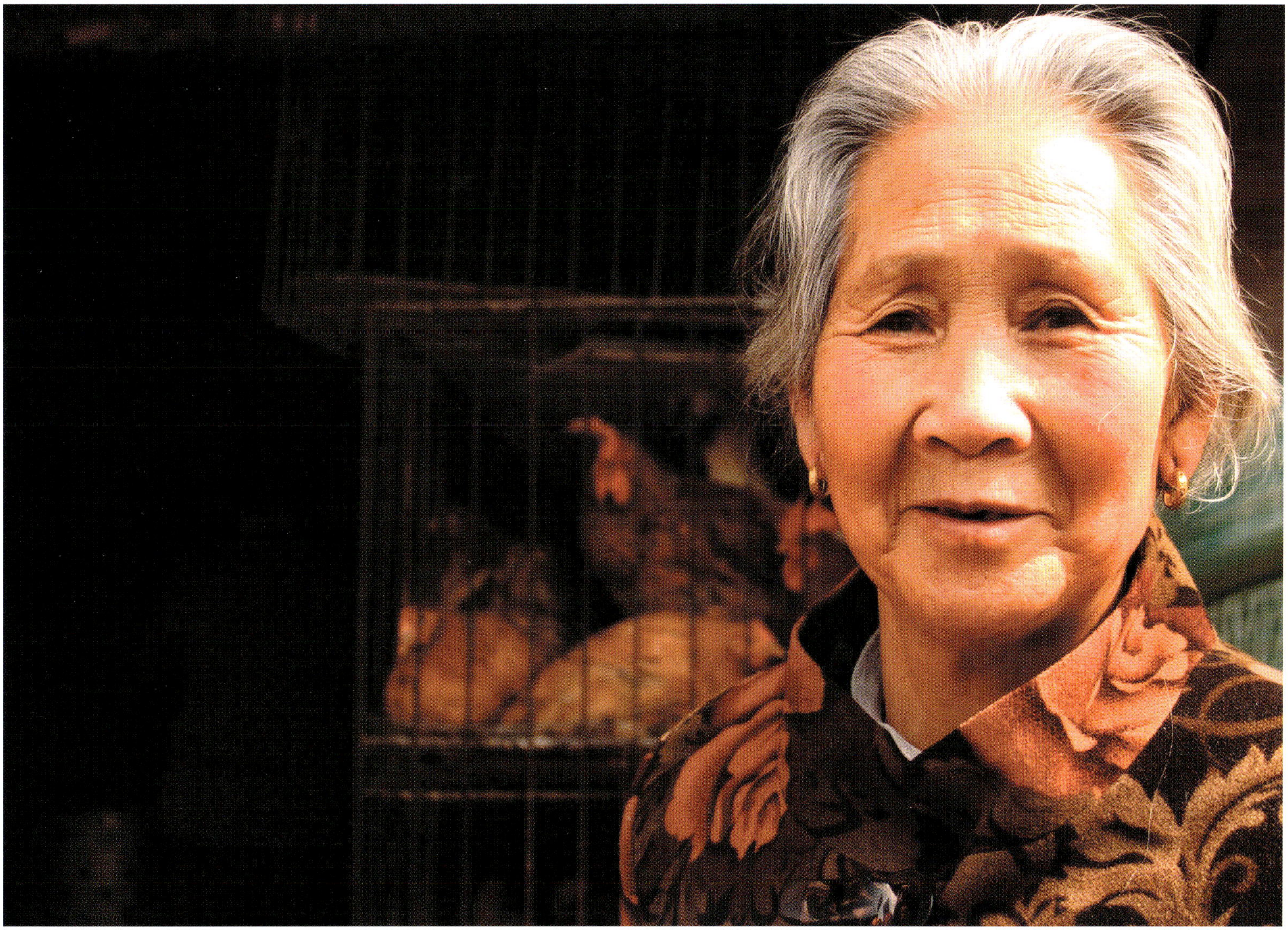

How to get the most out of this book

Divided into seven chapters, this book sets out how to get great results when shooting portraits outdoors. Read in its entirety, it covers all the ways in which light can be used and manipulated to best effect, from choosing the time of day to adding artificial lights and creating mood through filtration and reflection. Alternatively, you can dip into the book at any point. Each spread is self-contained, concentrating on a particular aspect of outdoor portrait photography. As such, the book can be used as a problem solver for specific areas of interest, for example, how to effectively balance flash with daylight.

The text

The main (or, in some cases, sole) picture on each spread is accompanied by four paragraphs of text, with the headings, The concept, The location, Composition and Lighting and technique. These explain the background to the picture and the thought process of the photographer as he or she set out to achieve it. The image is analysed to pinpoint its strengths, and we look at compositional devices and see how the location was chosen and used to best effect. The technique and lighting employed are described in straightforward, easy-to-understand language, with specific photographic terms explained in the glossary at the back of the book.

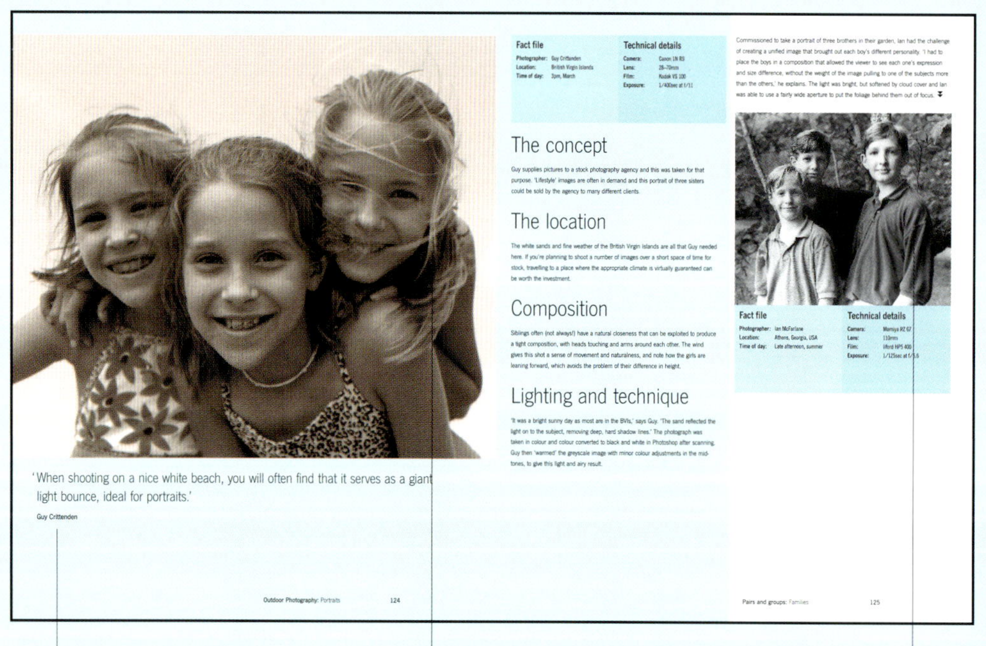

'When shooting on a nice white beach, you will often find that it serves as a giant light bounce, ideal for portraits.'

Guy Crittenden

Fact file

Photographer: Guy Crittenden
Location: British Virgin Islands
Time of day: 3pm, March

Technical details

Camera: Canon 1N RS
Lens: 28–70mm
Film: Kodak VS 100
Exposure: 1/400sec at f/11

The concept

Guy supplies pictures to a stock photography agency and this was taken for that purpose. 'Lifestyle' images are often in demand and this portrait of three sisters could be sold by the agency to many different clients.

The location

The white sands and fine weather of the British Virgin Islands are all that Guy needed here. If you're planning to shoot a number of images over a short space of time for stock, travelling to a place where the appropriate climate is virtually guaranteed can be worth the investment.

Composition

Siblings often (not always!) have a natural closeness that can be exploited to produce a tight composition, with heads touching and arms around each other. The wind gives this shot a sense of movement and naturalness, and note how the girls are leaning forward, which avoids the problem of their difference in height.

Lighting and technique

'It was a bright sunny day as most are in the BVIs,' says Guy. 'The sand reflected the light on to the subject, removing deep, hard shadow lines.' The photograph was taken in colour and colour converted to black and white in Photoshop after scanning. Guy then 'warmed' the greyscale image with minor colour adjustments in the mid-tones, to give this light and airy result.

Commissioned to take a portrait of three brothers in their garden, Ian had the challenge of creating a unified image that brought out each boy's different personality. 'I had to place the boys in a composition that allowed the viewer to see each one's expression and size difference, without the weight of the image pulling to one of the subjects more than the others,' he explains. The light was bright, but softened by cloud cover and Ian was able to use a fairly wide aperture to put the foliage behind them out of focus.

Fact file

Photographer: Ian McFarlane
Location: Athens, Georgia, USA
Time of day: Late afternoon, summer

Technical details

Camera: Mamiya RZ 67
Lens: 110mm
Film: Ilford HP5 400
Exposure: 1/125sec at f/5.6

Outdoor Photography: Portraits 124

Pairs and groups: Families 125

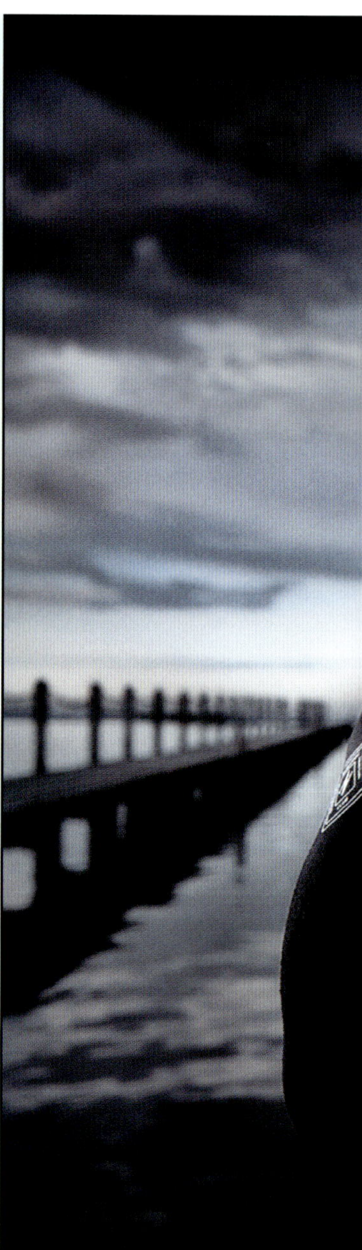

Quotations

The photographers' own words refer to their picture and explain what they were trying to achieve, any problems they encountered and tips they can pass on.

Inspiration

The pictures are intended to provide a source of inspiration and ideas and can be enjoyed in their own right by professionals, students and all followers of portrait photography who appreciate quality imagery.

Supporting pictures

These are used to further explore the theme of the spread. They are accompanied by a caption explaining technique, plus technical details and fact file panels.

Fact file

Information in this panel includes the photographer, the location and timing of the shot. A fact file accompanies every picture in the book.

Technical details

Camera, lens, film and exposure are included in a panel alongside every picture. This helps the reader understand how the choice of equipment may affect the result.

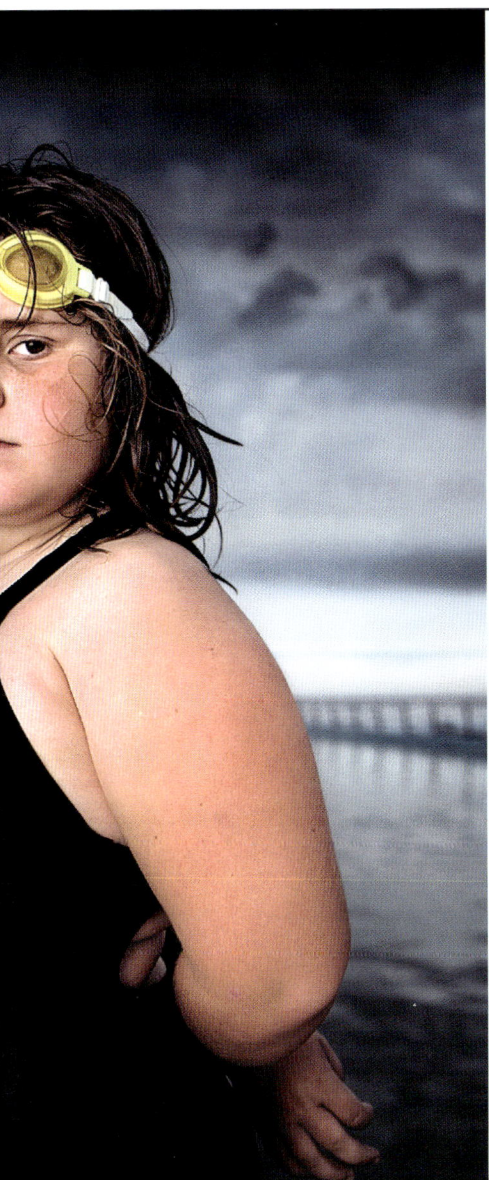

'Samantha not only impresses me with her swimming abilities, but with the way she holds herself and the pride she exudes beyond her years.'

Michael Hall

Fact file

Photographer:	Michael Hall
Location:	Narrabeen Rockpool, NSW coastline, Australia
Time of day:	Late afternoon, late summer

Technical details

Camera:	Hasselblad 503SW
Lens:	50mm
Film:	Kodak 160vc
Exposure:	1/250sec at f/8

Sun behind clouds

Flash in softbox

Medium format camera

The concept

This was personal work for Michael, part of an on-going series of portraits he is producing. 'Samantha, who was eight years old at the time this was taken, is in the same class at school as my middle son, Samuel,' he explains. 'She also belongs to the North Narrabeen Amateur Swim Club where we meet every Saturday morning for friendly races.'

The location

The point of the portrait was to portray Samantha as the keen swimmer she is and so it was a natural choice to place her against the background of water. The place also exudes atmosphere, especially in this light.

Composition

Michael made sure he took the portrait while Samantha was still wet from the swim and placed her centrally in the frame, side on with her head turned towards the camera. This is a striking, solid pose, emphasising the child's pride and confidence, which shines through in her face. The position of the arms can be difficult to get right in a three-quarter-length portrait, as the subject often holds them awkwardly, but folding them behind the back like this solves the problem and helps reinforce the tightness of the composition. The position of the two platforms in the sea either side of her helps to frame her figure and provide perspective by leading the eye into the background.

Lighting and technique

Michael planned the portrait in advance, waiting for a stormy afternoon to give those atmospheric clouds. The subject was lit with a large softbox, slightly to the left of the camera and exposed to one and a half stops more than the ambient light. The strong contrast between her face and skin and the darker, brooding background add a great sense of drama and power to the image. Some Photoshop retouching of the contrast was undertaken to boost the existing effect.

Mood: Creating drama 19

The pictures

Each spread is illustrated with one or more images, by the same or different photographers. The images have been chosen not only for their impact and quality but because they illustrate a particular technique or aspect of lighting.

Diagrams

These show the direction of the sun, position and type of camera and any additional equipment that was used, such as reflectors and flash, or tungsten lighting units.

Information

The written information explains how the pictures were achieved, thus giving the reader the background knowledge and confidence to try a similar effect for themselves.

Michael Trevillion/Trevillion Picture Library

Chapter 1: **Mood**

The mood of a portrait is often dictated by circumstances. A person's expression, or the way the light happens to catch them may be what inspired you to grab the camera, focus and shoot before the moment has gone. Often, though, you will want to exert an influence over this through planning.

Mood can be described as the overall 'feel' to an image. It may be so subtle, you can't put a label on it, or it could be completely contrived to make a point. People have a multitude of emotions and photography can attempt to enhance these, not just by capturing a frown or a smile, but by the use of light and colour, the way shadows fall, the timing of the shot and the angle of the camera to the subject.

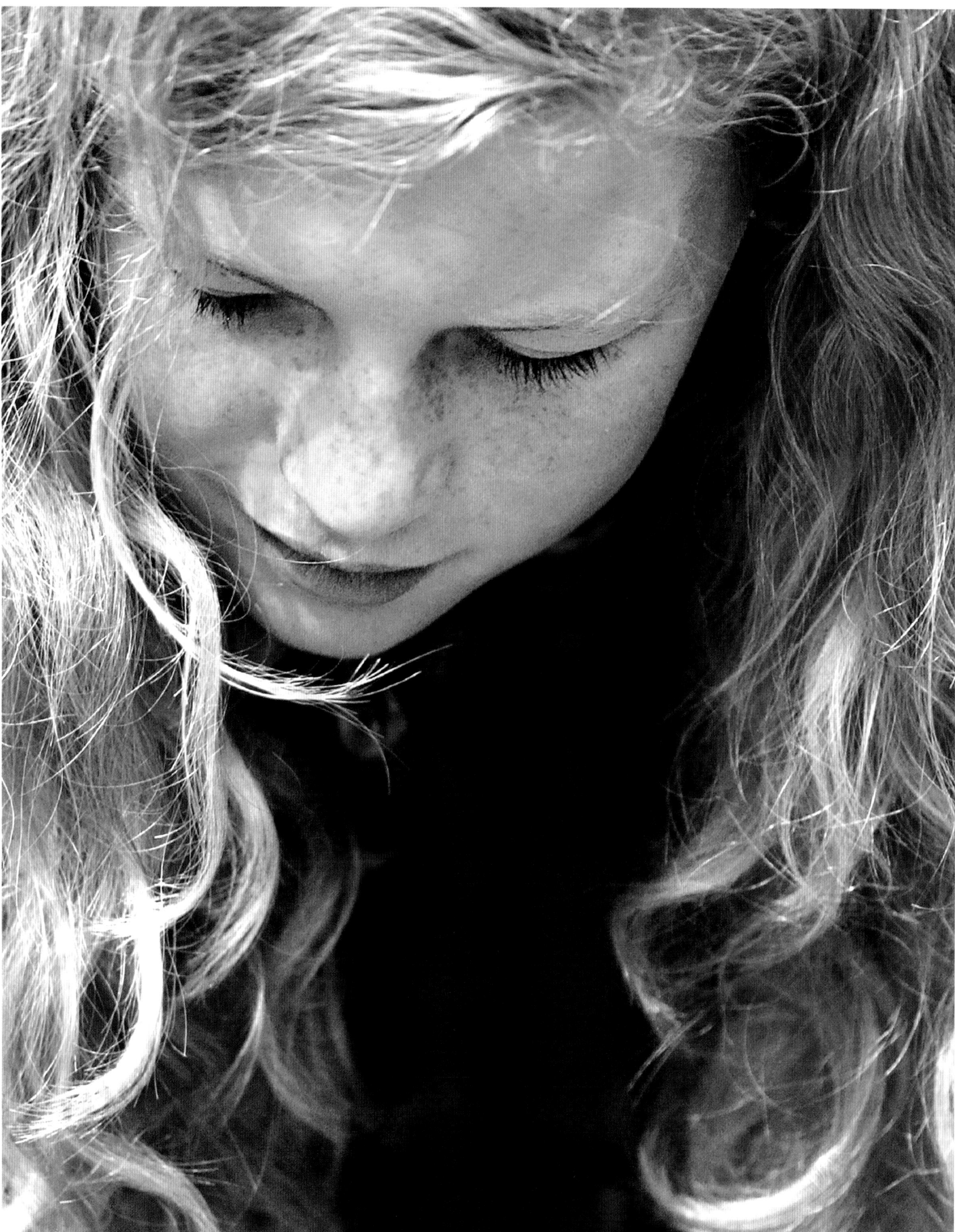

Fact file

Photographer: Trine Sirnes Thorne
Location: Koster Island, Sweden
Time of day: 1.30pm, July

Technical details

Camera: Canon EOS 300D (digital)
Lens: 180mm
Film: n/a
Exposure: 1/1600sec at f/3.6

Sun

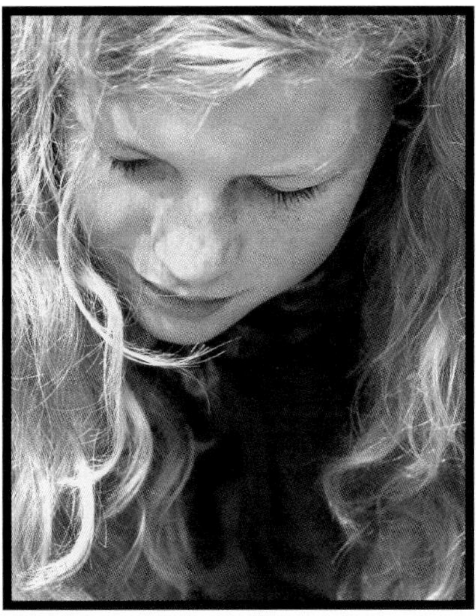

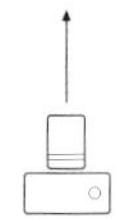

35mm camera

'I walked around the group of children from a distance, shooting a lot of photos over a period of time until they forgot I was there.'

Trine Sirnes Thorne

The concept

Trine bought herself a new Sigma EX 180mm f/3.5 recently and she set herself a goal of using it to explore the field of outdoor portraiture. A summer holiday with a large group of friends gave her the ideal opportunity. 'This was one of the results,' she says. 'It helped having such a beautiful crowd to choose from.'

The location

'Each summer we go camping on a small island in Sweden. It's totally primitive with no water or electricity, just us, our tents, gas and the sea. We make furniture from driftwood and have a great time. This year there were about 20 people altogether, many of them children or teenagers.'

Composition

The girl's striking hair was what caught Trine's eye when she was composing this shot. Using the fixed focal length telephoto lens, she moved her own position until she had a tight crop in the viewfinder, with the hair effectively providing a frame around the face. Fortunately, she was wearing a dark top, which provides an important strip of contrast down the centre of the image.

Lighting and technique

The subject and her friends were playing a game in a sandpit and, with the sun shining directly above them, the light was harsh. Often this would have created problems with too much contrast and heavy shadows. Here, the girl's natural pose with her head down, shielded most of her face from the strong rays, leaving attractive highlights on her nose and hair, and providing an uplifting summery glow to the portrait.

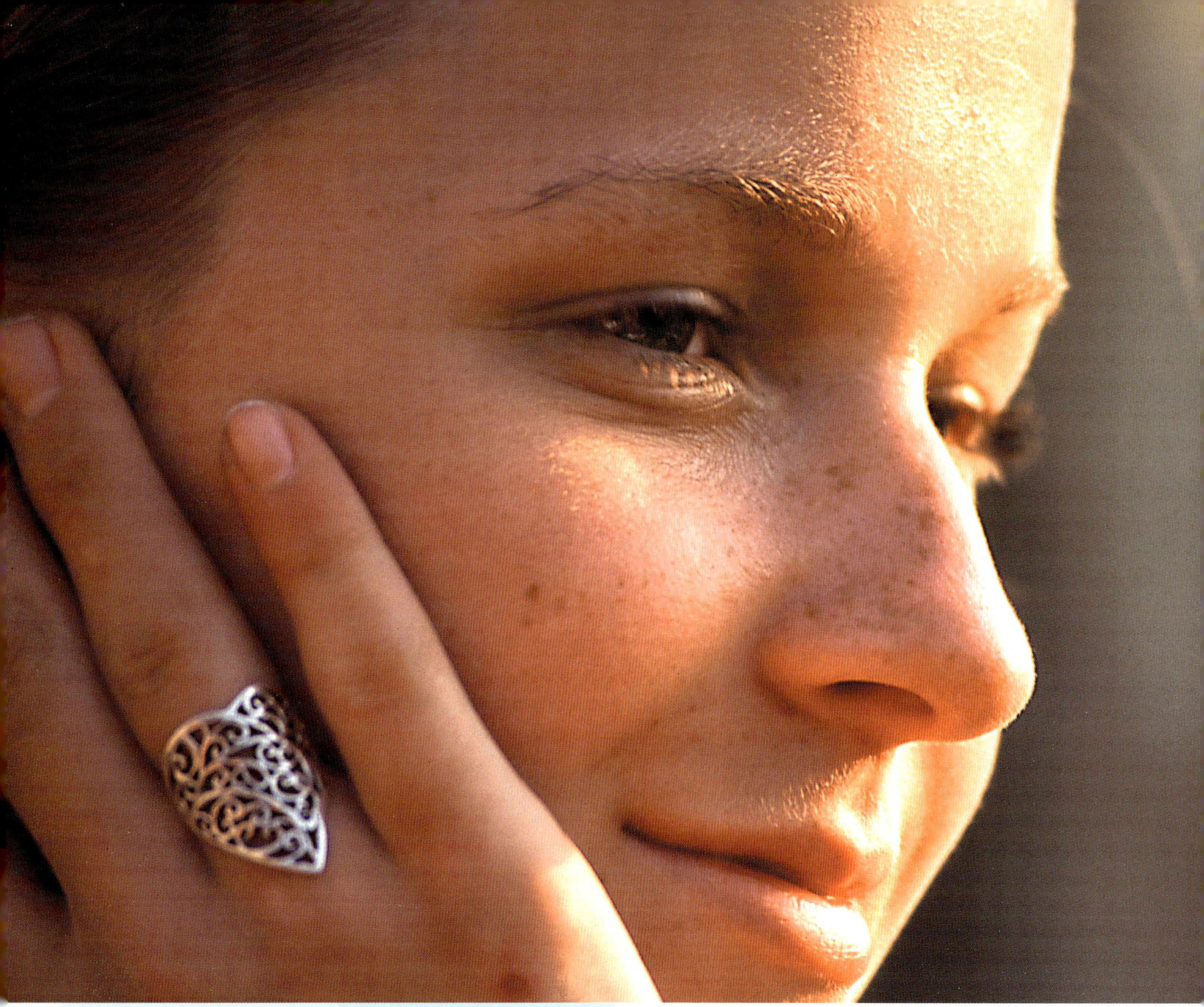

Fact file

Photographer:	Arthur Sevestre
Location:	Rannoch Moor, Scotland
Time of day:	4pm, August

Technical details

Camera:	Minolta Dynax 7
Lens:	50–500mm
Film:	Fuji Sensia
Exposure:	1/200sec at f/4

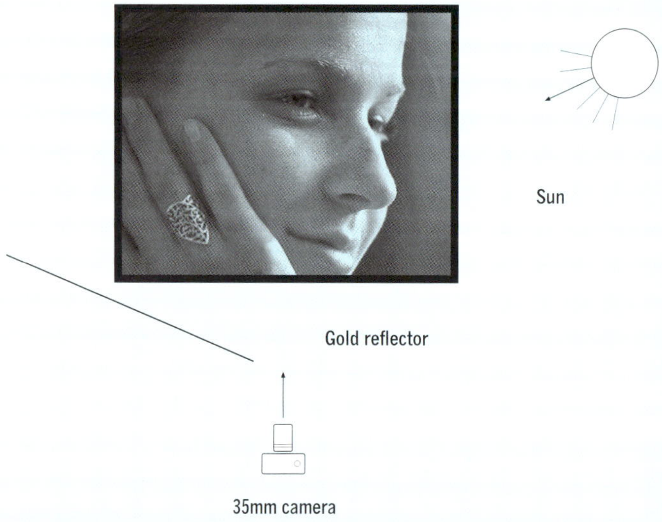

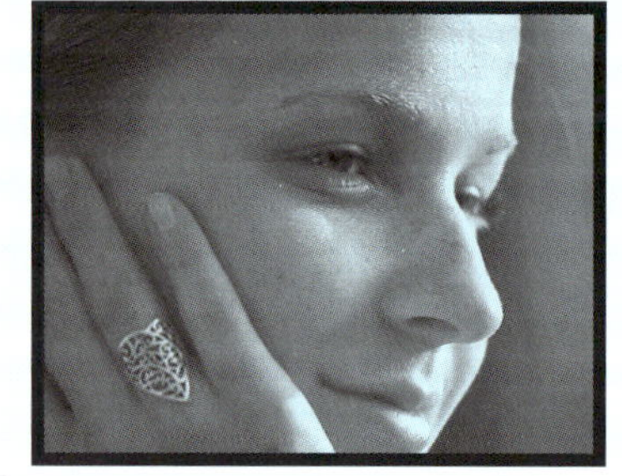

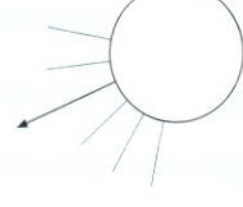

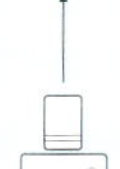

The concept

This portrait of Arthur's sister was prompted by a ring she had just bought while on holiday. 'It seemed like a nice idea to take a picture of her, including the ring. Especially as the late afternoon light was so good, providing interesting shadows and highlights,' he recalls.

The location

Taken on the campsite where they were staying, Arthur didn't want the background to intrude, so he chose an uncluttered space of a colour that would complement the face and used a shallow depth of field to throw it out of focus completely.

Composition

'I was after a simple portrait, featuring the new ring of hers. I wanted to get up close and personal without making the mistake of including too much cheek – which tends to make the model look big, or even fat. Placing the hand over part of the face like that takes away that problem.'

Lighting and technique

'The light that attracted me so much was also slightly tricky because it would have been easy to blow out the highlights,' explains Arthur. 'I positioned my sister in such a way that the light would highlight her features, while keeping the largest part of her face in shadow. A gold Lastolite reflector was used from the left corner, low down, to bounce some light back into those shadows and keep them a warm tone. I spot-metered the small area of highlight in the middle of the frame and overexposed by about 0.7 stops. Then, having locked the exposure, I aimed at several parts of her face to compare the brightness. To keep detail in all parts, I wanted the highlights to be below 2.5 stops (pure white) and the shadows above –2.5 stops (pure black). It turned out that a spot meter reading from the even-toned part of her cheek in the middle of the image was perfect.'

Misty took this shot with a photo contest in mind and wanted to create a solitary and thoughtful mood. The clothing, pose and location all add to this, as does the glow of early morning light around the model. Fill-in flash was used to lighten up the shadow areas at the front.

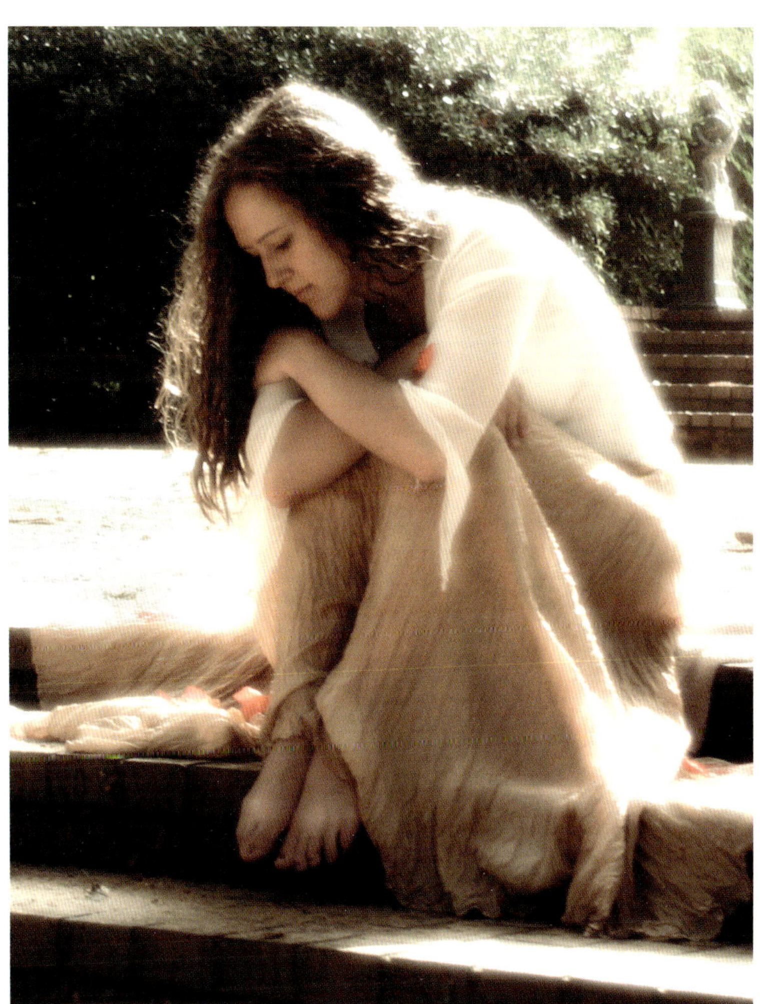

Fact file

Photographer: Misty Morris
Location: Hopeland Gardens, South Carolina, USA
Time of day: Early morning, April

Technical details

Camera: Canon D60 (digital)
Lens: 28–300mm
Film: n/a
Exposure: 1/90sec at f/11

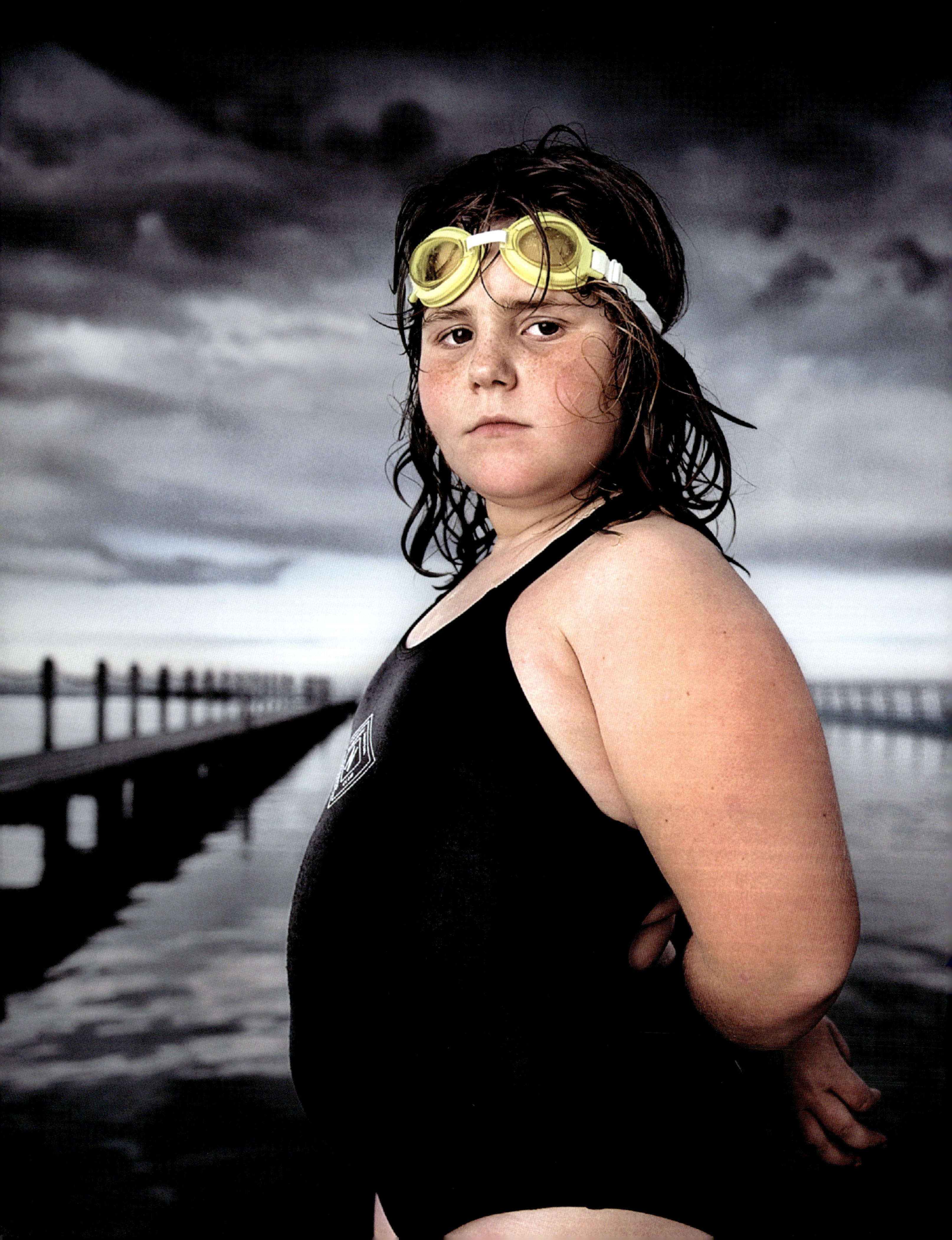

'Samantha not only impresses me with her swimming abilities, but with the way she holds herself and the pride she exudes beyond her years.'

Michael Hall

Fact file		**Technical details**	
Photographer:	Michael Hall	**Camera:**	Hasselblad 503SW
Location:	Narrabeen Rockpool, NSW coastline, Australia	**Lens:**	50mm
		Film:	Kodak 160vc
Time of day:	Late afternoon, late summer	**Exposure:**	1/250sec at f/8

The concept

This was personal work for Michael, part of an on-going series of portraits he is producing. 'Samantha, who was eight years old at the time this was taken, is in the same class at school as my middle son, Samuel,' he explains. 'She also belongs to the North Narrabeen Amateur Swim Club where we meet every Saturday morning for friendly races.'

The location

The point of the portrait was to portray Samantha as the keen swimmer she is and so it was a natural choice to place her against the background of water. The place also exudes atmosphere, especially in this light.

Composition

Michael made sure he took the portrait while Samantha was still wet from the swim and placed her centrally in the frame, side on with her head turned towards the camera. This is a striking, solid pose, emphasising the child's pride and confidence, which shines through in her face. The position of the arms can be difficult to get right in a three-quarter-length portrait, as the subject often holds them awkwardly, but folding them behind the back like this solves the problem and helps reinforce the tightness of the composition. The position of the two platforms in the sea either side of her helps to frame her figure and provide perspective by leading the eye into the background.

Lighting and technique

Michael planned the portrait in advance, waiting for a stormy afternoon to give those atmospheric clouds. The subject was lit with a large softbox, slightly to the left of the camera and exposed to one and a half stops more than the ambient light. The strong contrast between her face and skin and the darker, brooding background add a great sense of drama and power to the image. Some Photoshop retouching of the contrast was undertaken to boost the existing effect.

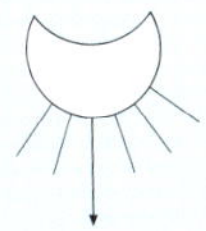

Sun behind clouds

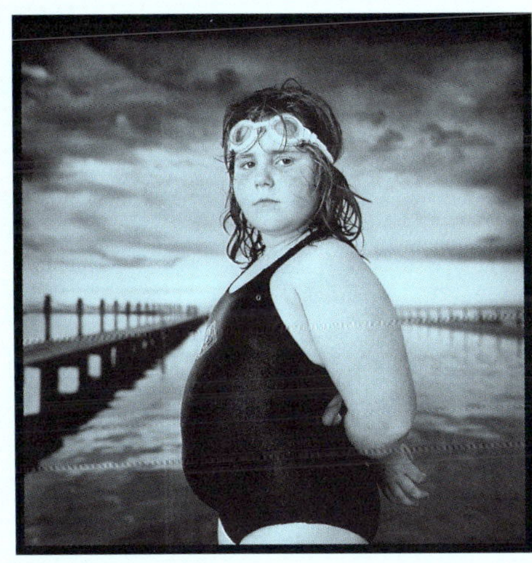

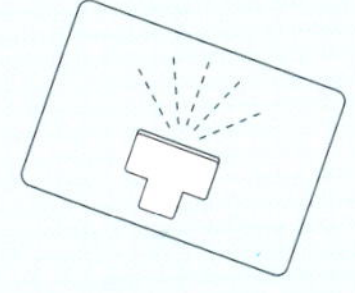

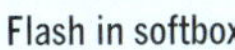

Flash in softbox

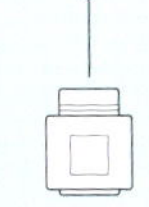

Medium format camera

‘Perfect pictures are like ying and yang. They have contrast, of which one part cannot exist independently.’

Igor Sarzynski

Fact file

Photographer: Igor Sarzynski
Location: Sopot, Poland
Time of day: Late afternoon, August

Technical details

Camera: Canon EOS 50E
Lens: 28–70mm
Film: Agfa APX 400
Exposure: 1/250sec at f/8

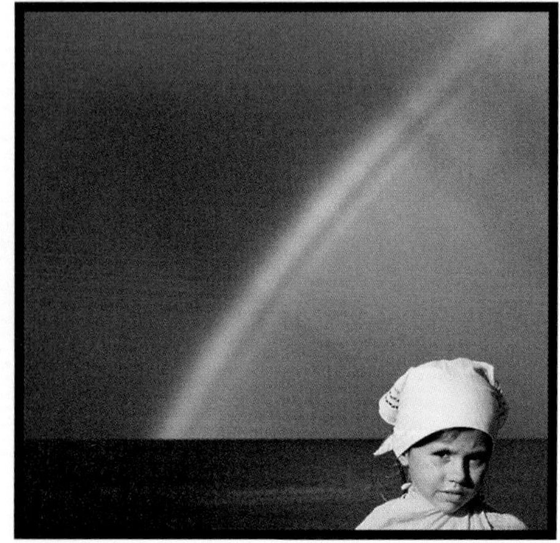

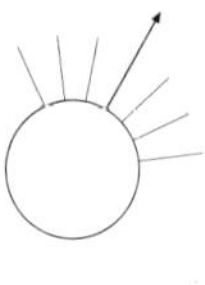

sun

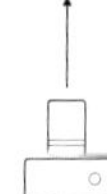

35mm camera

The concept

This is a personal picture of Igor’s young sister. It wasn’t planned in advance but he had his camera with him, looking in particular for images with strong contrast between light and shade. ‘I saw the bright face of my little sister, lightened by the setting sun with a dark, stormy sky in the background,’ he recalls. ‘When I raised the camera to my eye, a rainbow slowly started appearing. I waited for a couple of minutes and then made the picture.’

The location

‘This was somewhat accidental. We were out for a walk on the beach and were caught by heavy rain. We took shelter and then returned to the seashore when it stopped.’

Composition

Igor felt that including too much of his sister’s bright figure would make the whole composition unbalanced. Instead he decided to include a small, but very strongly lit part as a contrast against the large dark area of the background. With Photoshop he cropped the image further on the right hand side, and the position of the small child, almost overpowered by the big forces of nature, adds to the great sense of drama. The position of the rainbow in the frame is effective in separating the light and dark areas.

Lighting and technique

‘The sun was quite low on the horizon, a little behind my left-hand side,’ explains Igor. ‘It wasn’t very strong but had the nice orange colour that comes late in the day. I took a meter reading from a part of the sky that was most evenly balanced in tone. I prefer not to add artificial sources of light but I did use a polarising filter that allowed me to achieve the effect of a bright rainbow against a dark sky. The lens was set to 70mm to make the rainbow as large as possible.’

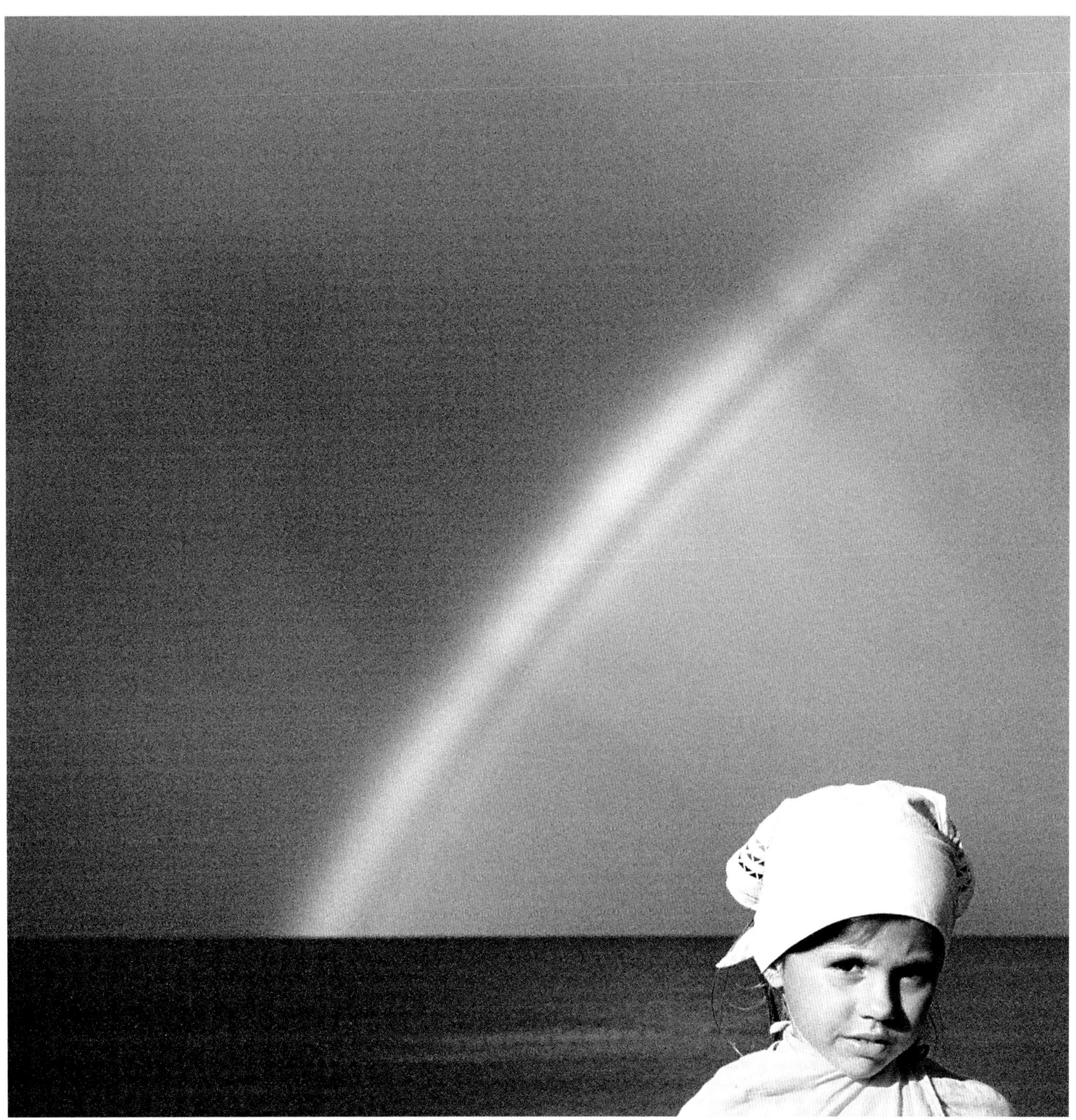

The concept

'The photo was taken on a terrace outside a restaurant while I was waiting to order, and fortunately I had my camera with me,' recalls Arthur. 'I saw this interesting man with a hat on sitting a few tables away and he immediately caught my eye. He was talking animatedly to the other people at his table most of the time, but would occasionally pause and look away thoughtfully. That was the moment I wanted to capture – a bit of the character of a man I had never met before and will probably never meet again.'

The location

Arthur felt that the location added little to the picture and so used a long lens with a wide aperture to throw it out of focus. The white restaurant table was useful, though, as it acted as a reflector for the subject's face.

Composition

The man's hat particularly appealed to Arthur and he felt the tone and texture of it went well with the sweater. 'In this composition, they are nicely mirrored in shape, even with the dark bands of his shirt and in the hat. This only works because of the tight crop, and I think that makes it more personal, too.'

Lighting and technique

The sun was right in front of the camera, high in the sky and not easy to work with, as passing clouds meant the light was constantly changing. 'At this moment the sun was just covered by thin cloud – without it, the contrast would have been too much to capture detail in both the hat and the face. I took a spot meter reading from the brightest part of the man's cheek and underexposed by 0.7 stops with the aim of getting the exposure as good as possible on the face.'

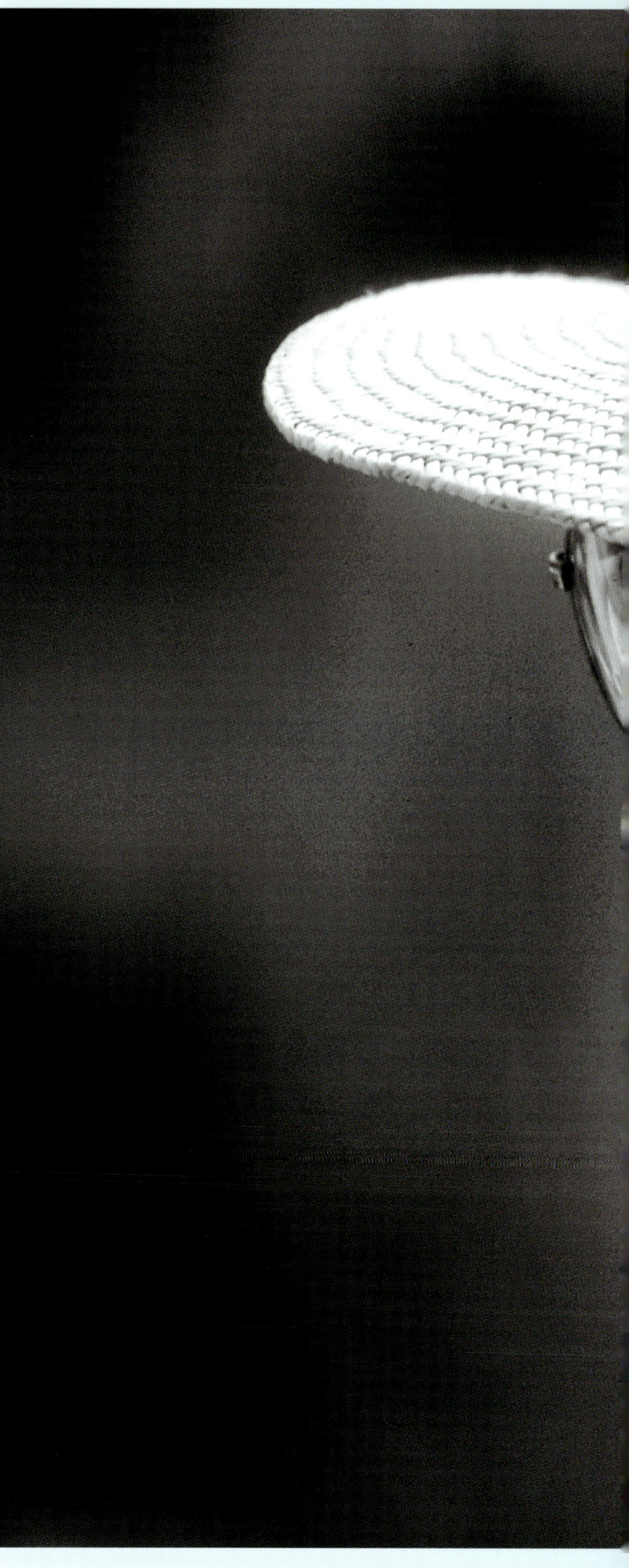

Fact file

Photographer:	Arthur Sevestre
Location:	Zierikee, the Netherlands
Time of day:	1pm, May

Technical details

Camera:	Minolta Dynax 7
Lens:	50–500mm
Film:	Fuji Provia 100f
Exposure:	1/40sec at f/4

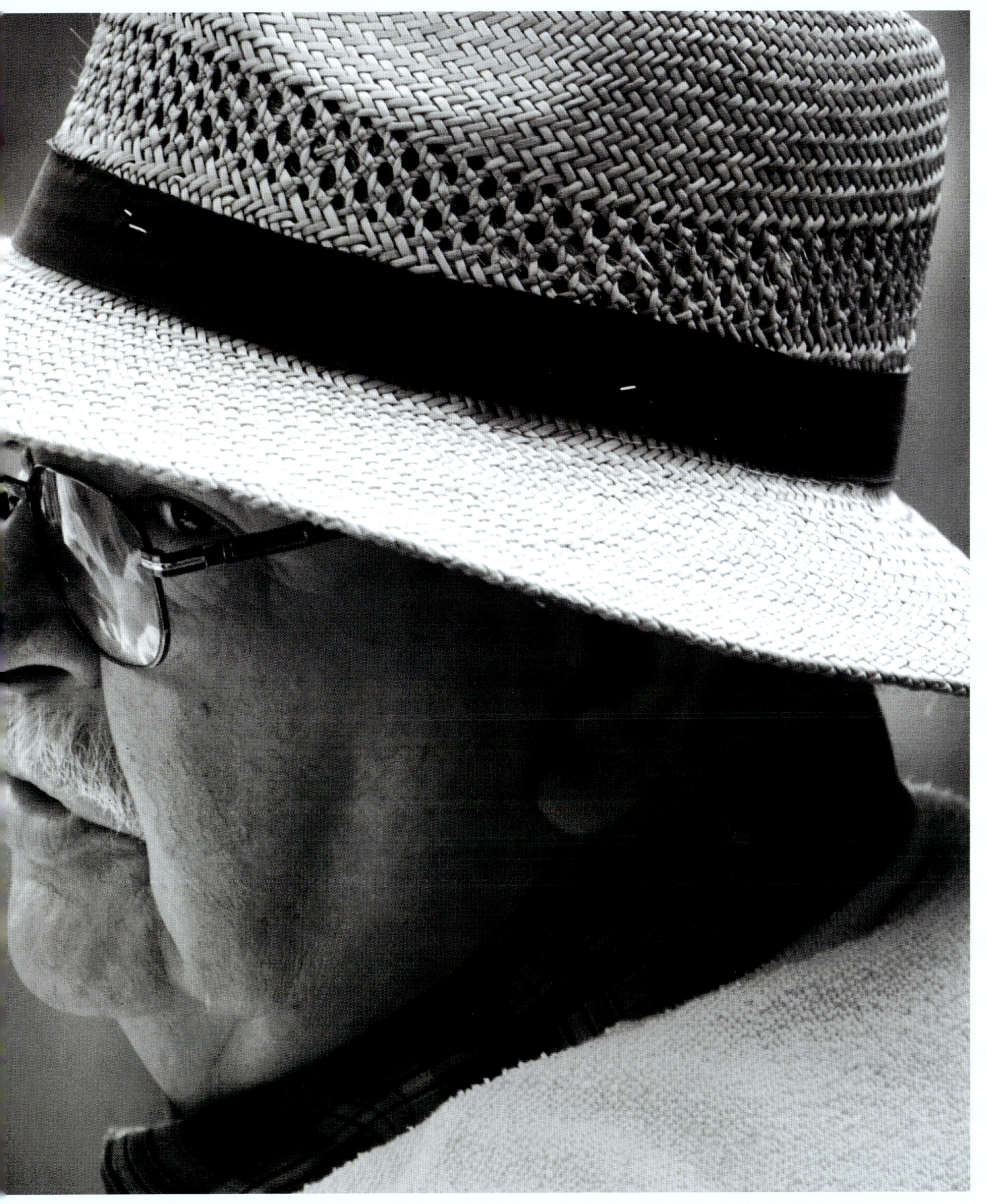

Fact file

Photographer:	Piotr Kowalik
Location:	Lublin, Poland
Time of day:	Midday, August

Technical details

Camera:	Canon EOS 50E
Lens:	70–200mm
Film:	Fuji Velvia
Exposure:	f/4, fill-in flash

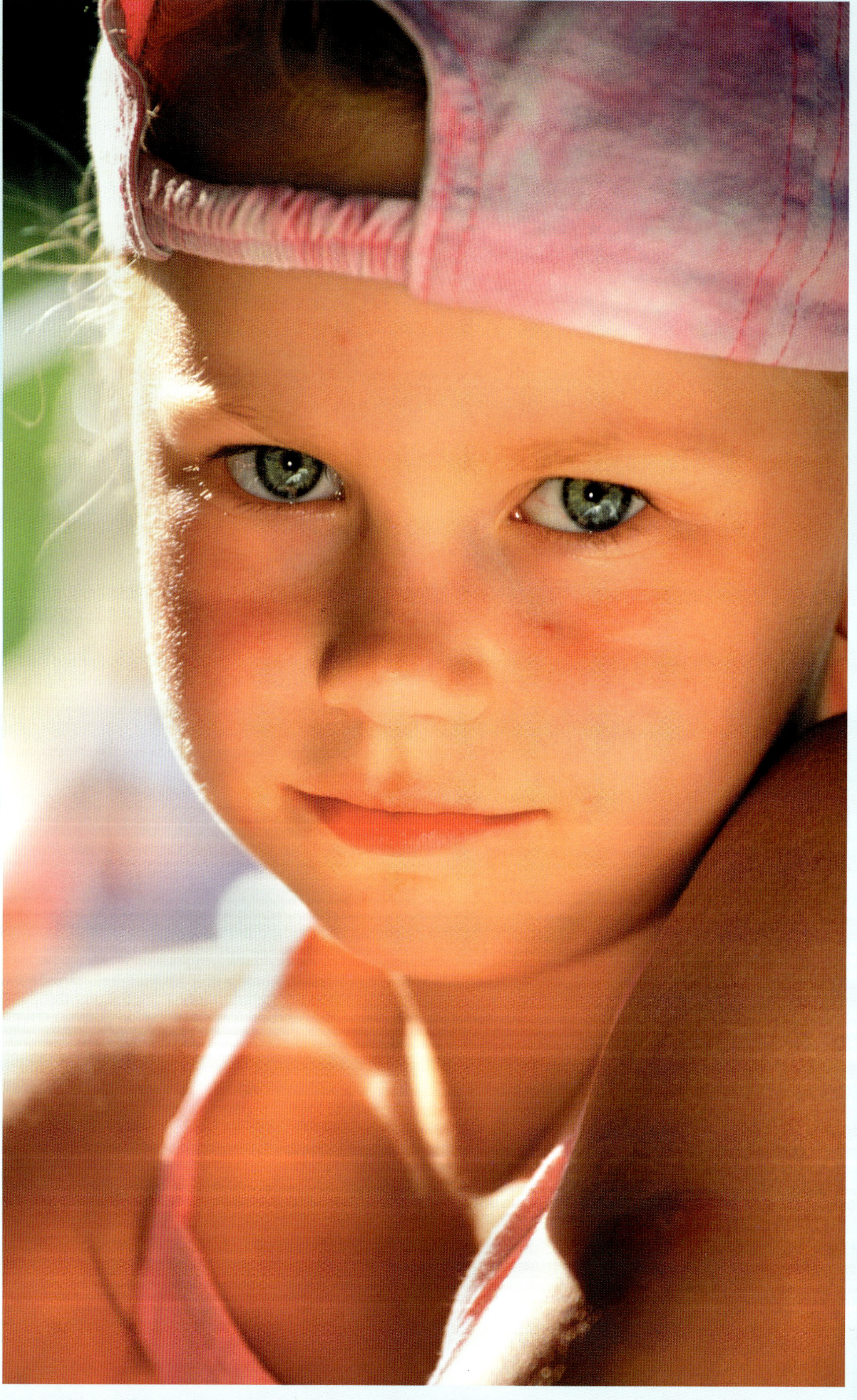

The concept

'This is one of those images you just capture when on holiday – as long as you are taking pictures of people,' says Piotr. 'I met this lovely young model while travelling round Poland during the summer. When I pointed the camera towards some other people, she immediately paid attention, so I asked permission from her mum to take some shots.'

Composition

Piotr wanted a simple composition, but controlled the lighting carefully so that the child's striking eyes had maximum impact. The pose was unforced, but he ensured that the angle of her arms created 'lead-in' lines from the bottom left corner to keep the shot looking tight and organised.

Lighting and technique

The strong backlight provided attractive highlights around the child's figure but meant that Piotr needed equally strong and even light to fill in the shadows. With no reflector to hand, he improvised using a white plastic bar table, which he moved to just below the model's head. 'The angle of the table was important to ensure the reflected light fell more intensely around the nose and eyes.' Piotr also used an 81C warm-up filter and soft fill-in flash to complement the highlights created by the sun. 'When taking light readings for this subject I had to consider both the backlight and the power of fill-in needed and try to avoid underexposure,' he explains. 'I used the built-in evaluative meter on my camera and bracketed either side of the suggested exposure. One stop overexposure on the camera was enough to keep the highlights bright enough, while the flash was set at -1/2 a stop to avoid destroying the natural mood of the image.'

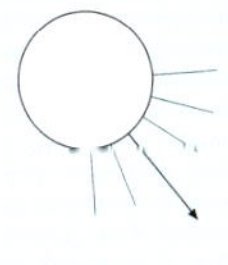

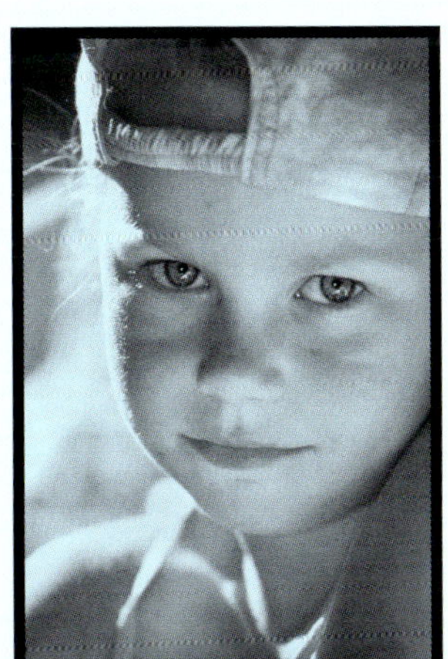

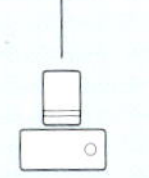

Fact file

Photographer:	Misty Morris
Location:	Florida, USA
Time of day:	4–5pm, May

Technical details

Camera:	Canon D60 (digital)
Lens:	28–300mm
Film:	n/a
Exposure:	1/500sec at f/5.6

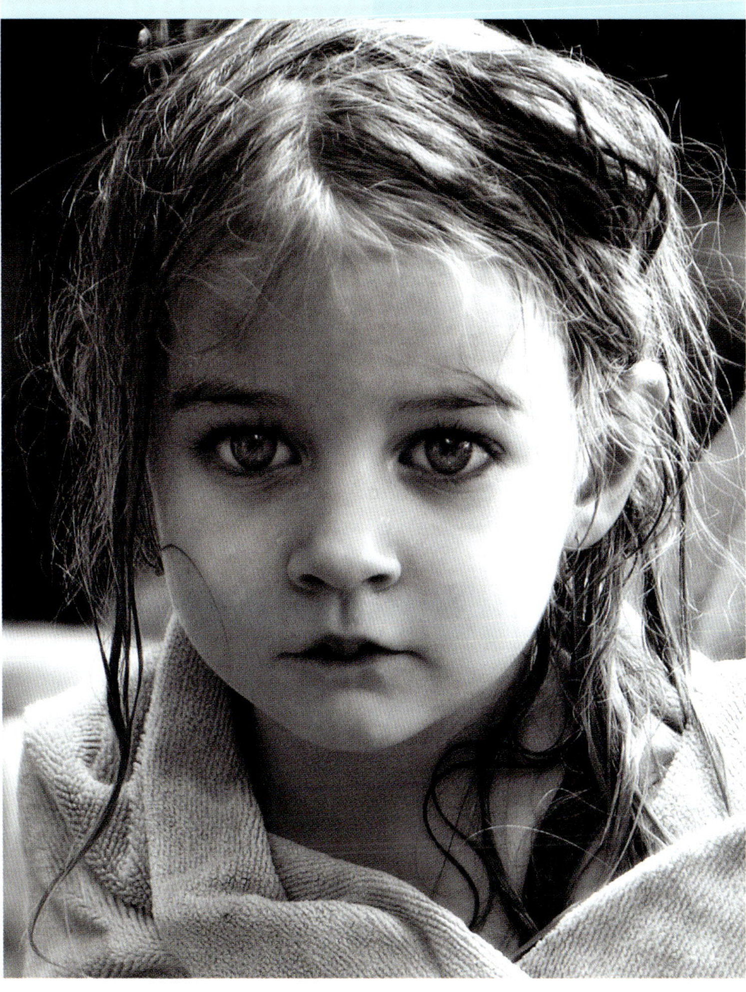

'This particular child had done her best to avoid me throughout the day, but as she sat shivering after a late-afternoon swim, she no longer cared about me or my camera,' says Misty. 'I like this shot better than any of the ones I chased her around for.' The sun was to the right of the camera and, to add a little more sparkle to the eyes, Misty used fill-in flash, softened with a Lumiquest diffuser.

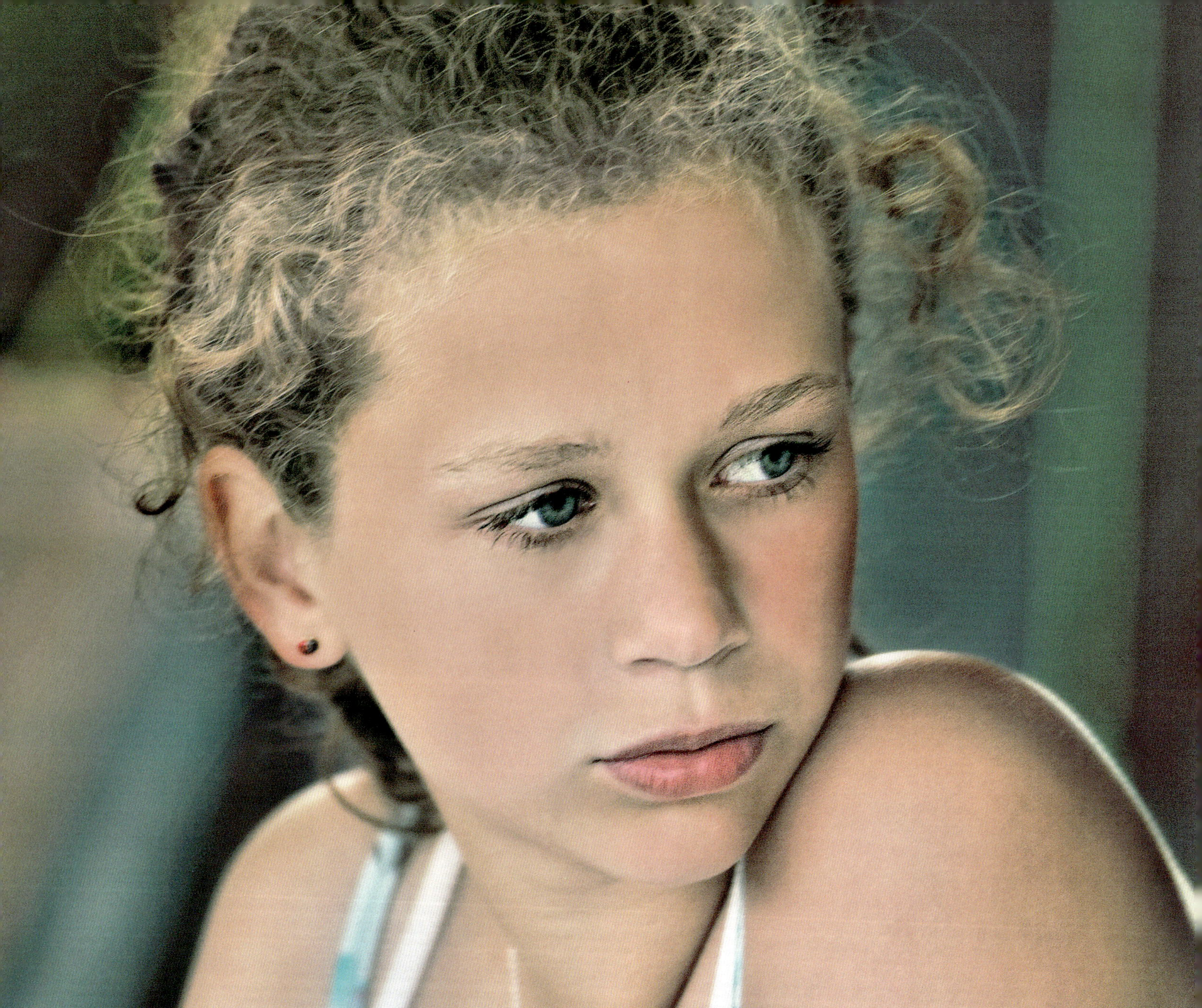

Fact file

Photographer:	Trine Sirnes Thorne
Location:	Koster Island, Sweden
Time of day:	12.30pm, July

Technical details

Camera:	Canon 300D (digital)
Lens:	180mm
Film:	n/a
Exposure:	1/80sec at f/3.5

'I have two preferences when it comes to portraits. I like them to reflect the true personality of the subject, and I prefer natural light whenever possible.'

Trine Sirnes Thorne

The concept

This is one of many outdoor portraits that Trine took on holiday with a group of friends. Another from the same trip is shown on pages 14–15.

The location

The group was camping and this shot was taken in front of Trine's tent. 'That particular day, a lot of the kids were sitting around our table doing their thing – writing, drawing, talking and so on,' she says. This girl wasn't asked to move her position or pose as Trine prefers to capture her subjects as naturally as possible.

Composition

The muted pastel colours are really what make this shot stand out. In some respects, Trine was just lucky that the colours of the tent in the background perfectly complemented the girl's skin tones, eyes and even the strap of her top. Even so, she was careful to choose a viewpoint where the tent colours were broken up in this way, giving vertical, diagonal and horizontal lines to add interest to the image. The effect is quite subtle because Trine used a wide aperture to make the subject stand out sharply against the slightly hazy background.

Lighting and technique

Although the sun was shining strongly and, at 12.30pm, was virtually overhead, the subject was sitting in the shade of a canopy, resulting in much softer and more even light.

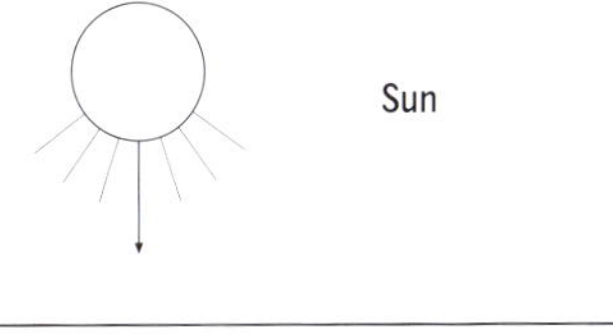

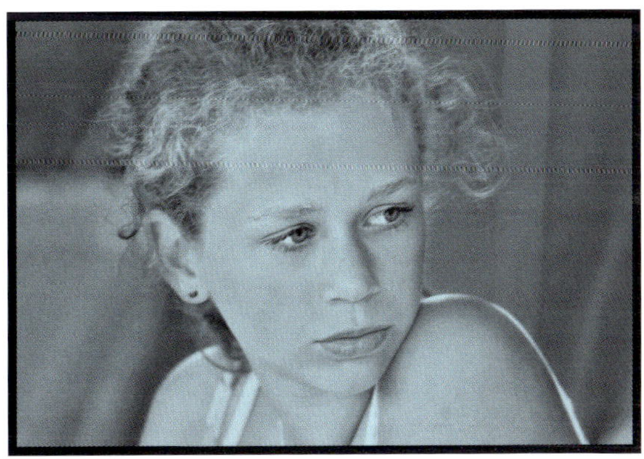

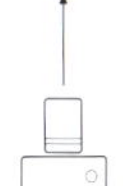

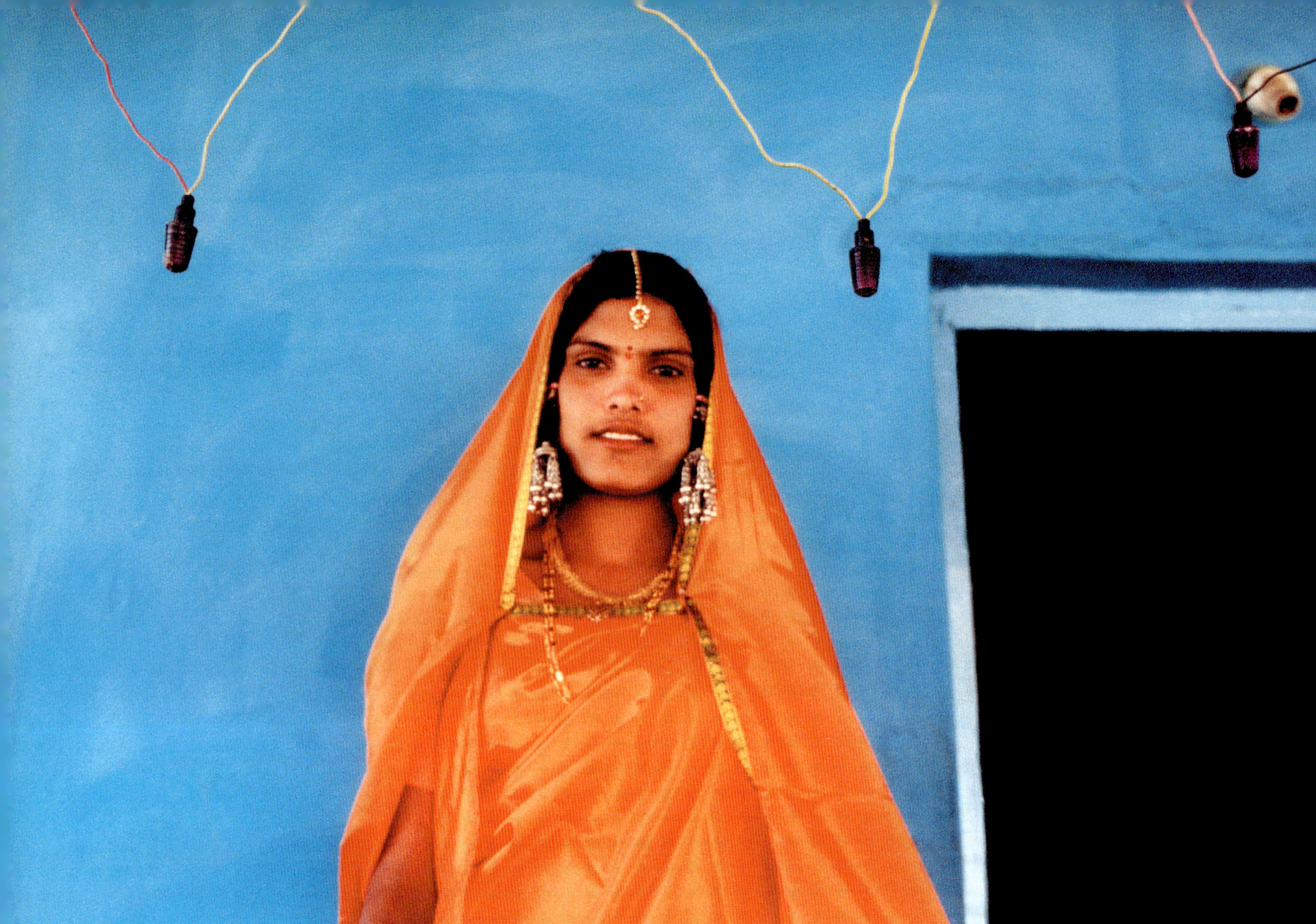

The concept

Aaron was given a GSE grant by Rotary International to take photographs in the Karnataka region of India. 'My intention was to simply document the people, character and day-to-day life of the area and to communicate a sense of the place to a Western audience,' he explains.

The location

One afternoon Aaron was taken to a small village where the young women were preparing to dance in a local festival. 'The second I saw this bright orange costume and golden jewellery, gleaming against the contrasting blue building, I rushed over to take a photograph. As soon as I raised the camera, I was also struck by the zig-zag pattern created by the string of lights and the way this echoed the shape of the costumed woman herself. I felt it would contrast well with the flat solidity of the wall behind, bringing a bit more graphic texture to the image.'

Composition

'When I do portraiture, I generally like to position the camera a little below the subject's eye-level in order to exaggerate their presence,' Aaron explains. 'I usually steady the camera and then wait for about 10 seconds, without saying anything, before clicking the shutter. This gives the subject a little more time to grow more comfortable with the camera, to make genuine eye-contact and to adjust their immediate "photo-face" into a more natural pose. I also try to find backgrounds that are not too busy and use wide-angle lenses so that I'm as close to the subject as I can be. I try to invade his or her personal space a little bit, giving the photograph a greater sense of intimacy.'

Lighting and technique

At midday, the light was high in the sky and very harsh. To avoid too much contrast, Aaron stood in a shaded area and the subject was under the cover of a porch. 'The earth below was a light reddish colour, so as the sun reflected off it, a warm tone was dispersed evenly. I metered directly at the centre of the frame, around the woman's face.'

Fact file

Photographer: Aaron Schuman
Location: Shimoga, Karnataka, India
Time of day: 1pm, January

Technical details

Camera: Nikon F3
Lens: 28mm
Film: Kodak Portra VC 400
Exposure: 1/125sec at f/11

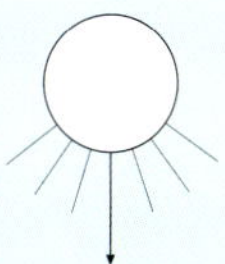

Porch providing shade

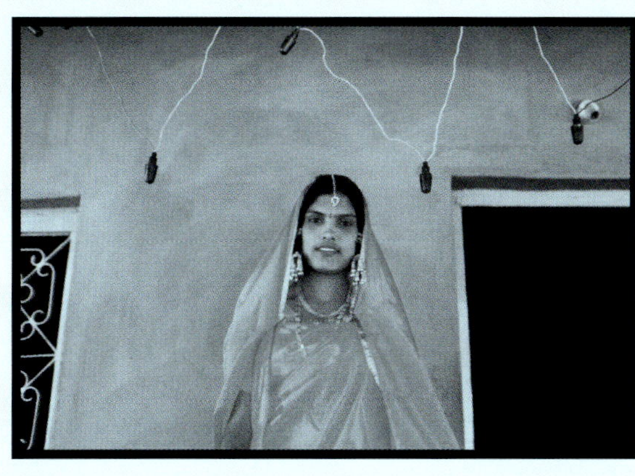

Ground reflecting light on to subject

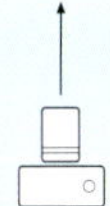

'Throughout my trip I was often struck by the overwhelming saturation of colour in India and tried my best to capture moments where certain colours were exaggerated to the highest level.'

Aaron Schuman

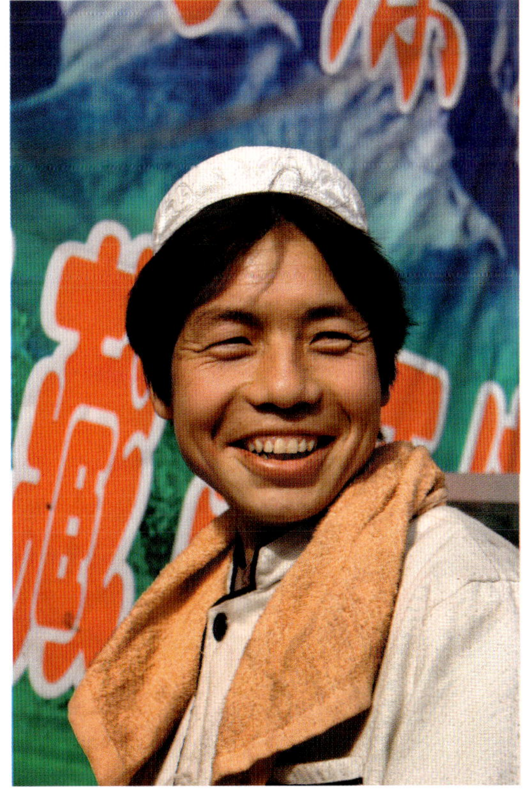

Jean met this man in a market and wanted to take a formal portrait of him, that also captured his sense of fun. The market itself was too busy to provide a suitable background and, while Jean could have blurred it with a shallow depth of field, he chose instead to position the subject against a colourful billboard. Far from being distracting, the colours, boosted with fill-in flash, add a sense of vibrancy and life to the portrait. ◀◀

Fact file

Photographer: Jean Schweitzer
Location: Lanzhou, Gansu Province, China
Time of day: 2pm, March

Technical details

Camera: Canon 300D (digital)
Lens: 18–50mm
Film: n/a
Exposure: 1/400sec at f/6.3

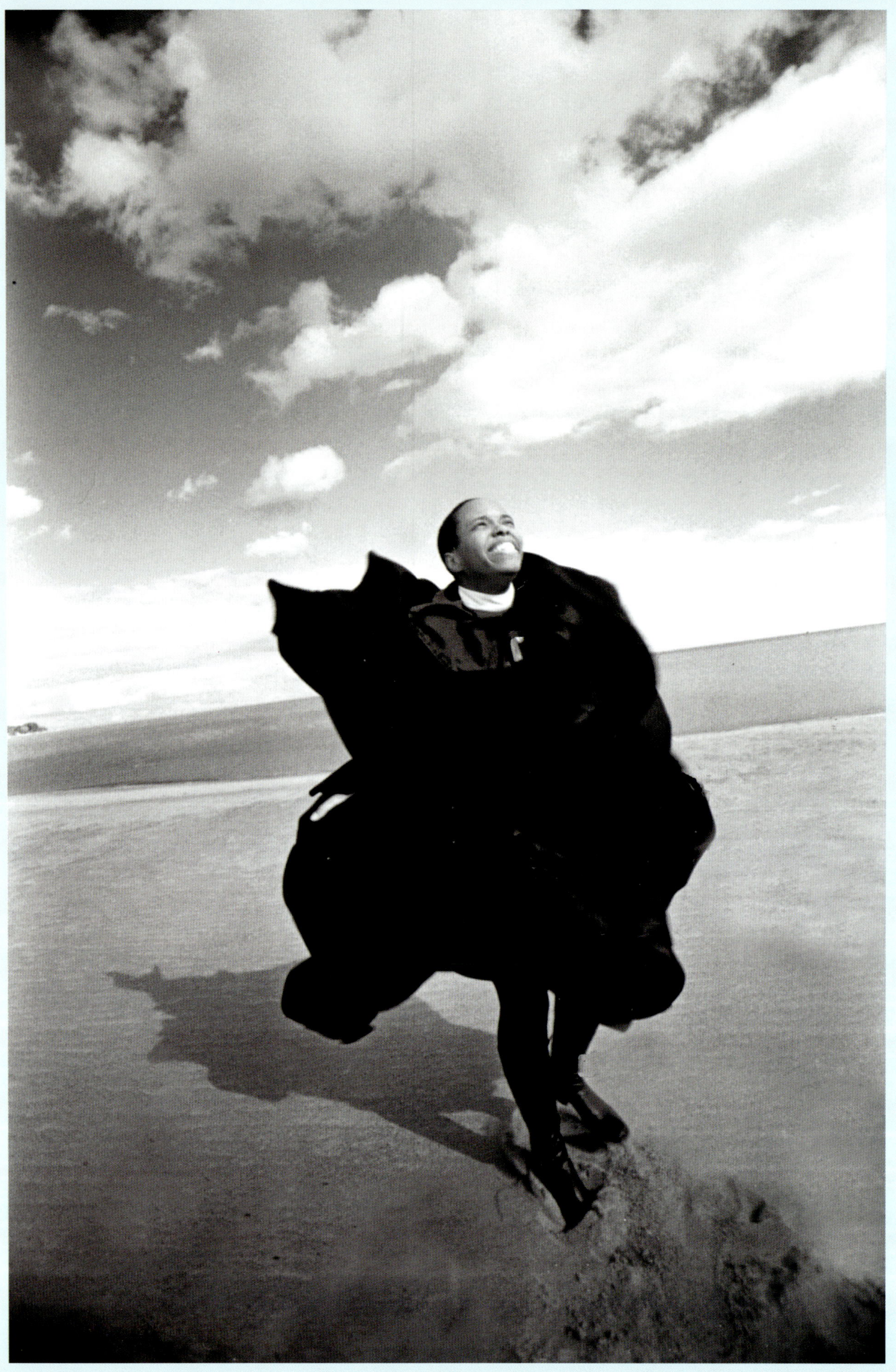

Fact file

Photographer: Jim Allen
Location: Kew Beach, Toronto, Canada
Time of day: 4.30pm, August

Technical details

Camera: Nikon F90
Lens: 20mm
Film: Kodak Tri-X ISO 200
Exposure: 1/60sec at f/8.5

The concept

This lively portrait was for a first CD cover and promotional material for the singer Kelley Lee. With this kind of commission, Jim usually asks the subject plenty of questions to try and find out about their personality. 'In this case there were not a lot of initial clues,' he explains. 'After one or two meetings I noticed that the energy was there, but a shyness was evident. I suggested that we rent a cape from a costume store and go down to a large beach. I remembered a movie that was shot by Bruce Weber about Chet Baker called "Let's Get Lost", where the camera moved in circles around the main figure. It really taught me a lot about creating motion and emotion on one frame.'

The location

Jim uses this beach a lot for this kind of action photo. It was ideal for this shot, providing the sense of space he was after and allowing him and Kelley Lee the freedom to move around. 'I wanted her to let go of her inhibited self,' he says.

Composition

Although shot on the move, this image was carefully designed to give a sense of uplifting emotion. The slightly elevated camera position, the tilted horizon and the angle of the subject's head, looking skywards, all serve to give the impression that Kelley Lee is reaching out to the world in a joyful way. The cloak, billowing in the wind, was chosen to provide an interesting shape against the horizon line and even the clouds obliged on the day by forming diagonal lines up to the top corner of the frame. The exaggerated perspective of the 20mm wide-angle lens has the effect of opening up the space.

Lighting and technique

The shoot was timed for a particular time of day when the sun was beginning to set and the subject's head was directed straight towards it in this particular frame. 'We were running around the beach, with me circling around the model, bobbing and weaving to change the camera angle,' recalls Jim. A red filter on the lens helped to boost contrast, separating the clouds from a darkened sky.

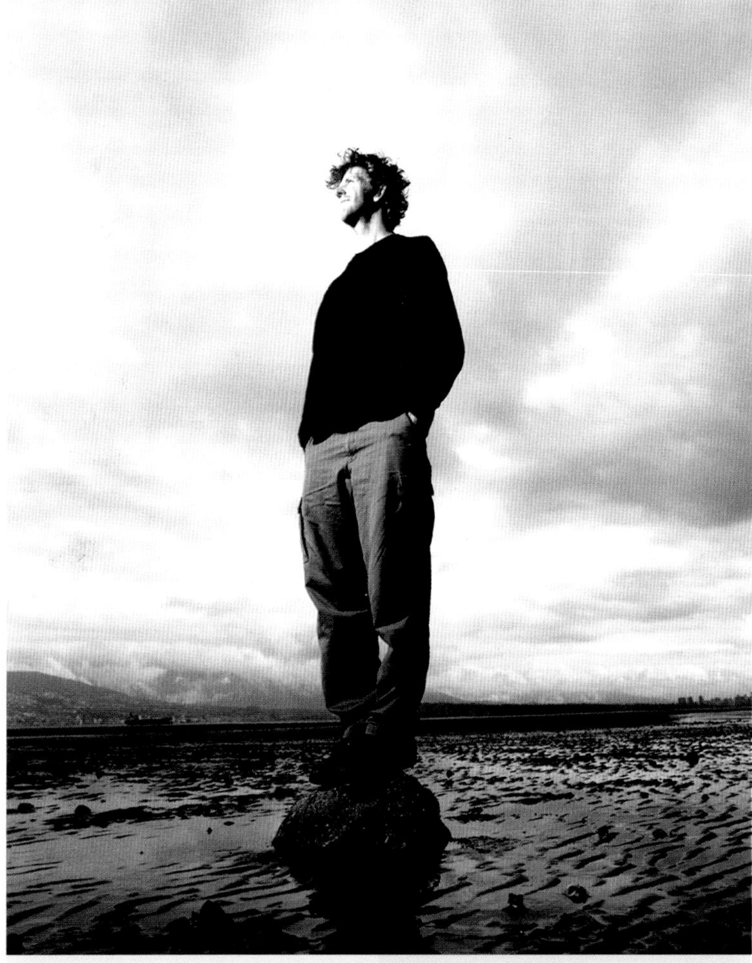

Fact file

Photographer: Jim Allen
Location: Wreck Beach, Vancouver, Canada
Time of day: Noon, July

Technical details

Camera: Hasselblad 500C
Lens: 40mm
Film: Kodak Tri-X ISO 200
Exposure: 1/60sec at f/8

A different kind of mood can be achieved by shooting from a low angle, especially when combined with a wide-angle lens. It works best, though, if there is plenty of interest in both the sky and the ground as there was in this portrait of Jim's assistant, taken while waiting for a shoot to begin. 'By placing the horizon line lower in the frame, two things happen,' he explains. 'The low tide is emphasised by the bend at the edges of the lens plus the mountains and deep clouds make the model appear taller – a looming figure on a small bit of rock. Also, by choosing the lower point of view, the puddles reflect the dramatic clouds.'

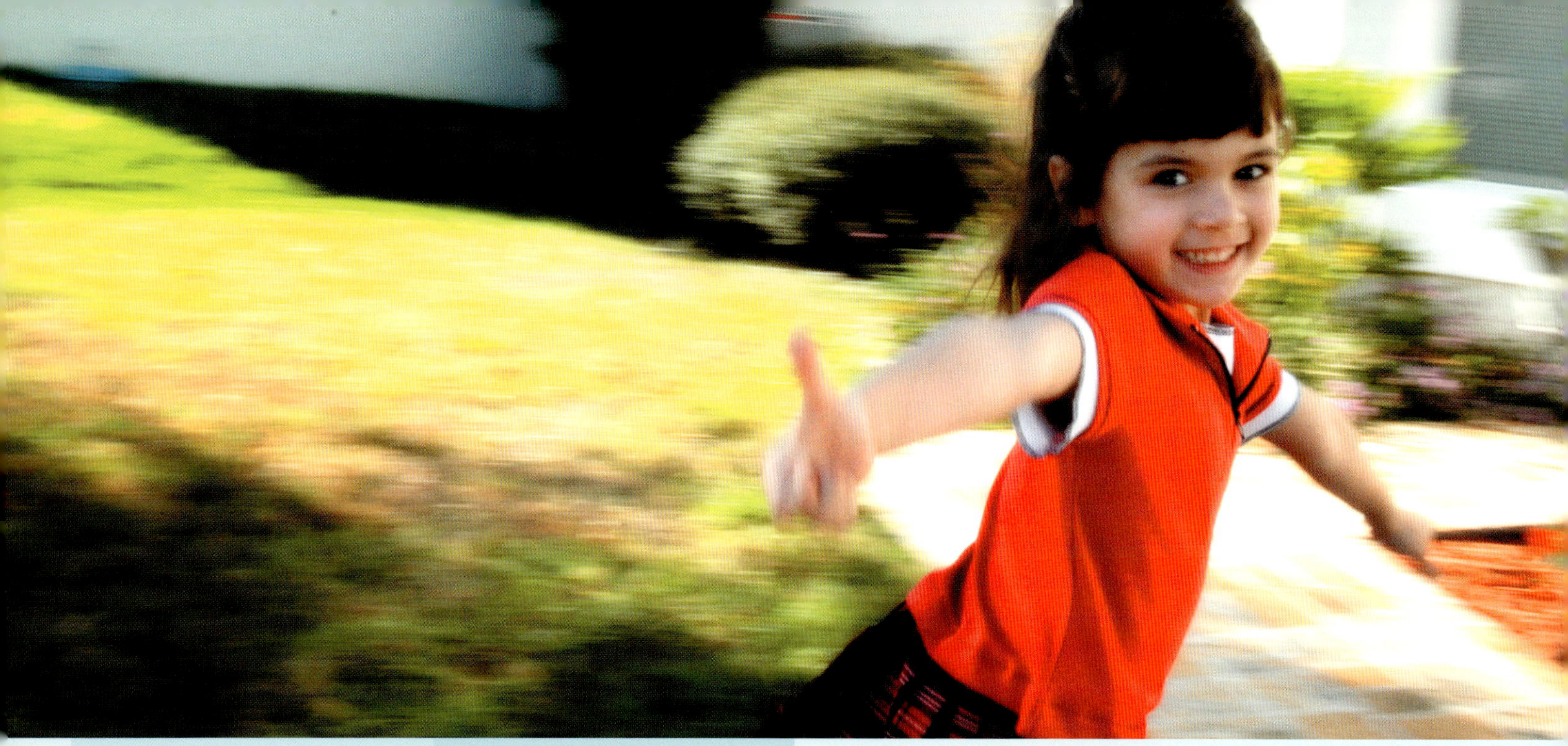

Fact file

Photographer: Alan Smilie
Location: Orlando, Florida, USA
Time of day: 9.30am, January

Technical details

Camera: Nikon D100 (digital)
Lens: 24–85mm
Film: n/a
Exposure: 1/80sec at f/13

'What better way to show motion than with a child who never seems to slow down.'

Alan Smilie

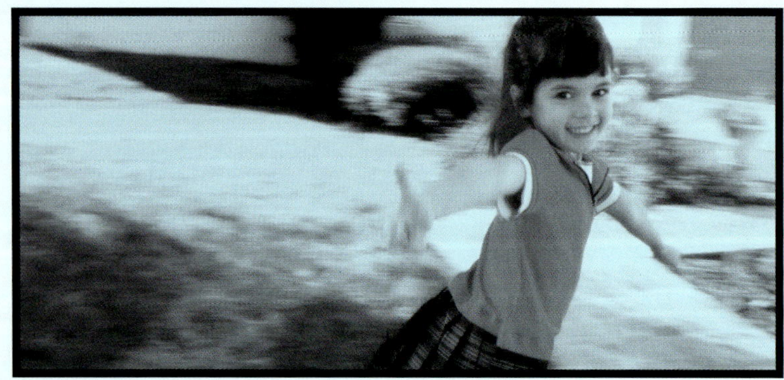

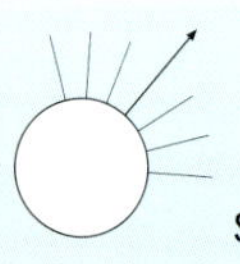

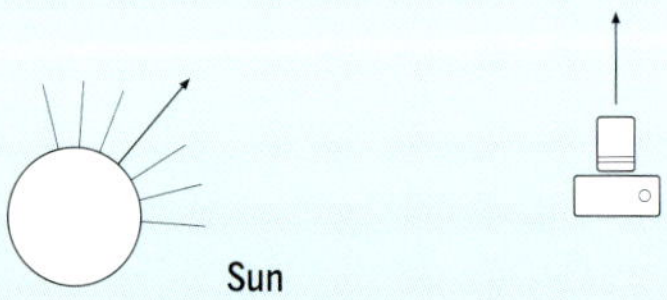

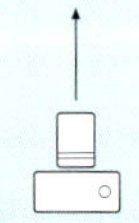

The concept

This was part of a personal experiment by Alan, using the technique of panning to show motion.

The location

Alan used the driveway outside his own house, mainly because of its convenience. 'Each morning on our way to work and school, I asked my daughter, Summer, to run up and down while I followed her with the camera,' he explains.

Composition

Composing a panned shot can be a bit hit and miss and requires plenty of practice and editing of pictures to ensure a good result, particularly if the subject is travelling at high speed like a sprinter. This child was moving a little more slowly and Alan was able to direct her to smile at the camera and stretch out her arms, the two things that give the shot such a joyful mood.

Lighting and technique

Panning involves using a slow shutter speed and tracking the moving subject with the camera, pressing the shutter at the appropriate moment during the pan. The idea is to keep the subject relatively sharp while blurring the background, and the amount of blur will depend on the shutter speed selected and the speed of the subject. Trial and error is the best way to decide what works best for a particular subject. This was taken on a sunny morning with no additional lighting. The image was cropped and the colours enhanced in Photoshop.

Fact file

Photographer:	Christel Sundebäck
Location:	Gothenburg, Sweden
Time of day:	Mid-afternoon, October

Technical details

Camera:	Canon A1
Lens:	50mm
Film:	Fuji NPS160
Exposure:	1/60sec at f/5.6

Taken with a fairly slow shutter speed, the slight blur on the child as she has a fit of giggles adds to the natural, uplifting quality of the picture. 'Children are so full of life, totally unaware of the camera's presence, which makes it easy to capture their moods and emotions,' says Christel. 'Out for a walk with my nieces on a cloudy day with very nice, soft light, I couldn't resist taking some portraits. Capturing a happy, smiling moment that was completely unforced gives me a lot of satisfaction.'

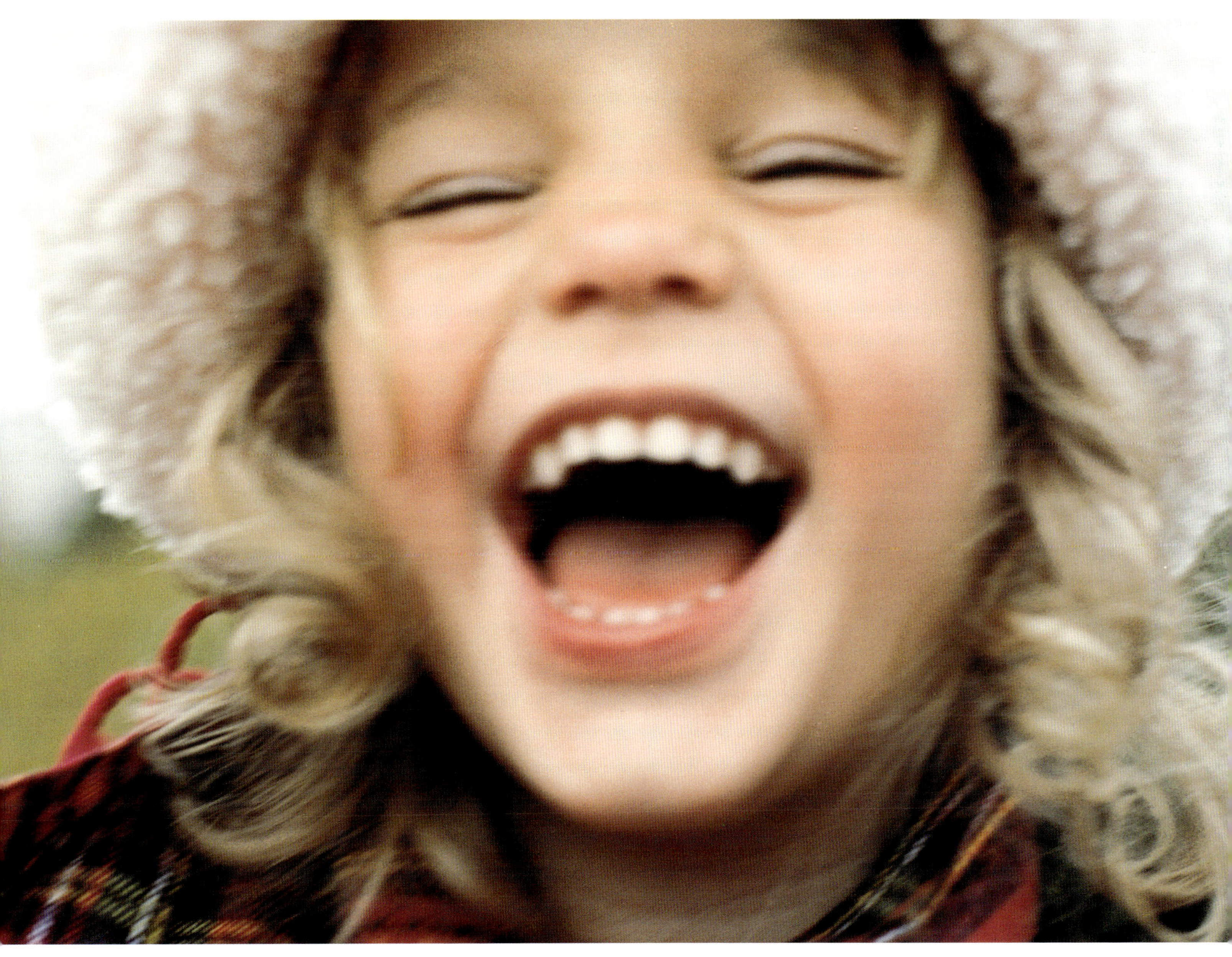

Fact file

Photographer: Brad Kim
Location: Downey, Los Angeles, USA
Time of day: 4.30pm, December

Technical details

Camera: Canon EOS 10D (digital)
Lens: 200mm
Film: n/a
Exposure: 1/250sec at f/4

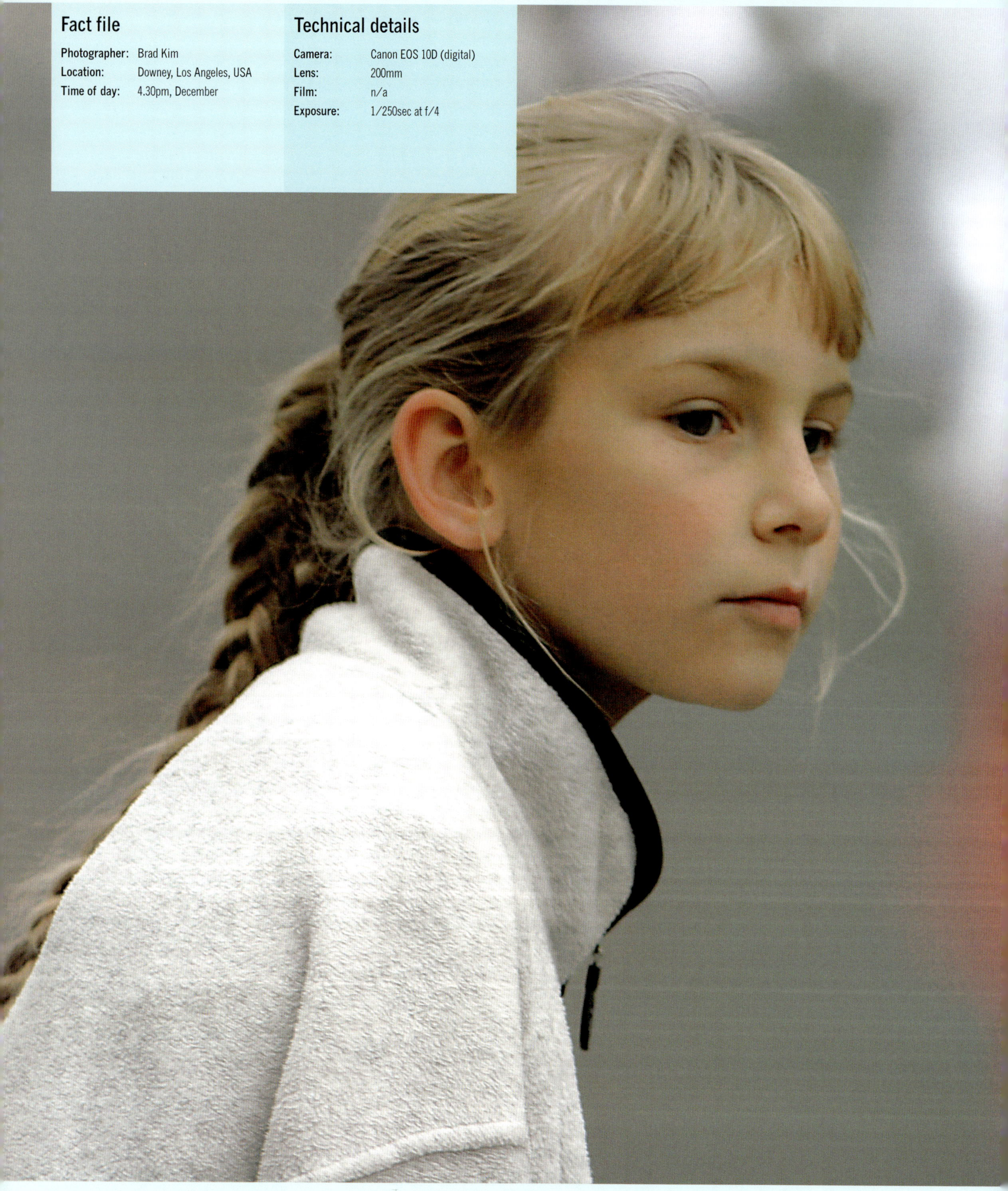

'This was the last frame I took of this subject and, the moment I released the shutter, I felt I had made the shot I wanted. It was the only one in which she was leaning forward.'

Brad Kim

The concept

'I learned from a local newspaper that there would be a Christmas parade in Downey and decided to go down there to take some photographs of people as a personal project,' recalls Brad.

The location

'In Southern California the winter weather is mild and you only see a white Christmas on cards. Nevertheless, many towns and cities start to hold Christmas parades as soon as December comes, to promote the festive mood and boost their retail businesses. Small town local parades usually provide better opportunities for photographers as there is easier access to the subjects you want and a friendlier atmosphere.'

Composition

Brad was on the look-out for close-ups of both people involved in the parade and spectators. This girl was watching what was going on, hence the look of quiet concentration on her face. 'The subject's youthful beauty attracted my attention and I took about six frames of her.' The patch of red at the edge of the frame is from the trousers of a parader who, even with a shallow depth of field was too recognisable and distracting. 'I used Photoshop to blur him into the background – part of the beauty and convenience of digital image processing,' comments Brad.

Lighting and technique

The soft light of an overcast day is perfect for the contemplative mood of this image. Brad set the camera exposure earlier in the day, using the ISO 400 setting on the camera which, with aperture priority of f/4, he guessed would give him a shutter speed of at least 1/1000sec to freeze any movement. 'According to the exposure data for this shot, it was taken at 1/250sec at f/4 so, with a 200mm lens, I was lucky to get this without camera shake,' says Brad. 'In late afternoon the light changes rapidly so I should have checked my exposure settings.'

'This shot was taken while I was leading a photo tour to Thailand and Burma,' explains Jim. 'It's one of my favourite portraits, showing a young Nepalese girl, living in Burma. She was extremely shy and very frail, but the beauty of her face captivated me. I wanted to capture her innocence and vulnerability. Through my interpreter, I asked her to move into the shade to avoid the harsh contrast of direct sun. A large tree with a huge canopy of greenery provided the indirect light. I prefer out-of-focus backgrounds for many of my outdoor portraits because all of the attention is then focused on the subject. I am always careful to avoid distracting shapes and bold lines behind the subject that will compete for attention. I used a hand-held incident meter to read the soft, diffused light falling on the young girl.'

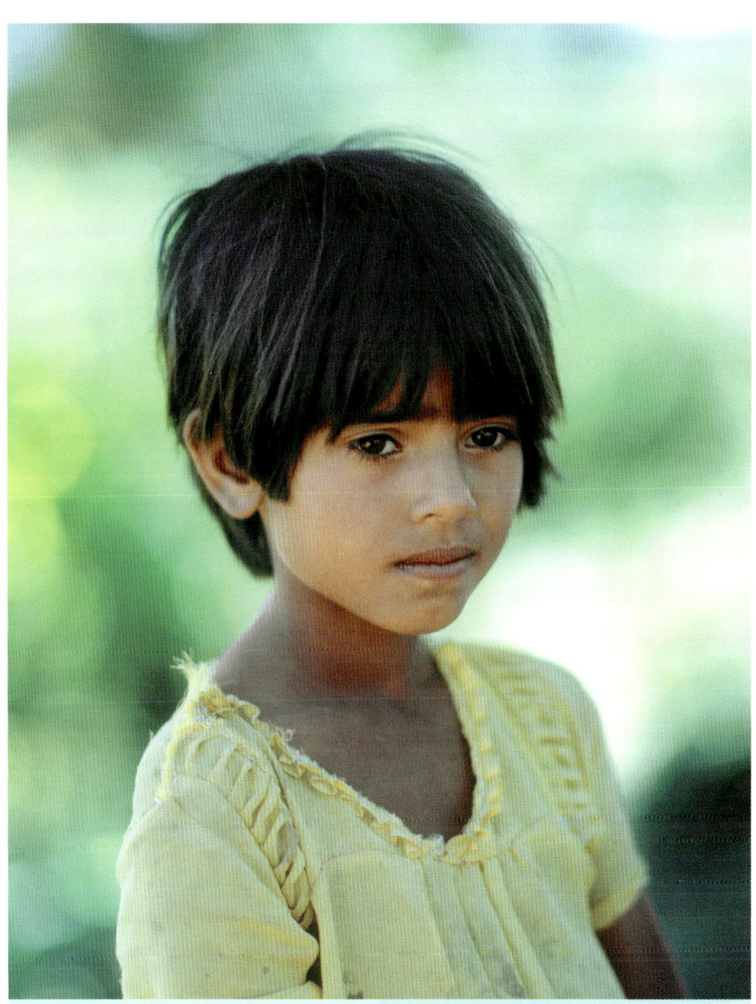

Fact file

Photographer:	Jim Zuckerman
Location:	Myanmar, Burma
Time of day:	Noon, February

Technical details

Camera:	Mamiya RZ 67 II
Lens:	250mm
Film:	Fujichrome Velvia
Exposure:	1/30 at f/4.5

Manuel Luís Cochofel

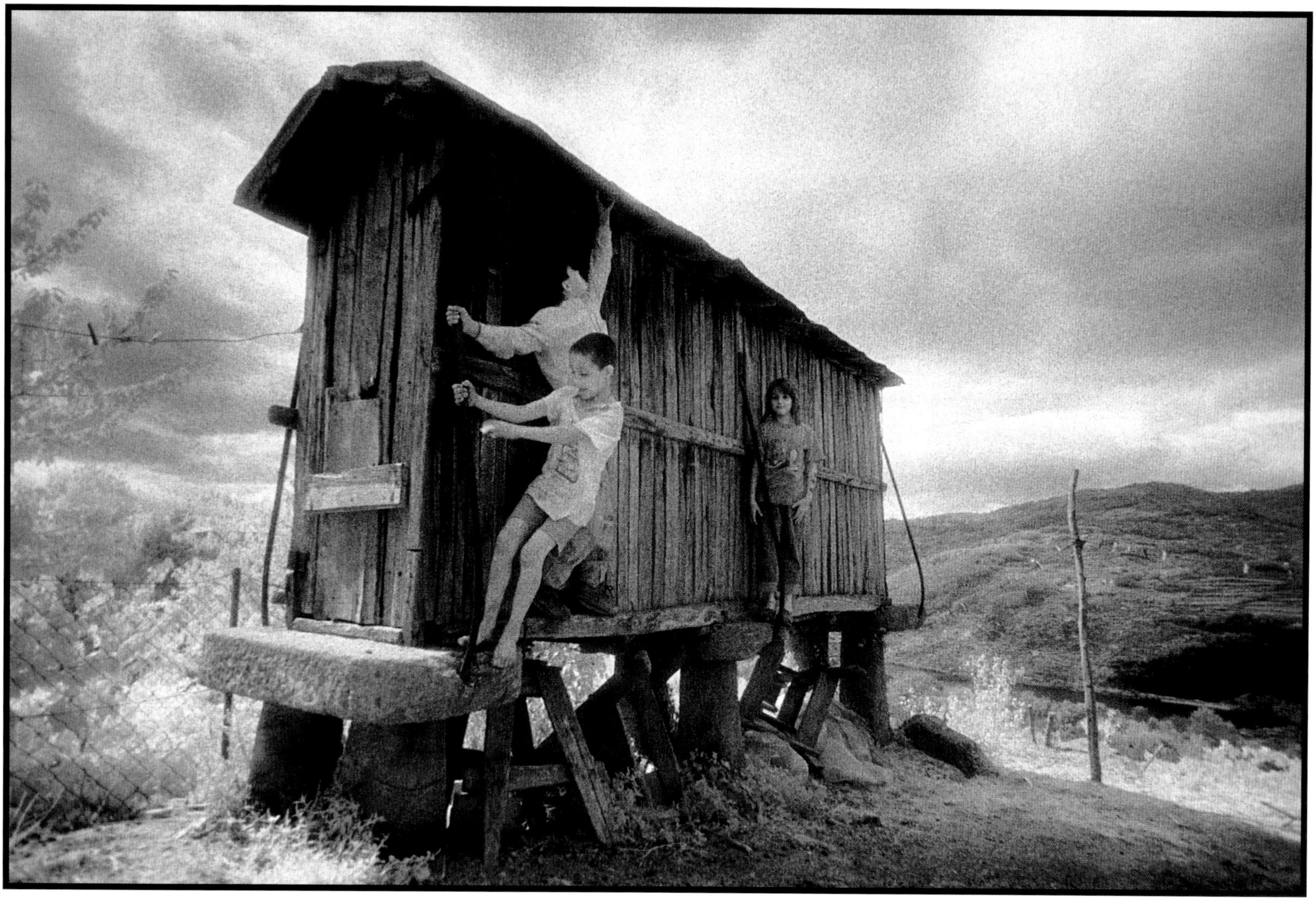

Chapter 2: **Setting**

It's easy to spend so much time concentrating on the subject of a portrait that little thought goes into the background. The danger of this approach is that distracting elements are mistakenly included and the whole effect is ruined. Another risk is that an opportunity to add strength and meaning to the image is wasted.

The setting of a portrait can be used to draw the viewer's eye into an image through perspective, line and contrast; it can help convey atmosphere and it can add details about a person's environment and way of life that will help the viewer's understanding of them. Think carefully about what you are trying to say through a portrait and, if you see your subject as part of a wider picture, compose carefully to achieve balance.

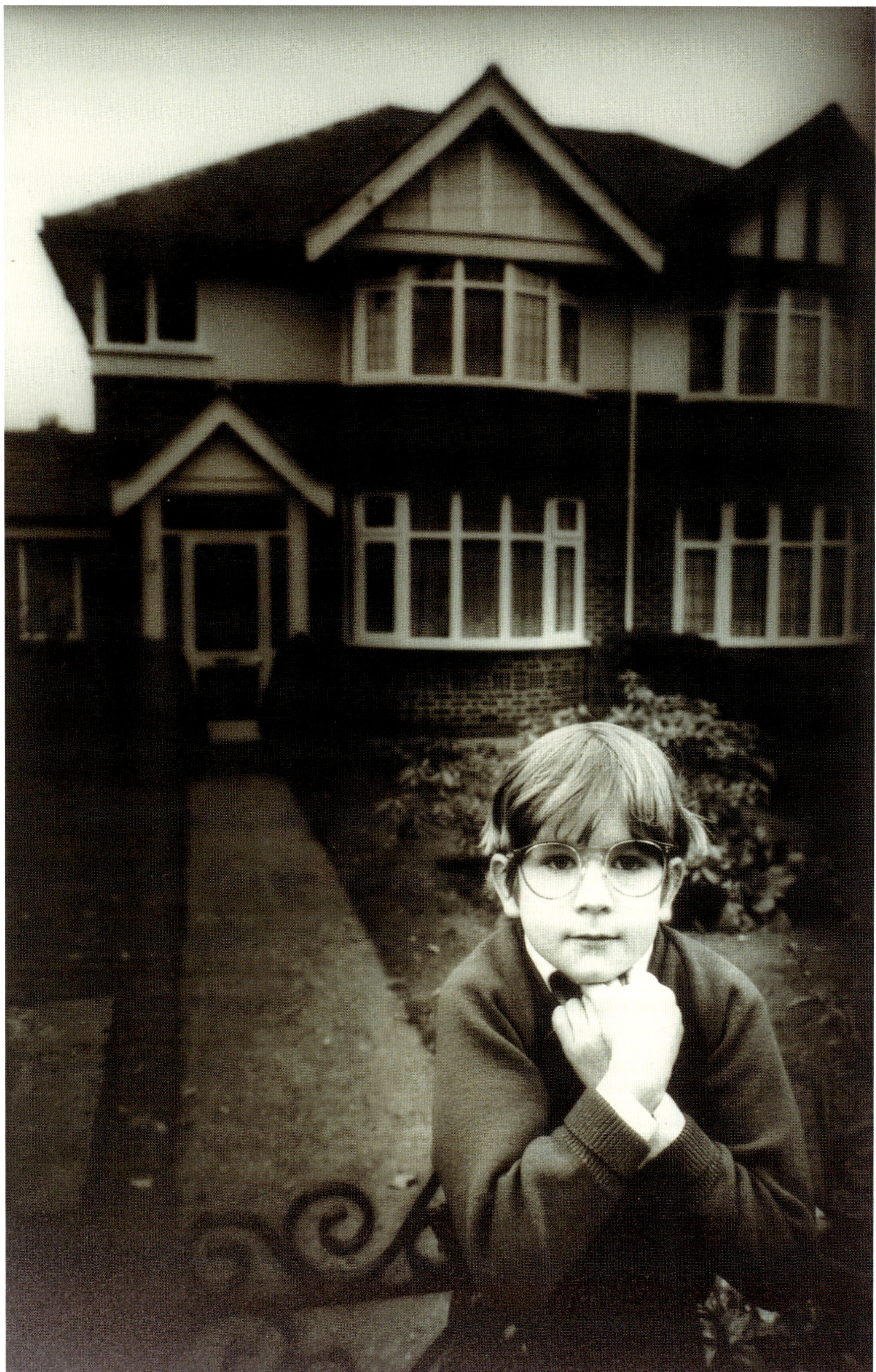

The concept

'This picture was an out-take from a commissioned shoot by the publisher, Headline, for the cover of a book about a schoolboy who was a bit of a loner and a fantasist,' explains Michael. The brief was very loose and it was up to him to think of a visual way of interpreting the story.

Fact file

Photographer: Michael Trevillion, Trevillion Picture Library
Location: Acton, London
Time of day: Mid-morning, October

Technical details

Camera: Olympus OM1
Lens: 50mm
Film: Kodak T-Max
Exposure: 1/125sec at f/11

The location

Michael wanted to show the boy – who was the art director's son – against a background of a suburban-looking house. He found this one by walking around some likely looking streets in West London, knocking on the door first to ask permission from the owner.

Composition

This house works perfectly for the picture because the straight path leads the eye into the image while the gate gives the idea of the boy confined to this setting, but with dreams of escape. 'We tried lots of variations on this shot, some with the boy running down the path, and the one that was used as the cover showed him sitting on a wall,' Michael explains. 'I often have a rough sketch in my mind of what I want to do but I rarely come back with that. New ideas come as you begin to shoot and you try things out. It's fairly instinctive really. I try not to think through it too much in case it spoils things!'

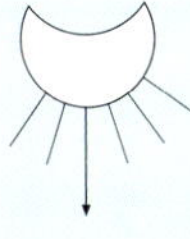

Overcast sky

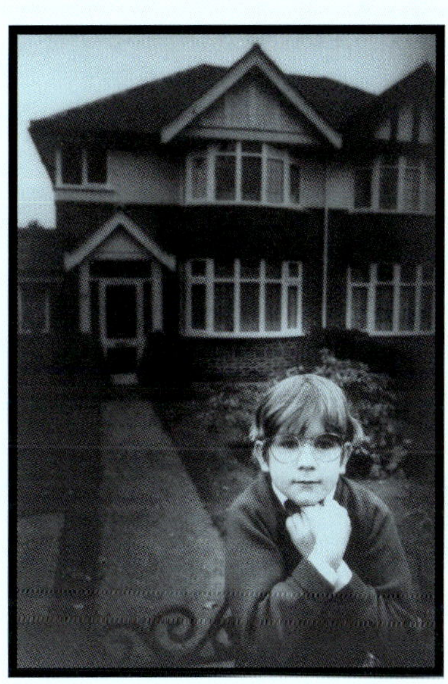

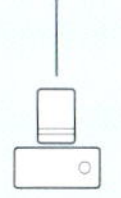

35mm camera

Lighting and technique

Michael chose a grey, overcast autumn morning for the shoot, the kind of light he prefers for portraits because of the lack of shadows. He trained as a printer before turning to photography and he did quite a lot of work in the darkroom to produce this final effect. 'The background was burned in and a little soft focus added and that has really made a difference to the way it would have looked as a straight print.'

'Everything I do in the darkroom could be done on Photoshop, but I enjoy playing in the darkroom with the radio on and the smell of chemicals. To me, it is a lot more pleasant than sitting in front of a computer screen.'

Michael Trevillion

> ‘As the screeching crows were concealed by the trees, they represented a hidden menace, which is what I tried to recreate in the image.’
>
> Paul Knight

The concept

This was a personal picture for Paul, who wanted to capture the feel of the location and mirror it in the personality of the model.

The location

‘In midwinter, partly as a result of the overhanging trees, the lane was consistently in twilight, giving the place an eerie feel,’ he explains. ‘However, what emphasised the overwhelming spirit of the location was the sound of crows screeching in the distance and so it was predominantly sounds that inspired the photograph.’

Composition

‘The picture almost composed itself,’ says Paul. ‘I used a wide-angle lens to give dynamics to the lane and, as I wanted a person in the shot, it naturally fitted that I shoot in portrait format. It became obvious that the model had to fill the lower half of the frame, leaving the top half to the strongest elements of the location.’

Lighting and technique

Paul took the picture during the brightest part of a particularly overcast day when the light was very flat. ‘I did this because I didn’t want any shadows, as I thought they would just add a confusing element to the image. Because there would not be very much contrast, I rated 400 ISO film at 200 ISO and used a red filter to boost it a little. I used a white board to reflect a little light back into the model’s face and handheld the camera about 15 centimetres above her head. Finally, as the light was even, I took a spot meter reading from her face, with the confidence that the film’s latitude could hold everything together.’

Fact file

Photographer: Paul Knight, Trevillion Picture Library
Location: Hertfordshire, England
Time of day: Midday, December

Technical details

Camera: Pentax ME
Lens: 24mm
Film: Ilford HP5 ISO 400
Exposure: 1/30sec at f/2.8

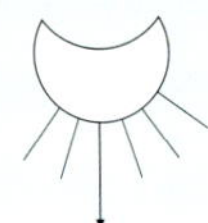

Sun behind clouds

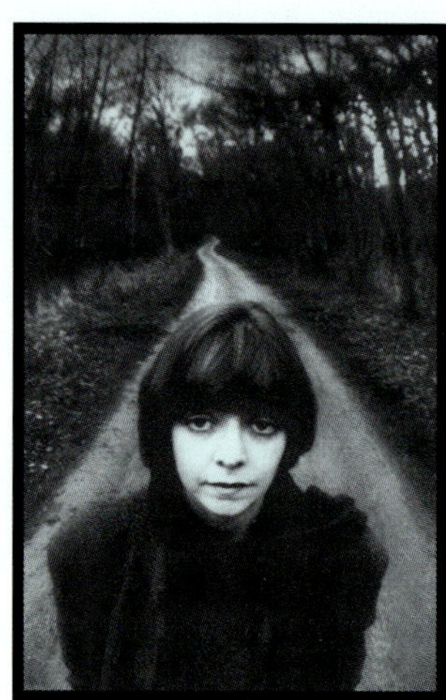

White reflector board

Medium format camera held above model’s head

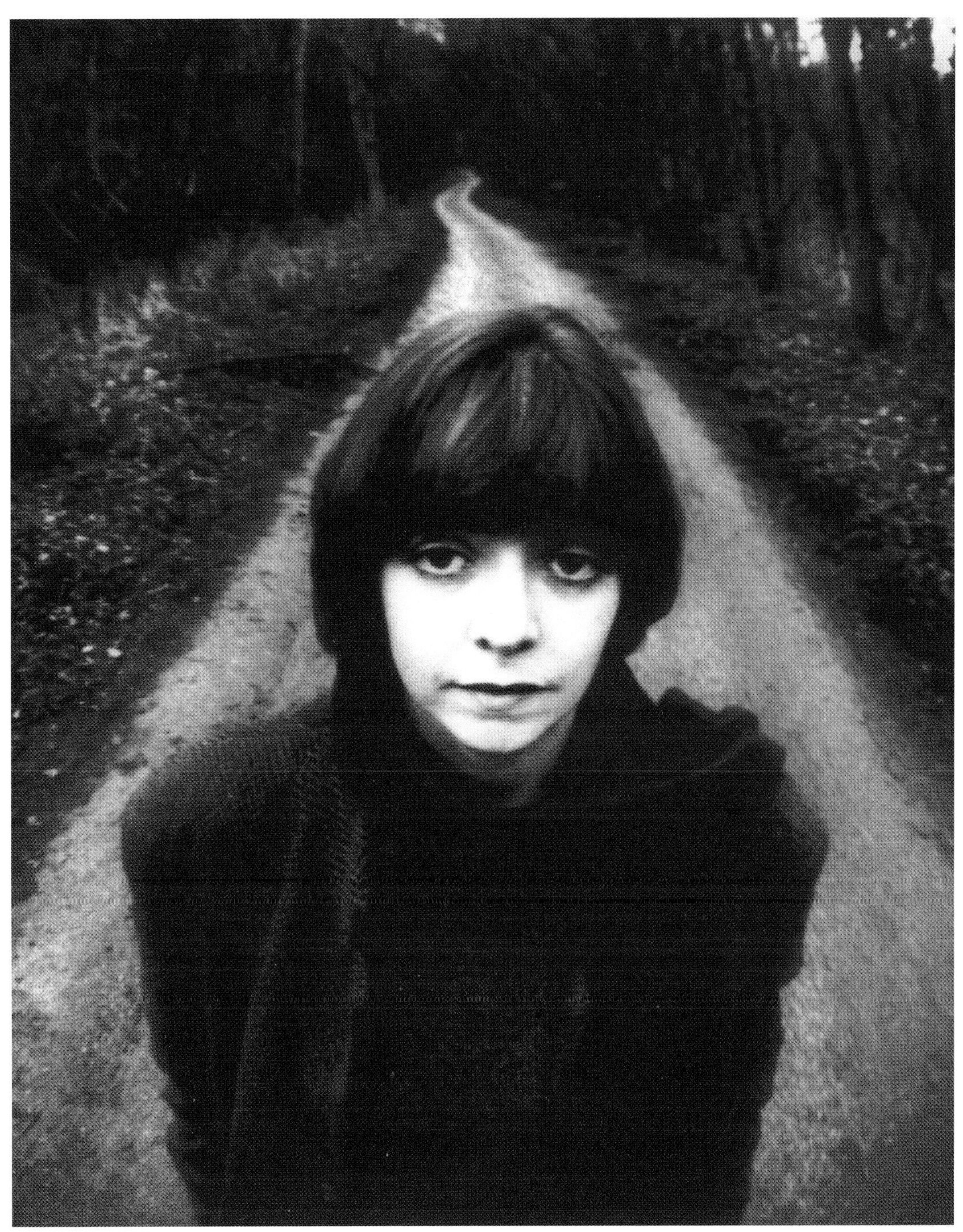

Fact file	
Photographer:	Michael Hall
Location:	Gore, Southland, New Zealand
Time of day:	Early morning, midwinter

Technical details	
Camera:	Nikon F4
Lens:	28mm
Film:	Kodak E100s
Exposure:	1/15sec at f/4

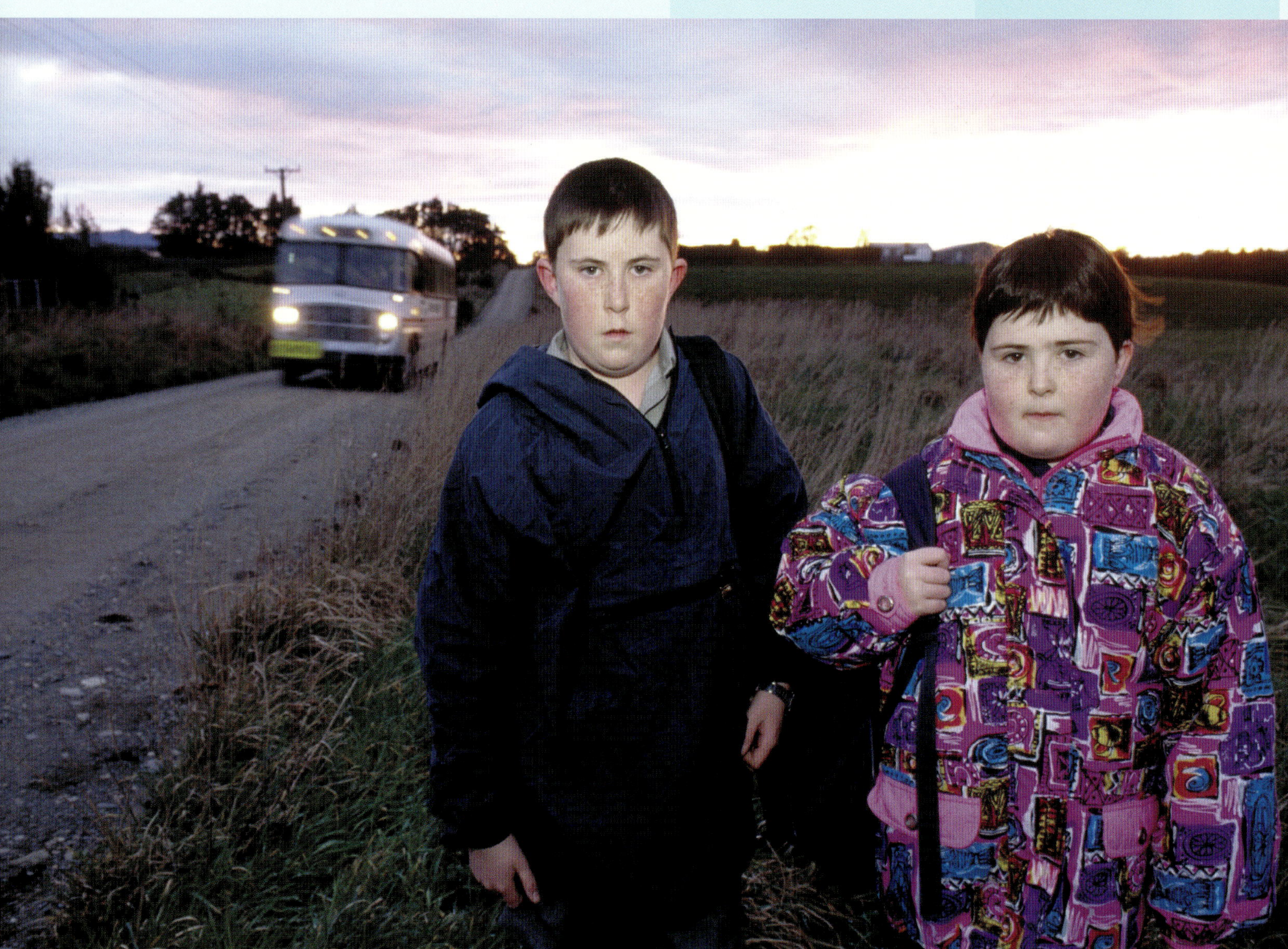

'I was flying by the seat of my pants that morning, trying to drive my own vehicle, shoot good pictures and keep one step ahead of the bus driver.'

Michael Hall

The concept

Michael was commissioned for this shot by The Public Trust, an organisation in New Zealand that handles wills, personal insurance and similar areas, for its annual report. 'That particular year they wanted to portray a small town/rural angle,' he recalls. 'I travelled to a place called Gore and in the afternoon managed to hitch a ride on the school bus. Early next morning I travelled the same route in my own vehicle in front of the bus, stopping when an image presented itself.'

The location

'The Public Trust is one of the oldest companies in the country and the reason, initially, for choosing Gore as the location, was that its oldest client lived there. I think she had just turned 102 and had been with the trust some 80 odd years. The other reason for going there was that it is a small town, with a population of 5000, and about as remote as you can get.'

Composition

Michael had this brother and sister in mind for the main subjects when he saw them on the bus the previous day. Their direct eye contact immediately engages the viewer and the picture also tells a story. They are clearly waiting for the bus, and in need of it in such an empty landscape at this early hour. The bus appears here in just the right part of the frame, with the road leading the viewer's eye up to it and beyond.

Lighting and technique

The timing of this shot was crucial, as the bus was on the move, and Michael had to work fast but stay cool to achieve it. 'I only had a loose arrangement with the driver to allow me to take pictures,' he says. 'He had a job to do also, and I figured he wouldn't be prepared to give up any time for me. As it was still early in the morning and the subjects were effectively backlit by the sunrise, I had no choice but to use on-camera flash. It's my least favourite way of lighting a portrait, but in this instance, I think it fits in with the mood of the image.'

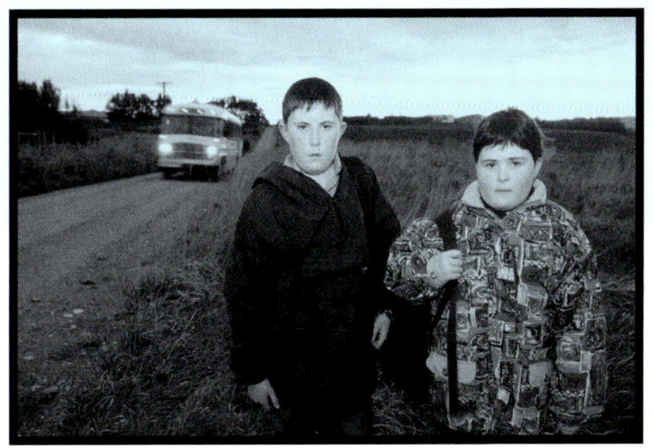

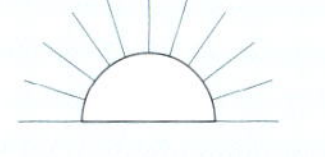

Sun below the horizon

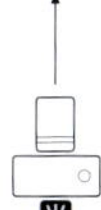

35mm camera with flash

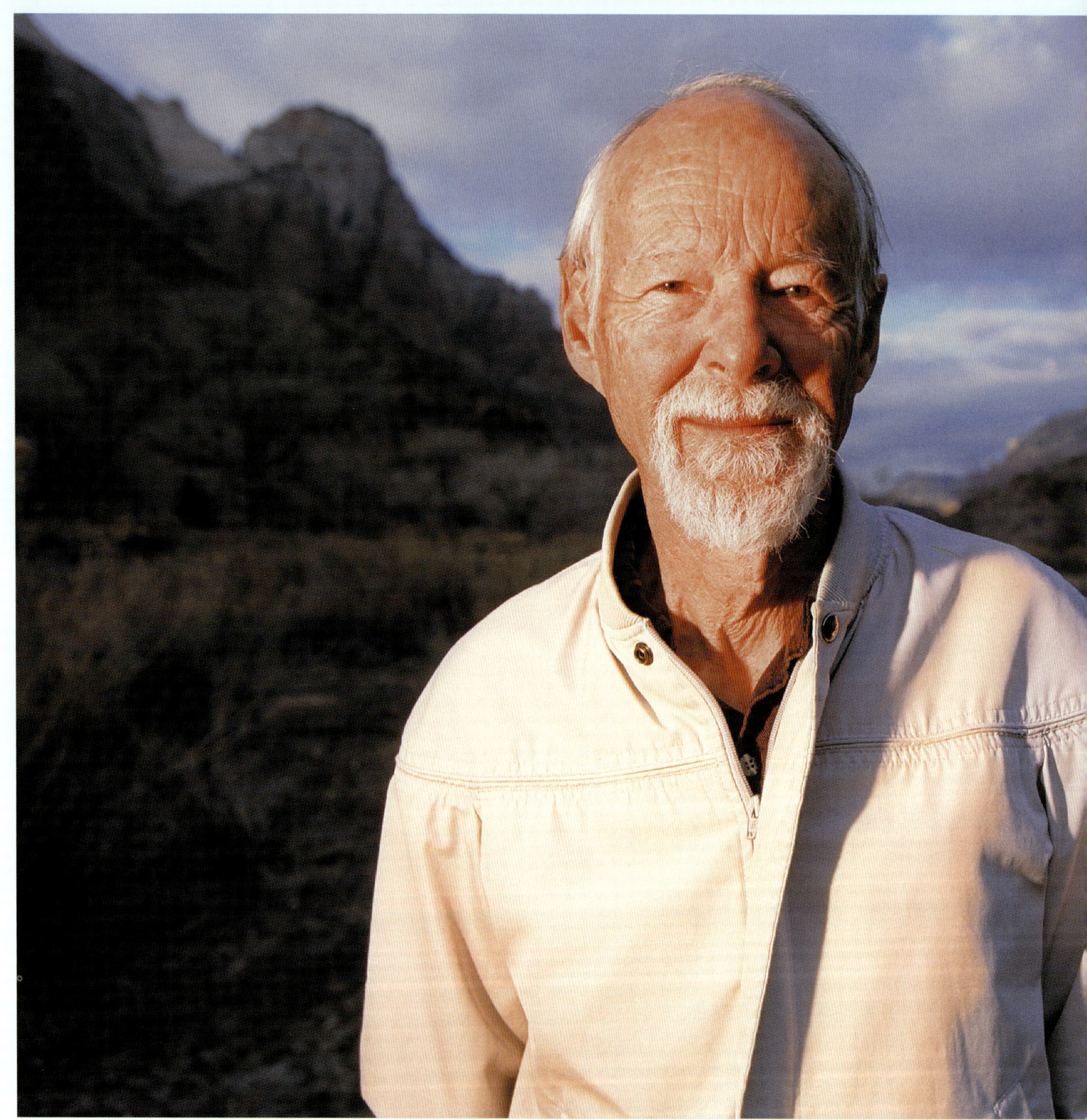

‘Portraiture offers a great opportunity to push the envelope, bend the rules and fiddle with technique to tell a person’s story. But photographers really need to connect with their subjects to pull it off.’

Lin Alder

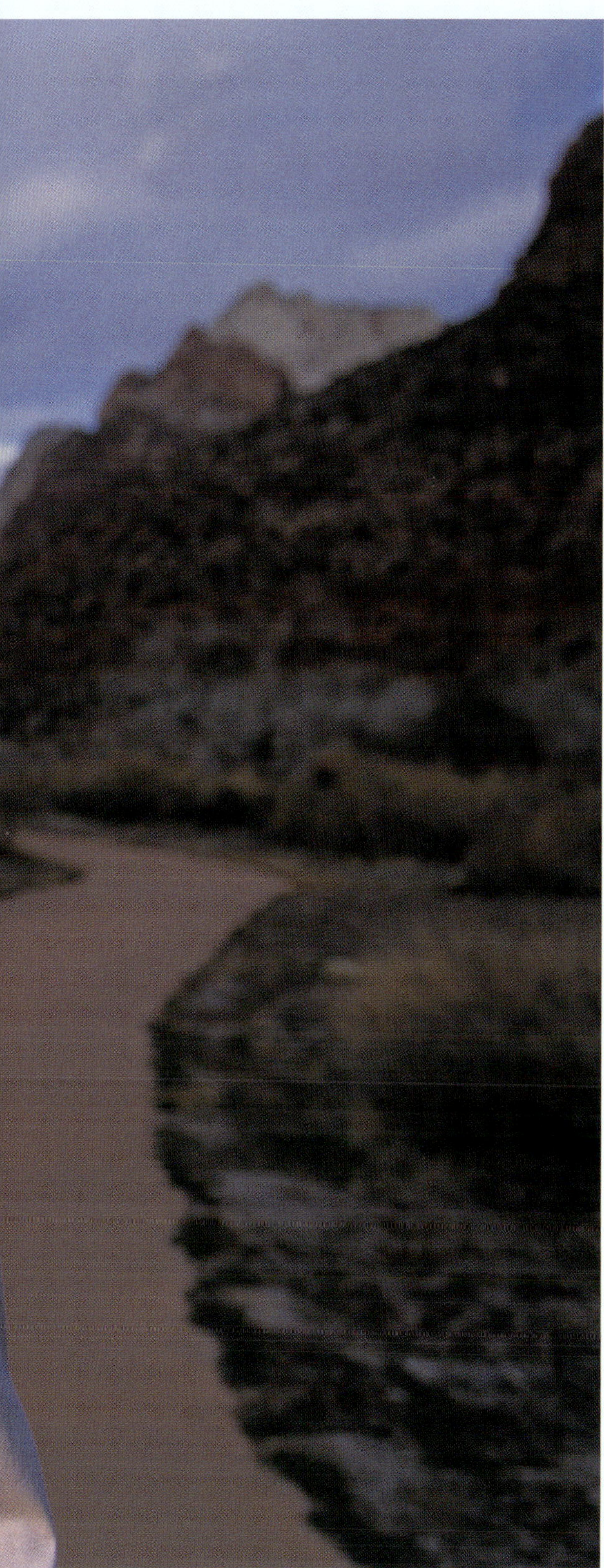

The concept

Lin was commissioned by a magazine to take this portrait. It was for a story about recreation in the southern Utah region and the subject, John Donnell, was profiled because of his spare-time interest in building trails for hiking, biking and other activities.

The location

The background shows the Pa' Rus trail in Zion National Park. It was near to the subject's home and a favourite spot of his. It also, fortunately provided a stunning background for a portrait.

Composition

Just because it's called 'portrait format' doesn't mean you have to turn the camera on its side to take pictures of individuals. There are many occasions when the 'landscape' format will produce a more interesting composition, especially when the background gives meaning and relevance to the portrait. That is often the case for travel shots or, as here, when the landscape is a part of the subject's everyday life. Lin placed him so that sky, rather than mountains framed his head and the winding trail leads the viewer's eye into the photograph.

Lighting and technique

Lin planned the shoot for late afternoon because he wanted to use flash to make the subject stand out against fairly low natural light. On the day, the sky was overcast with dark clouds – an added bonus to give the shot more drama. Balancing the flash – a Nikon SB80DX used off-camera with a cord – with daylight requires some care and Lin took several bracketed exposures to ensure a good result. 'I used the Nikon matrix meter to establish the overall exposure and then underexposed by 1/3 of a stop,' he explains. 'I then took a series of exposures, bracketing for both the background and the flash in 1/3 of a stop increments over- and underexposed.'

Fact file

Photographer: Lin Alder
Location: Zion National Park, Utah, USA
Time of day: 5.45pm, October

Technical details

Camera: Nikon F100
Lens: 17–35mm
Film: Fuji Velvia
Exposure: 1/60sec at f/5.6

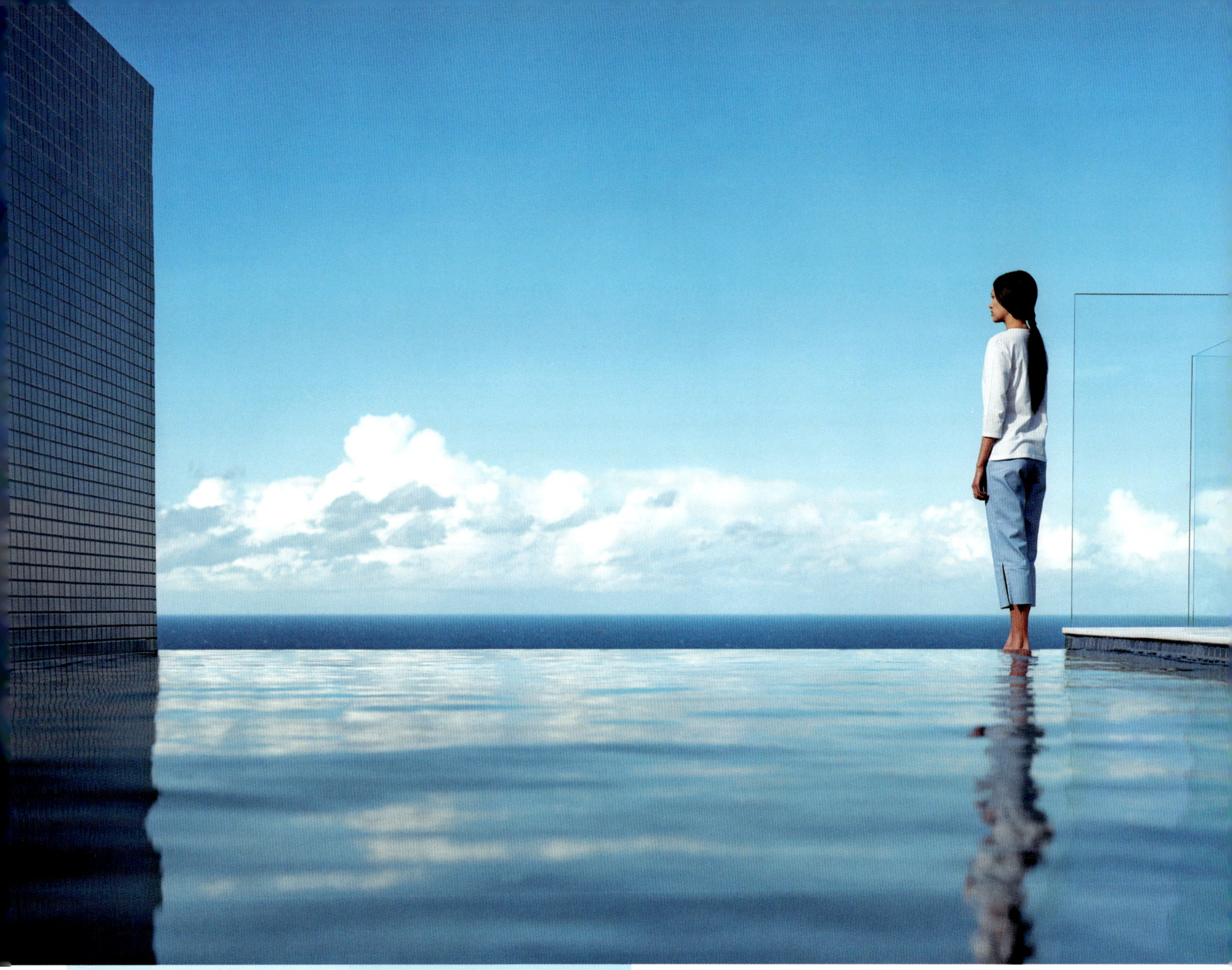

Fact file

Photographer: Michael Hall
Location: Dover Heights, Sydney, Australia
Time of day: Midday, late summer

Technical details

Camera: Wista zone 1v 4x5 field camera
Lens: 210mm
Film: Kodak 160VC
Exposure: 1/250sec at f/11

'The pool at the time of shooting was 13° Celsius. Even with a thick wet suit I was shivering by the end of the shoot.'

Michael Hall

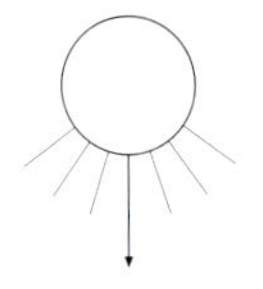

Sun

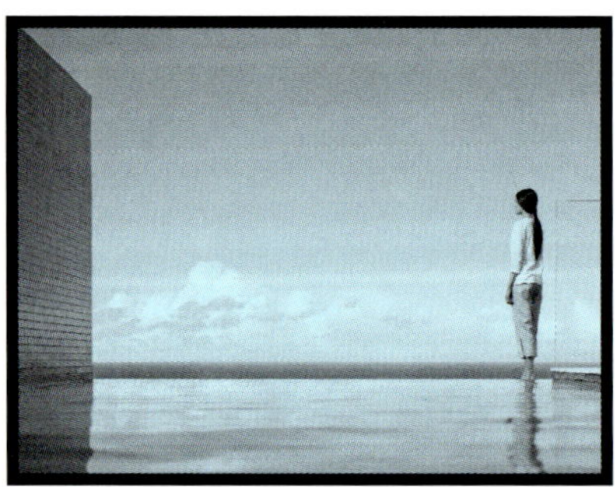

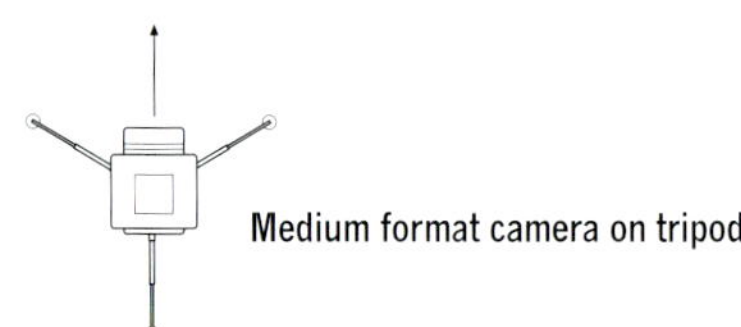

Medium format camera on tripod

The concept

This image was taken as part of a marketing campaign for one of the major digital camera manufacturers. The campaign required images that had a simple and pure atmosphere. The shot was taken using only available light, at midday, when the sun was at its highest point in the sky.

The location

'We chose this location for the clean, uninterrupted lines,' explains Michael. 'We needed a place that looked special and elegant, and the blue sky and water fitted the brief perfectly.'

Composition

Paring a composition down to just a few elements accentuates a feeling of space, especially when two of them are sky and water. The stillness of the water has resulted in mirror-like reflections, which also have the effect of expanding the space. The position of the model and the horizon line follows the rule of thirds, resulting in a balanced and harmonious composition.

Lighting and technique

'Because it was for a camera manufacturer the image had to have absolute clarity, so I took it on 4x5 sheet film,' explains Michael. 'I needed a low camera angle and ended up erecting the tripod in the middle of the swimming pool, which was as deep as the height of my shoulders. One can imagine the technical difficulty of erecting a carbon-fibre tripod and keeping it sand-bagged in place, mounting a field camera, focusing, pulling Polaroids and exposing film, all without causing ripples on the water. The base of the camera was literally a few centimetres above the surface of the water.' The shot was taken using only available light, at midday, when the sun was at its highest point in the sky.

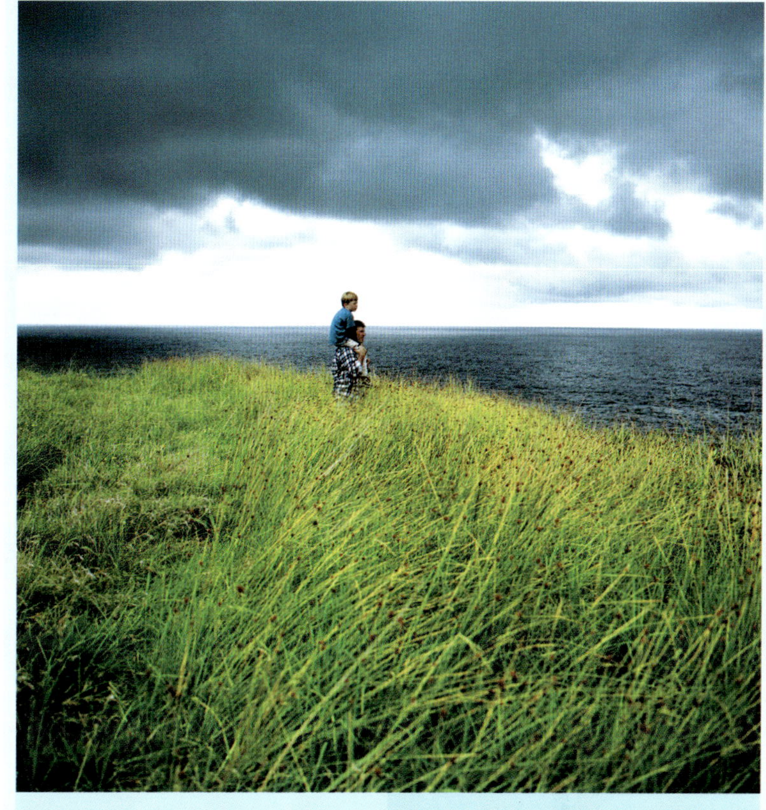

Fact file

Photographer: Michael Hall
Location: NSW, Australia
Time of day: Mid-afternoon, winter

Technical details

Camera: Hasselblad 503SW
Lens: 50mm
Film: Kodak 160 VC
Exposure: 1/30sec at f/5.6

There's no rule that says portraits have to be close up. These two figures occupy just a tiny proportion of the frame and yet the image is full of atmosphere and a sense of freedom and naturalness. Michael describes how it came about: 'Samuel is my nine-year-old son and Dave is paid talent. We shot this as part of a series of images for a bank brochure. Having travelled four-and-a-half hours south of Sydney the previous evening, we spent an ever increasingly gloomy day in Kangaroo valley looking for rural images. By mid-afternoon it was pouring with rain, so I pulled the plug and suggested we head for the coast. With no real objective in mind we came across this bluff looking out to the Pacific Ocean. It was stormy and electric and very changeable. By the time we parked the car and composed the shot, the magic of the light held for only a minute before turning dull and flat.'

'If you like flat, empty, deserted land, the island of Sal is the place to be.'

Rene de Haan

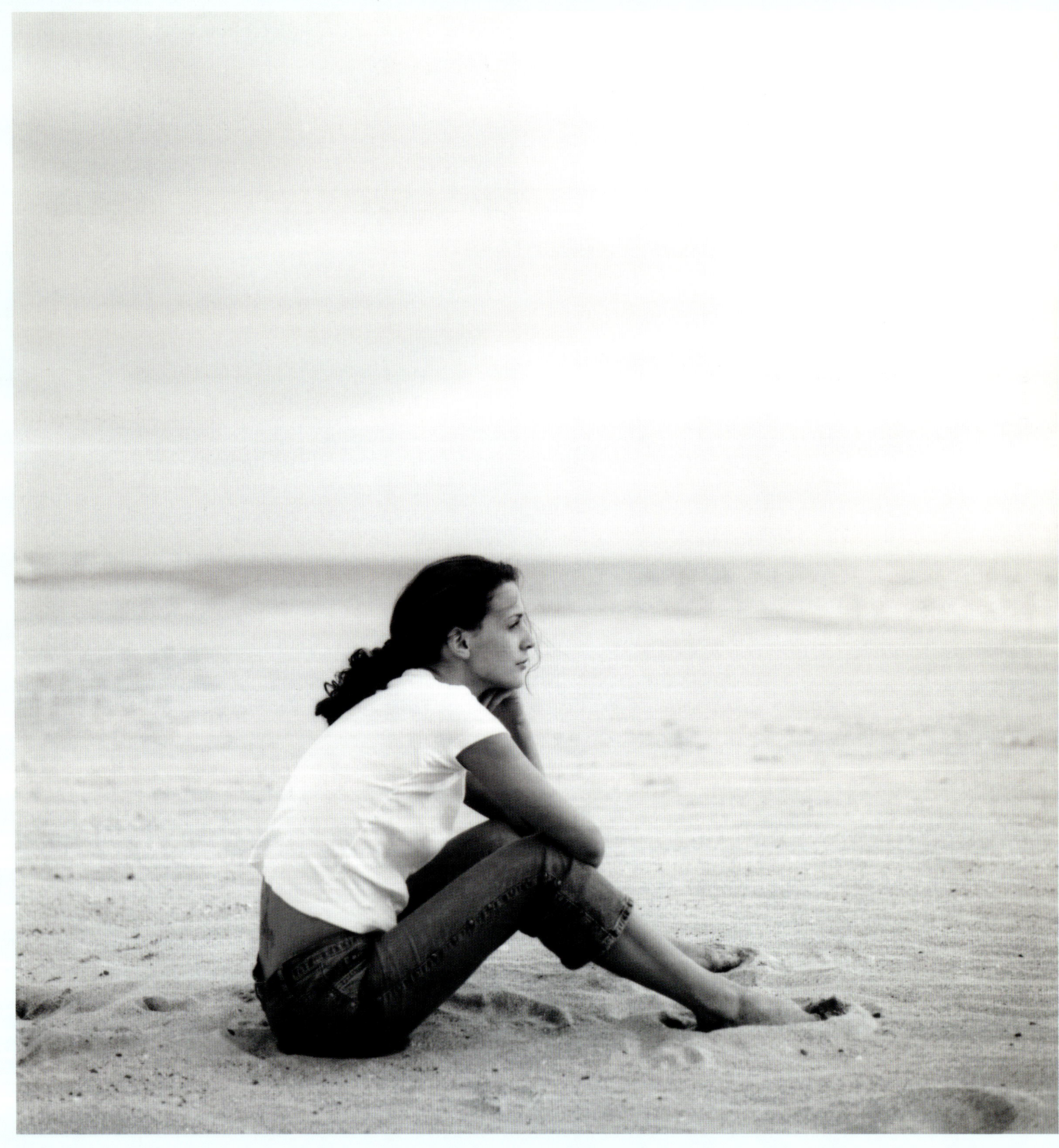

The concept

Rene went to the island with two models to do a series of nude images, but found the early morning and early evening light that he often finds most beneficial for photography turned out to be disappointing. 'It was usually cloudy until around 10am, then the sun would come out, only to disappear again at 5pm,' he recalls. 'This picture just happened by chance. On the first morning after arrival, Bianca and I went to the beach to check it out. She just sat in the sand, looking out to the sea. I liked the image, so took the picture.'

Fact file		Technical details	
Photographer:	Rene de Haan	**Camera:**	Hasselblad 500CM
Location:	Sal island, Cape Verde Islands	**Lens:**	80mm
Time of day:	9.30am, May	**Film:**	Ilford Pan-f
		Exposure:	1/250sec at f/4

The location

'There are not very many promising locations on Sal. It's very flat, pretty empty, barren land,' says Rene. 'I did not really know that beforehand. We went on a last-minute holiday trip and the Cape Verde Islands sounded really nice. Although the island was limited, I did make some really nice shots there, happily.'

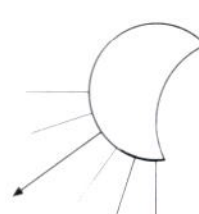

Sun behind dense cloud

Composition

In some ways, this image breaks some of the usual rules of composition. The horizon is almost dead centre in the frame, with the model's head nudging it from the bottom half of the image. Nevertheless, it works very well with the square format of the Hasselblad camera. The relatively small size of the model against a backdrop of wide sky and featureless beach gives the impression that she is alone in a vast empty space. In fact, the beach was not nearly as big as it looks, but the choice of lens and camera viewpoint can mislead the viewer to good effect.

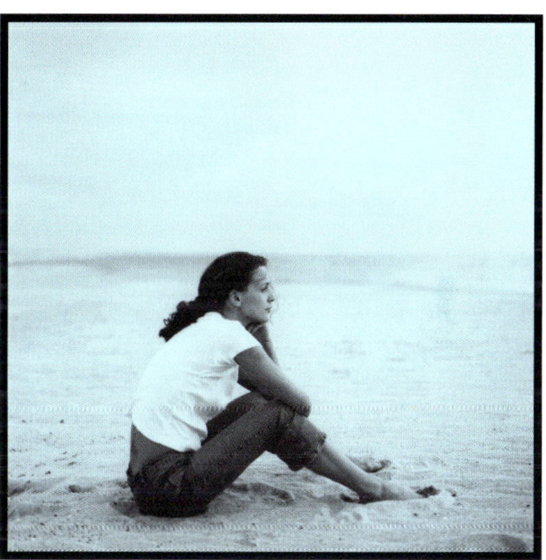

Lighting and technique

Because the sky was completely overcast, Rene didn't have to worry about the strength or direction of the sun. He took a meter reading from the model, as she was sitting, and her dark hair and jeans helped to counterbalance the overall light tones of the image, which could otherwise have fooled the meter into underexposing.

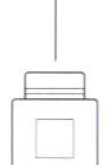

Medium format camera

‘For me photography is above all about capturing characters. If the subject is interesting, then the shot will be interesting.’

Matt Hoyle

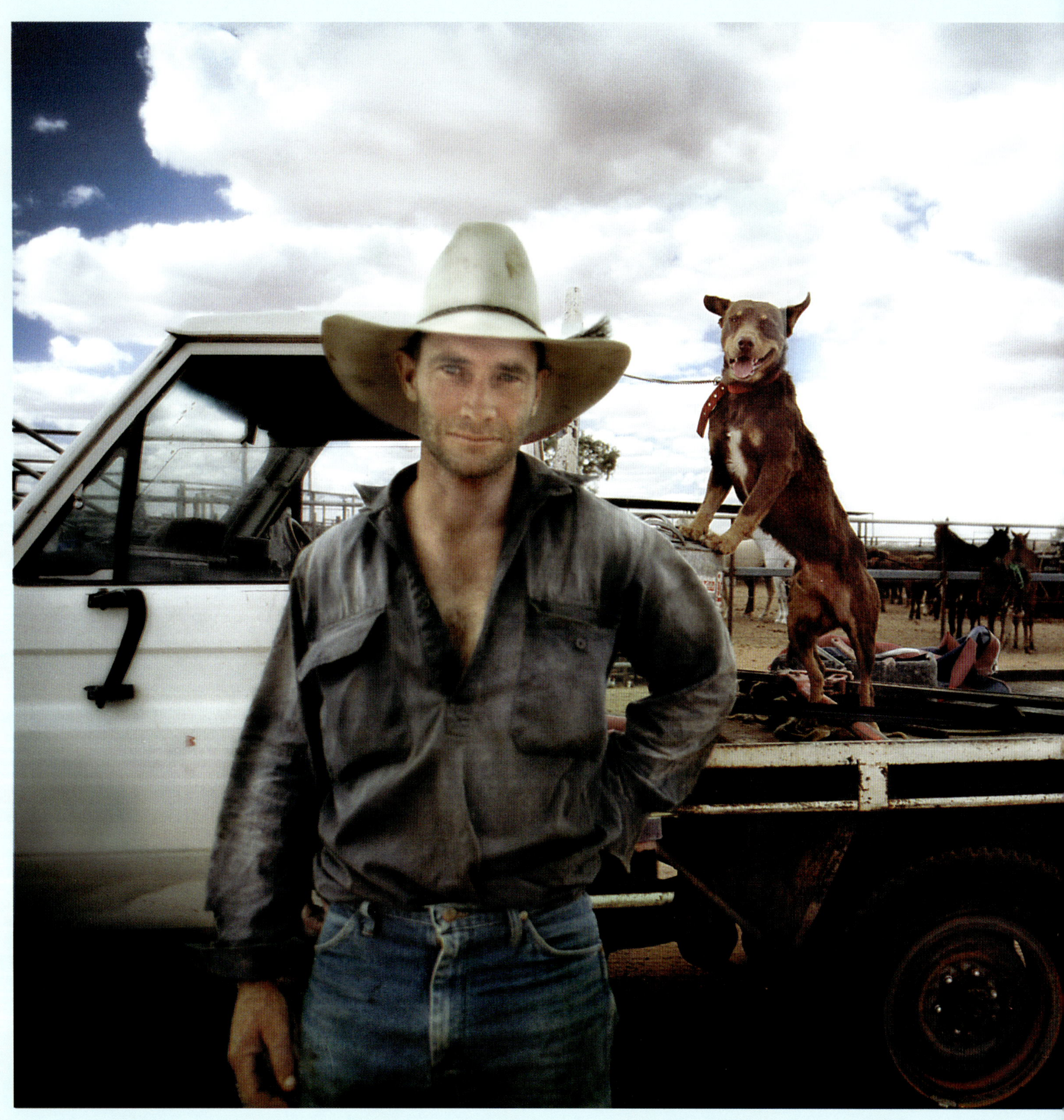

Fact file

Photographer: Matt Hoyle
Location: Windorah, Queensland, Australia
Time of day: Late afternoon, March

Technical details

Camera: Nikon F90
Lens: 35mm
Film: Fuji Velvia
Exposure: f/4 (aperture priority)

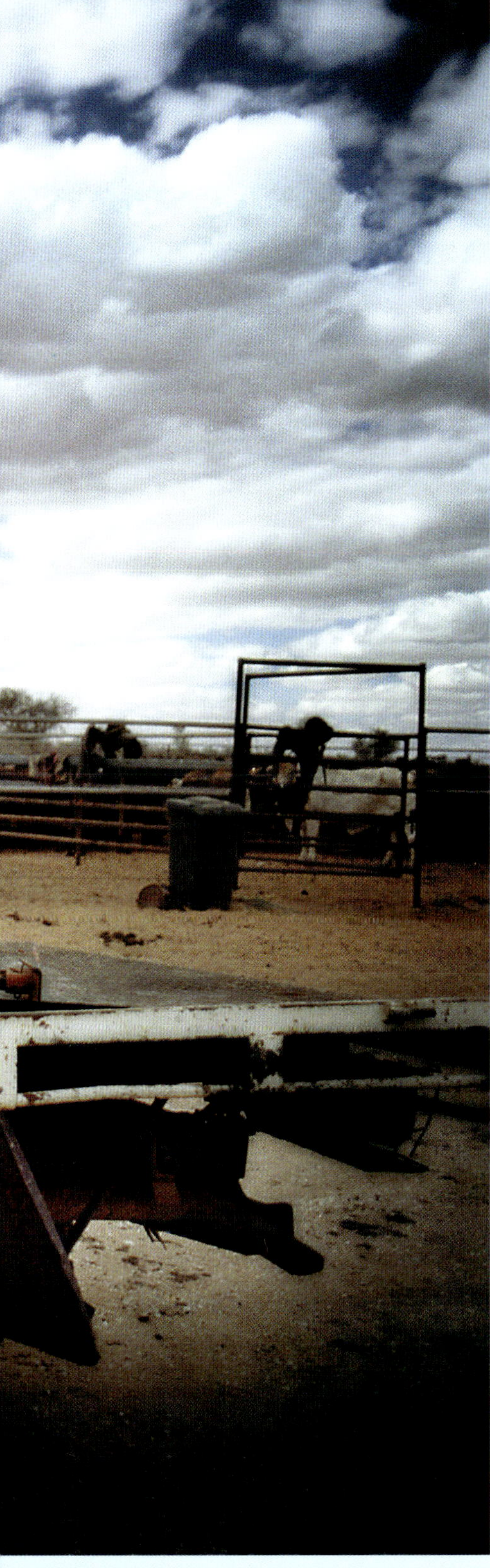

The concept

This was part of a self-commissioned series that Matt undertook, recording the lives of various people who live and work in the Australian outback. 'This man was the son of a cattle station owner and he himself had a son, so there were three generations of cowcockies – Australian cowboys – on the property. They used a helicopter and motorcycles to round up their stock.'

The location

'I went to the outback in south western Queensland to capture the unique saturated colours, the distinctive red earth and the gritty characters,' explains Matt.

Composition

Matt had spent the whole day with the cowcockies, beginning before sunrise to watch and photograph the herding. For this portrait, he wanted to show the character of the man, but in the context of the place where he lived and worked. The cattle in the background, the truck and the dog all help to tell the story. 'The dog is a blue heeler cattle dog and was very obedient, as is the nature of the breed. All the guy had to do was whistle for it to stand up like this,' he recalls.

Lighting and technique

'For the outback series, I preferred to shoot in the afternoon, when the sun painted the background red, but the colours were not over-saturated. Here the sun was behind some cloud, which softened the light. There was no flash or additional equipment used.'

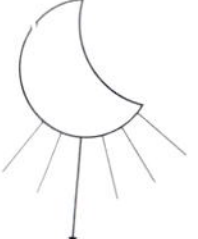

Low sun behind some cloud

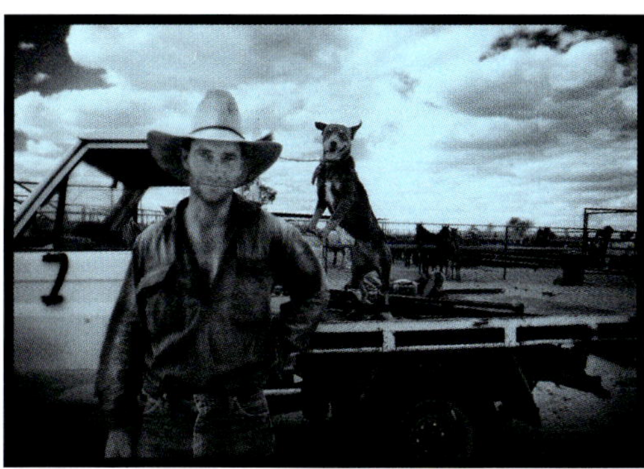

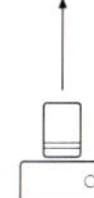

35mm camera

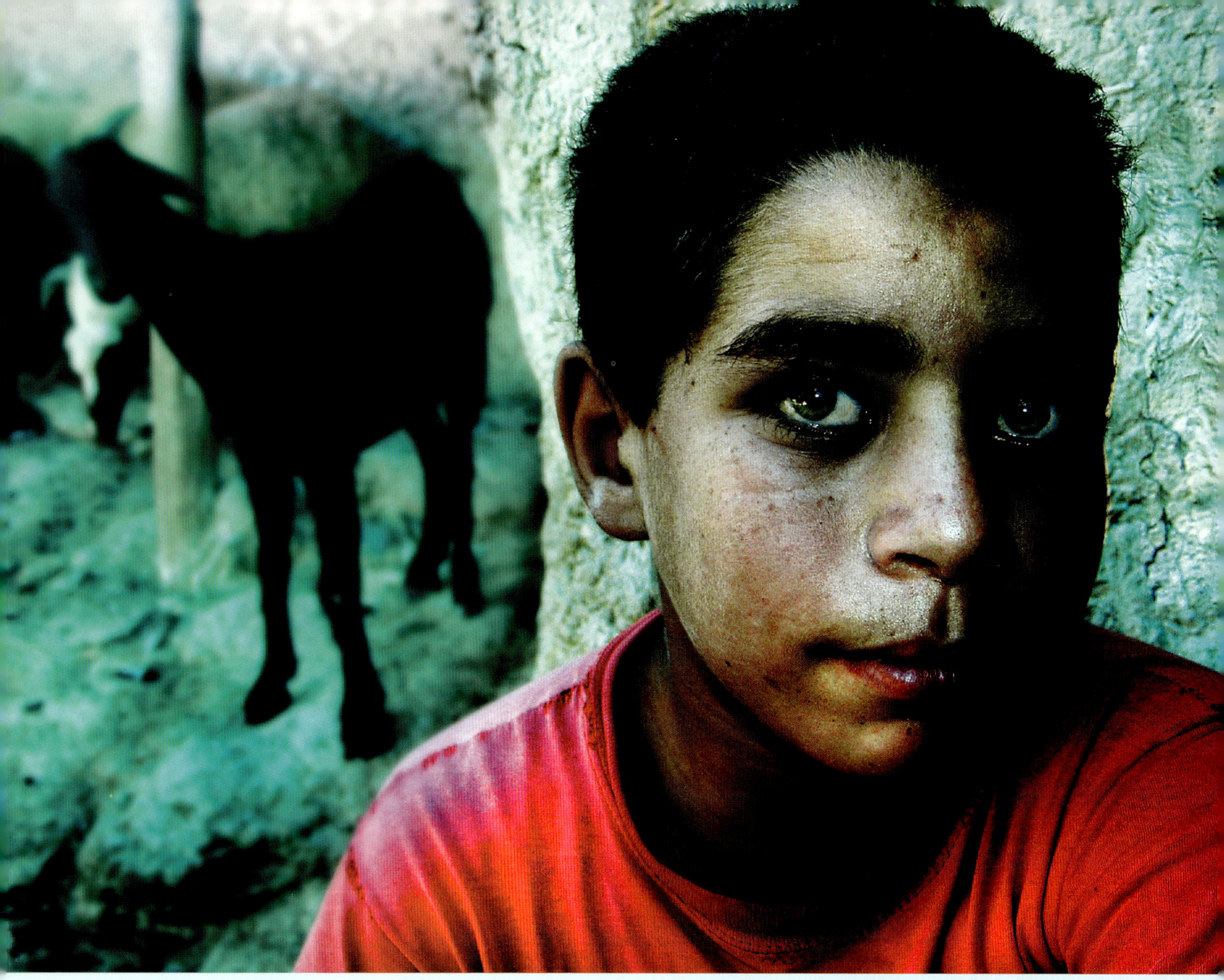

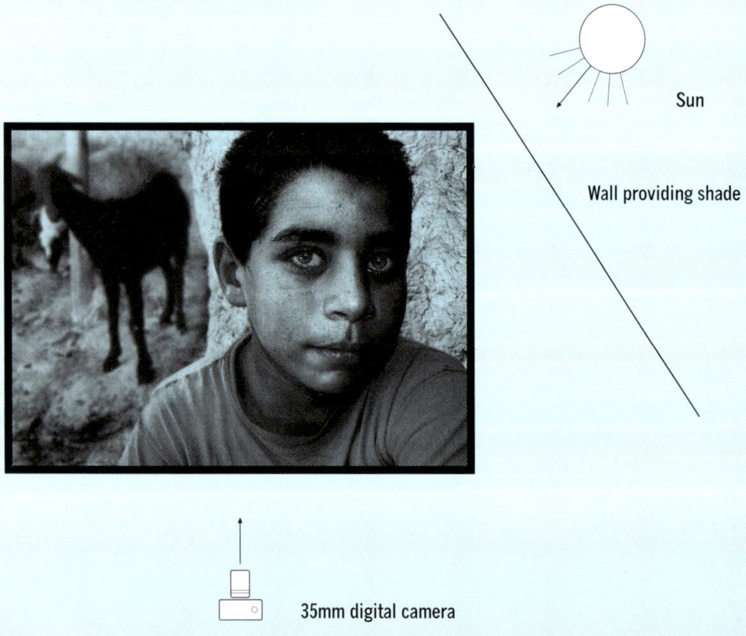

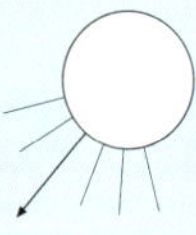

Wall providing shade

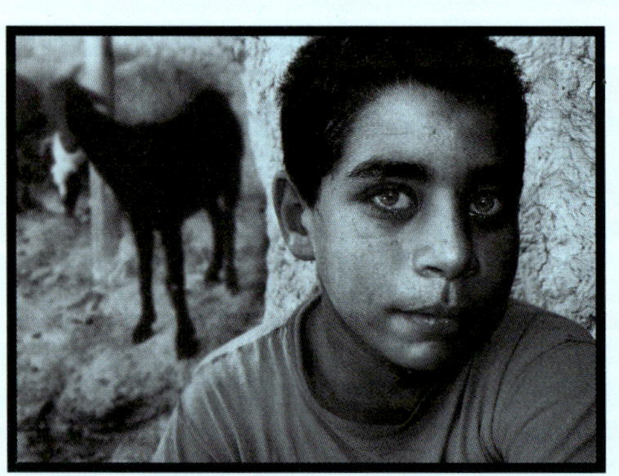

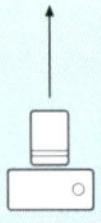

'When I saw Omar for the first time, I immediately noticed his bright green eyes and I really wanted to take some portraits of him.'

Nour Eddine El Ghoumari

Fact file

Photographer: Nour Eddine El Ghoumari
Location: Taza, Morocco
Time of day: 3pm, August

Technical details

Camera: Olympus E20 (digital)
Lens: 9–36mm
Film: n/a
Exposure: 1/60sec at f/3.2

The concept

This portrait of a young goatherd called Omar was taken while Nour Eddine was in Morocco visiting family. He had a digital camera with him and, when he came across this boy with his herd of goats, he asked him to pose for some pictures.

The location

The picture was taken on the outskirts of an ancient town in a rural part of north-east Morocco. Nour Eddine moved the boy nearer the wall, which provided shade against the bright sun.

Composition

Since the boy's eyes are so striking, Nour Eddine wanted him looking directly at the camera and he was also careful to compose the shot so the eyes were positioned according to the rule of thirds. Not only does this make for a pleasing and harmonious composition, but it also leaves space to the side of the subject to include details of the setting. In this case, the goat in the background reveals an important part of the boy's life.

Lighting and technique

Nour Eddine wanted to take his pictures quickly to allow the boy to get on with his job, so he used his camera on automatic. Fill-in flash brightened up the face as they were in the shadow of the wall. Looking at the picture a few months later, he felt this image could be improved and so he made some adjustments with Photoshop. The goat had stood out rather too sharply, distracting attention from the boy, so Nour Eddine created a layer and used the gaussian blur filter, then added a layer mask to recover the sharp face and T-shirt from under the blurred image. The boy's green eyes were saturated further with the sponge tool, and the background given a complementary green tone.

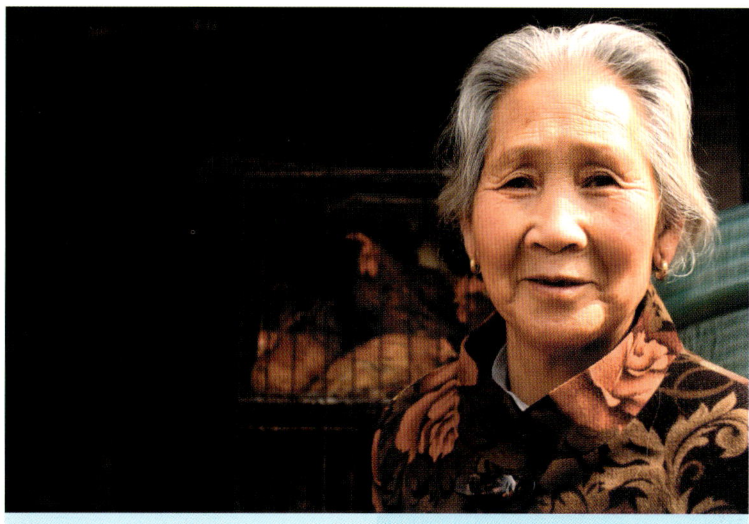

Fact file

Photographer: Jean Schweitzer
Location: Lanzhou, Gansu Province, China
Time of day: 3pm, March

Technical details

Camera: Canon 300D (digital)
Lens: 18–50mm
Film: n/a
Exposure: 1/250sec at f/4

While travelling in China, Jean was fascinated by a colourful market and tried to capture the atmosphere in a series of photographs. Here he wanted an environmental portrait of the smartly dressed old lady. 'I was especially keen to make the chickens visible in the background as they were surprising to see at a time when there were a lot of problems with chicken-related disease in Asia,' he says.

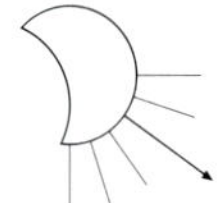

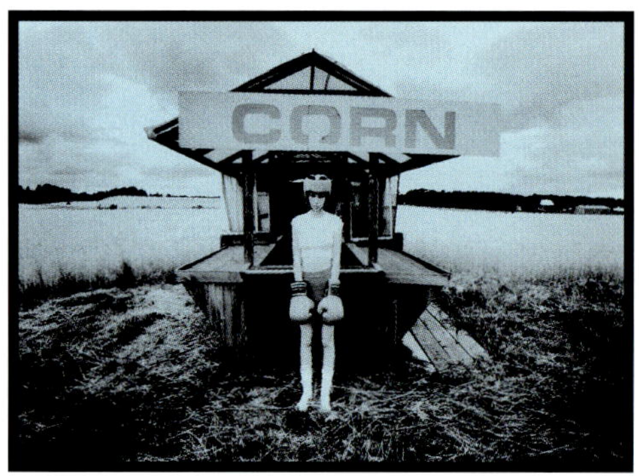

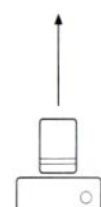

Fact file

Photographer: Jim Allen
Location: Markham, Ontario, Canada
Time of day: 11am, October

Technical details

Camera: Nikon F90
Lens: 28mm
Film: Kodak Tri-X ISO 200 (rated at 100)
Exposure: Not recorded

The concept

'This was personal work, which I always try my best to make surreal, or even a little bit comical,' says Jim.

The location

Jim was familiar with this quirky setting – an abandoned corn stall in a wild and unspoilt landscape – and had it in mind to use when the right opportunity came up.

Composition

Photography doesn't always have to be a serious business. Sometimes dramatic impact can be gained by placing a subject in entirely incongruous surroundings. The viewer can try to understand a link between the two, but in this case would be off the mark, as there was never intended to be one. The strangeness of this shot comes from placing the waif-like model, surprisingly wearing boxing gear, in front of an equally puzzling corn stall, apparently in the middle of nowhere.

Lighting and technique

As the light was overcast and the light very flat, I rated the film at ISO 100 and boosted the development to achieve contrast,' explains Jim. 'Using a red filter on the lens helped with that process. Surprisingly you achieve a negative with a long range of tones, which enables you to move the print up to a higher paper grade in order to achieve contrast while maintaining tonality.'

'What is this female boxer doing here? How silly can you get, I guess! Nice clouds...'

Jim Allen

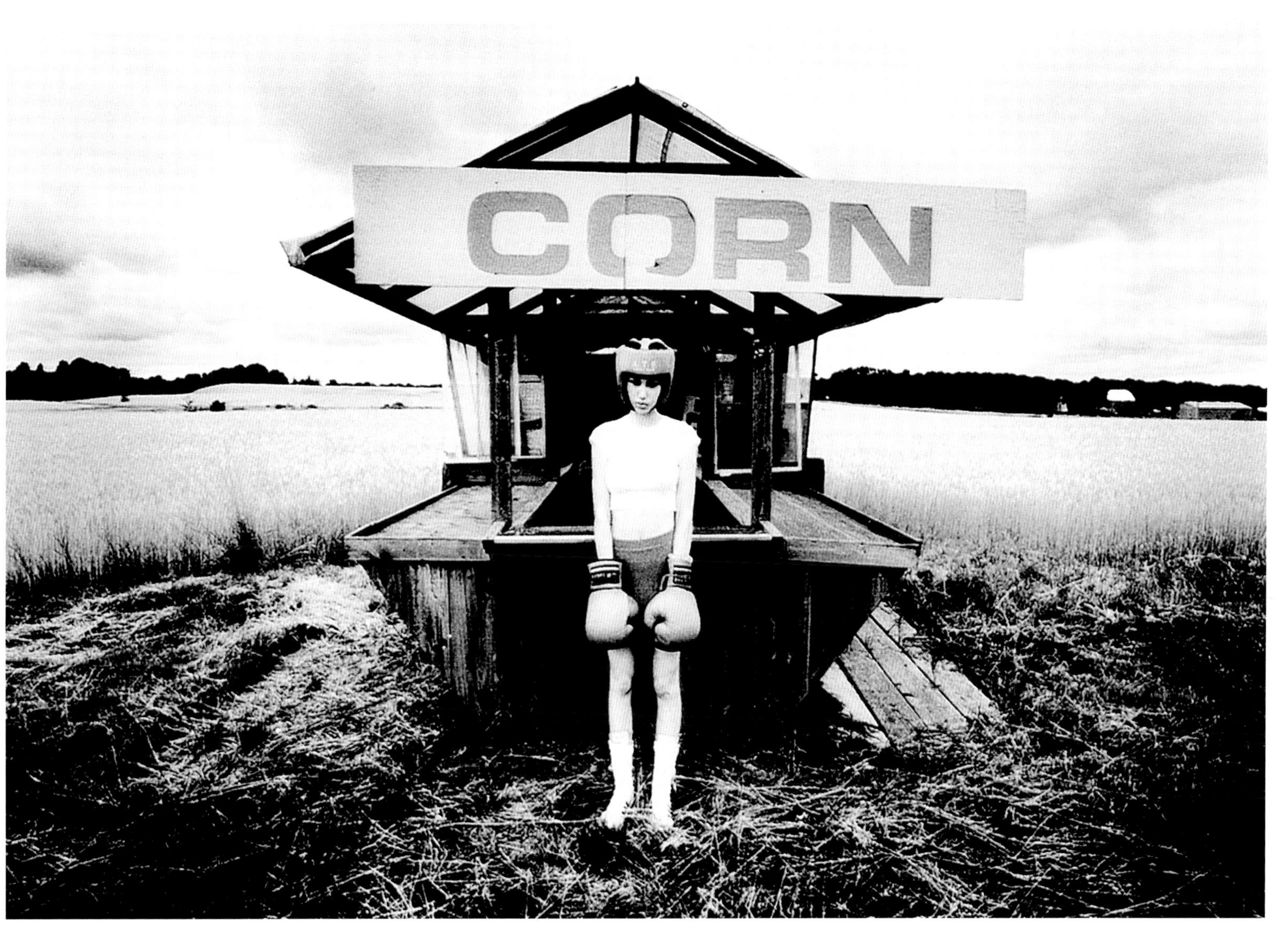
CORN

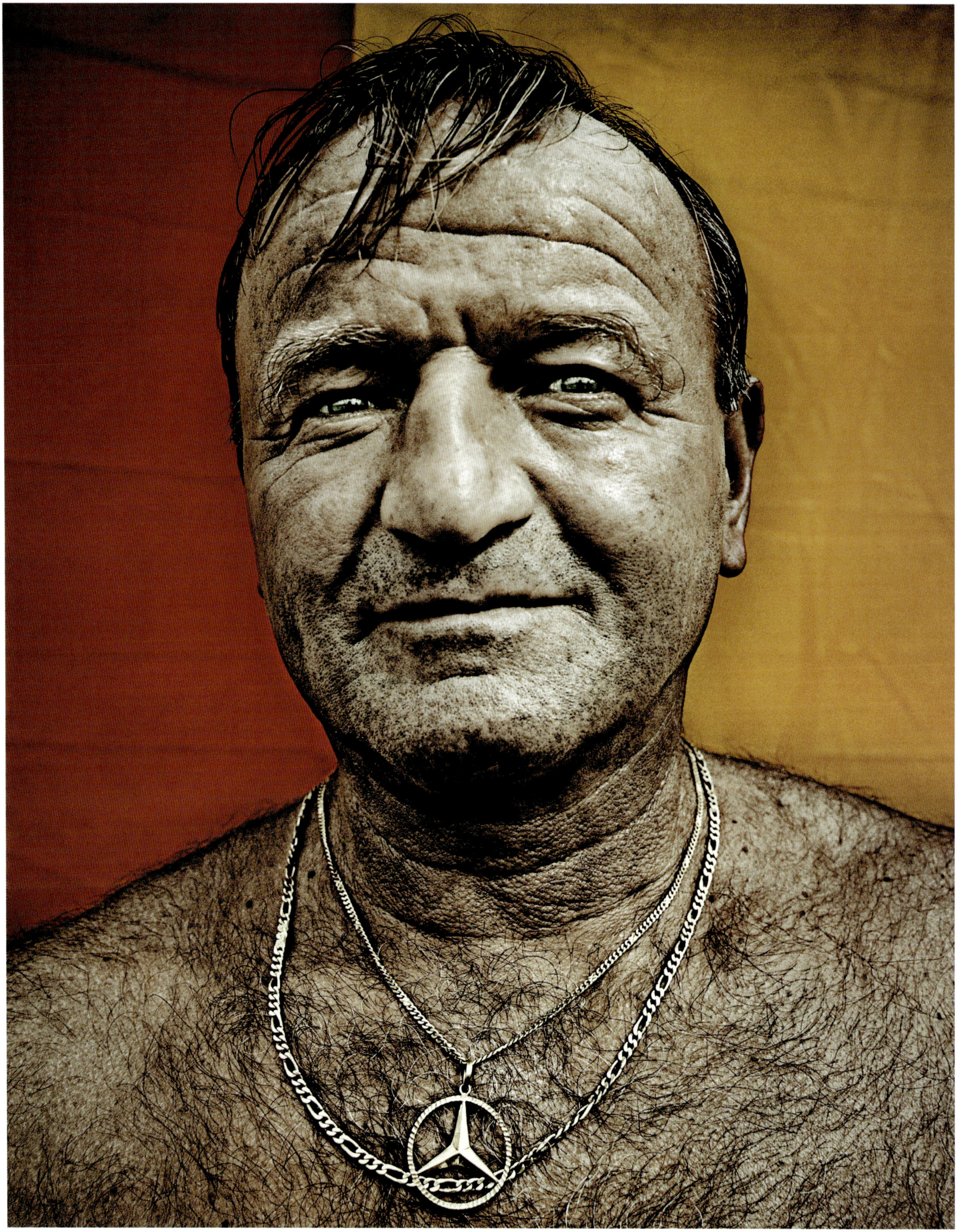

Michael Hall

Chapter 3: **Character**

Capturing a person's character is fundamental to portraiture and not as easy as it sounds. The dreaded passport photo proves that merely pointing a lens at a subject and clicking the shutter reveals nothing more about them than a passable record of their facial features.

This chapter looks at ways of using the camera to delve a little deeper – the power of close-ups and selective cropping, the effect of formal and informal composition, placing the subject within the frame and including texture to reveal the life behind the skin.

Fact file

Photographer:	Nikki Gibbs, Trevillion Picture Library
Location:	North Devon, UK
Time of day:	Late afternoon, spring

Technical details

Camera:	Nikon FM2
Lens:	50mm
Film:	Agfa 400
Exposure:	1/60sec at f/1.8

'Julia Margaret Cameron was a big influence on me at the time and her inspiration helped me to capture Jane's pre-Raphaelite looks.'

Nikki Gibbs

The concept

'This portrait of my friend Jane was a collaboration between myself and another great friend, printer Bill Rowlinson,' explains Nikki. 'Jane's parents lived in an idyllic cottage near Torrington, North Devon and I used to go down and stay with them when I could. After each trip I always came away with new images for my portfolio, but I hadn't yet taken a portrait of Jane that I was really pleased with.'

The location

Nikki was spoilt for choice with lovely settings to position her subject. 'The cottage was surrounded by miles of woodland and the garden ran down to a river. On summer days it was blissful being there in such beautiful and peaceful surroundings.' Eventually she decided on an ash arbour, which would make a perfect frame around Jane.

Composition

The appearance of the subject, her clothing and the classical, thoughtful pose give this portrait a timeless quality. Jane's looks and amazing long hair reminded Nikki very much of a pre-Raphaelite painting, and she wanted this to come across. 'The real challenge was to get Jane relaxed enough for her to lose any self-consciousness and work with me as I directed her through each pose,' Nikki recalls. 'However, it was short lived as it began to rain. The moment was gone, but thankfully caught on camera.'

Lighting and technique

'I wanted the lighting to be natural and diffuse to give an ethereal feel.
It was an overcast day, so I used the widest aperture, f/1.8, which was fine as I didn't want much depth of field. When I returned to London, I went round to visit Bill and showed him the contact sheet. He recognised the pre-Raphaelite look and immediately knew how to attain that image. He burned in the background so that the face and the hair would be dominant, and held back around the face where the shadows in the eyes and under the nose were unflattering. Then he hand-painted the hair with bleach to give it texture and also used a toning technique to show off the red colour. Jane's portrait ended up on the front cover of the British Journal of Photography as part of an interview with Bill Rowlinson, which was an unexpected reward.'

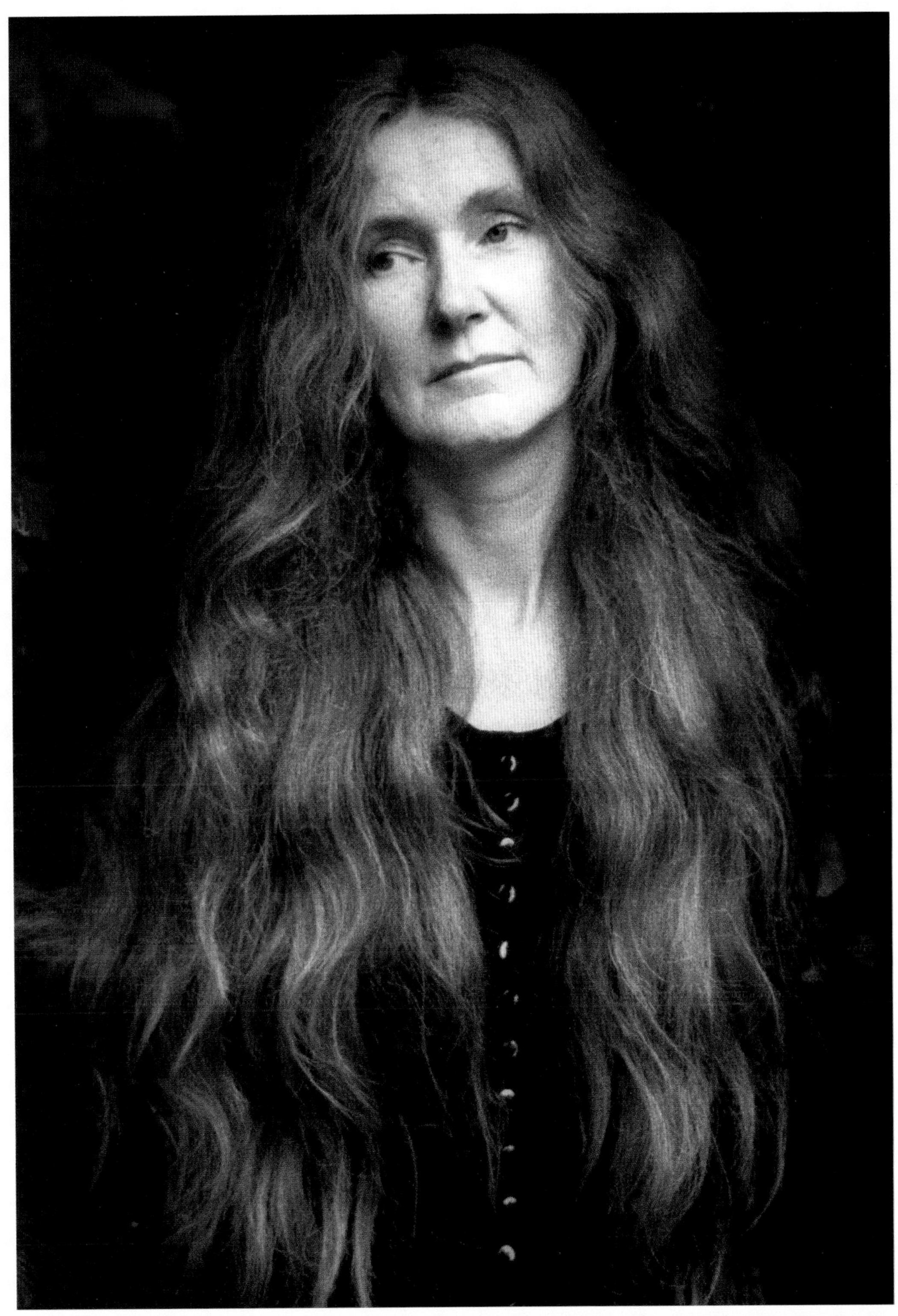

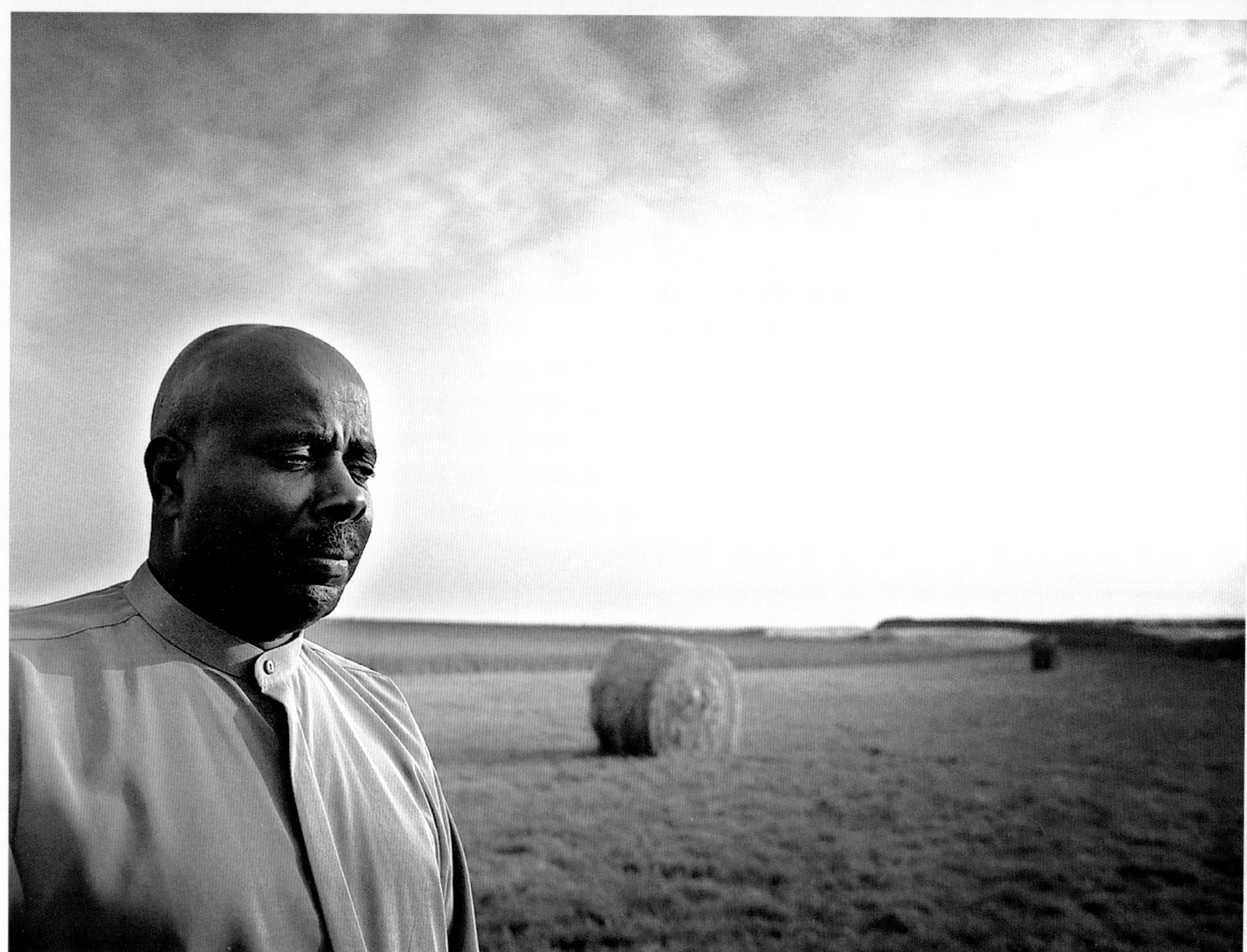

The concept

'Anthony was born near Augusta, Georgia and grew up on a farm without electricity or running water. He realised that the only way to escape was to join the US army and, although not a violent guy, he did what he was told, including several combat missions,' explains Steffen. 'My concept was to first show Tony as the sensitive, gentle farm boy he grew up as, and then as the self-confident, grown-up man he became after all those years and a long time in the army.'

The location

Steffen wanted a fairly simple location and he chose a freshly-ploughed field for both pictures. The first one shows more of it to provide the association with the farm on which Tony once lived.

Composition

'Placing the subject at the very edge of the frame, combined with the expression on his face was meant to stress the story I was trying to tell of the young farm boy lost in a big world,' explains Steffen. He also liked the position of the two hay circles, which adds to the agricultural feel and leads the eye towards the background.

Lighting and technique

The warm light of late afternoon in summer proved perfect for Steffen's purpose. He positioned the subject so the light mostly fell on the far side of his face, allowing some shadow to fall on the camera side to provide some modelling to the features.

Fact file

Photographer: Steffen Ebert
Location: Huettenberg, Germany
Time of day: Late afternoon, June

Technical details

Camera: Mamiya 645AF
Lens: 45mm
Film: Kodak T-Max 100
Exposure: 1/90sec at f/8

'To achieve touching, story-telling portraits, you don't need expensive equipment or fancy locations. What you need is an honest interest in the people you are photographing, to get closer and listen to what they have to say.'

Steffen Ebert

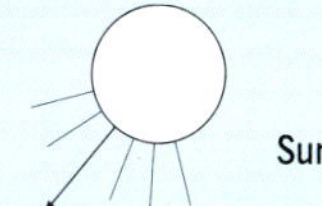

Sun

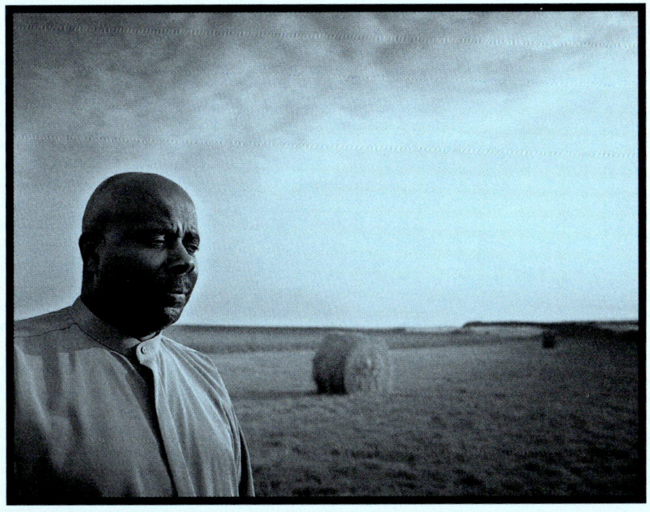

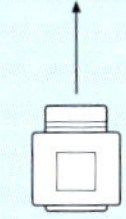

Medium format camera

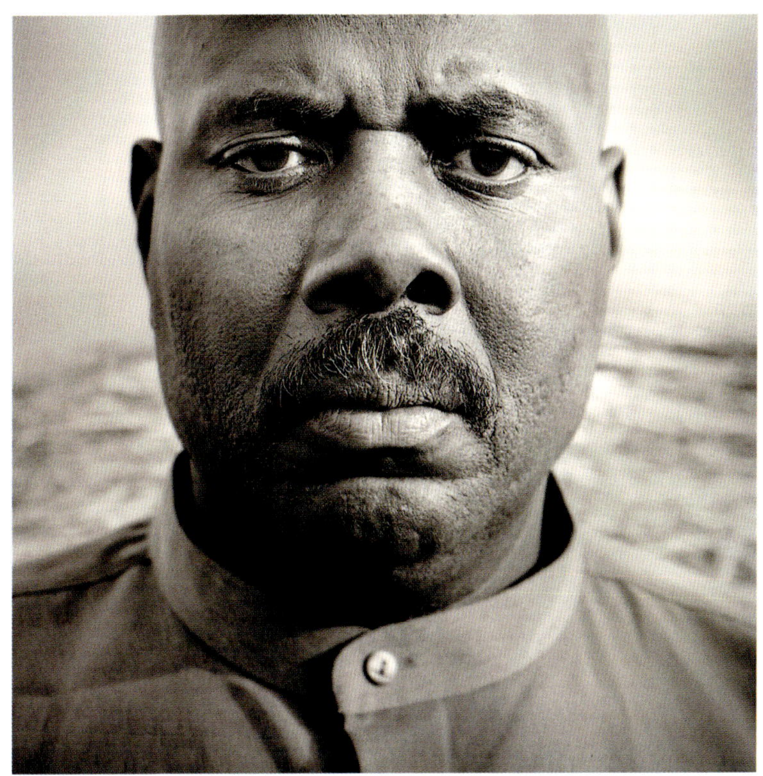

This second shot in the sequence shows what a difference a change in the camera angle, as well as the facial expression, can make to the way a person's character comes across. 'The direct and close approach used here was to support the fact that the farm boy finally became a strong, honest and grown-up man,' says Steffen. The frontal lighting, with fewer shadows, also helps the more straightforward, less contemplative mood to this shot.

Fact file

Photographer: Steffen Ebert
Location: Huettenberg, Germany
Time of day: Late afternoon, June

Technical details

Camera: Hasselblad 202FA
Lens: 80mm
Film: Kodak T-Max 100
Exposure: 1/500sec at f/2.8

'I knew that by showing only part of her face, that part would receive stronger attention when looking at the picture.'

Manuel Luís Cochofel

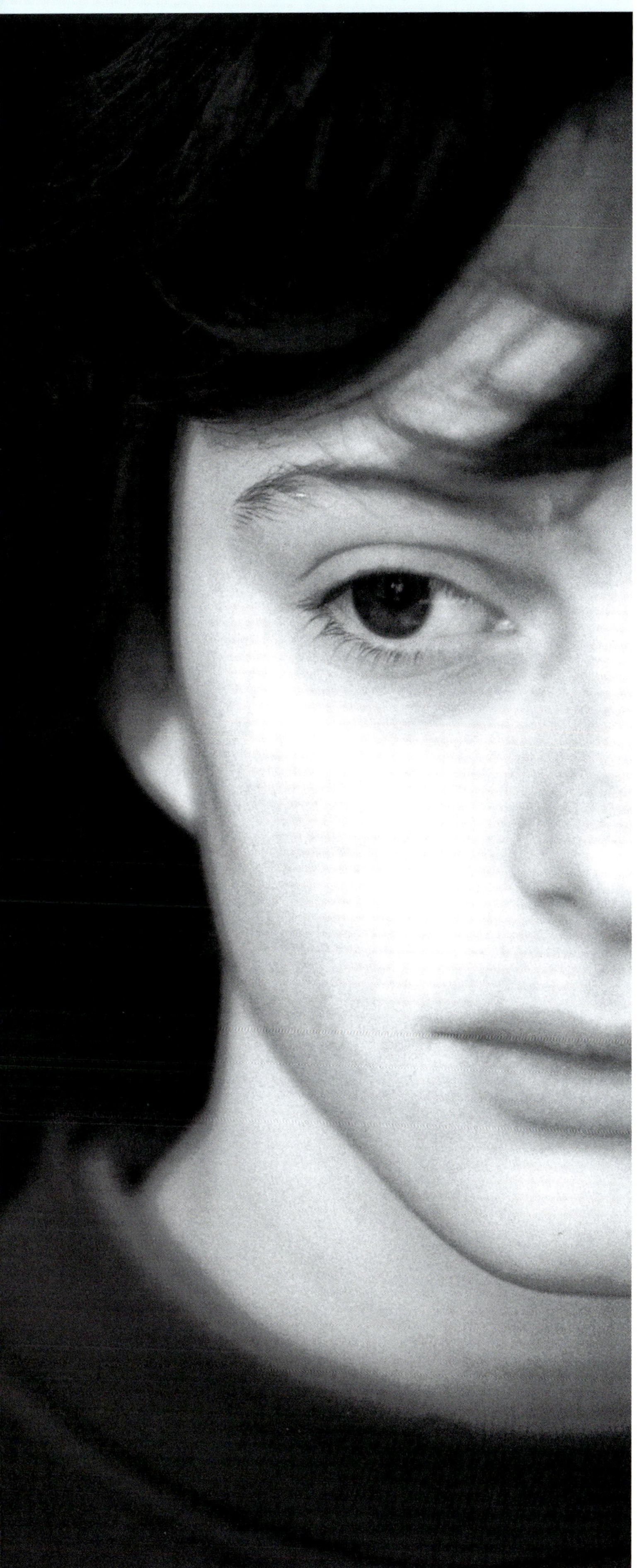

Fact file

Photographer: Manuel Luís Cochofel
Location: Public gardens, Lisbon, Portugal
Time of day: 1.30pm, May

Technical details

Camera: Pentax 67
Lens: 90mm
Film: Ilford Delta 400
Exposure: 1/125sec at f/2.8

The concept

'Carolina is a friend of mine and I simply wanted to photograph her,' explains Manuel. 'I find her very photogenic and asked her if we could do a photo shoot session. We met at this beautiful garden in the heart of Lisbon and I shot a few rolls.'

The location

Manuel wanted to use his heavy Pentax 67 medium format camera, but he prefers to hand hold it rather than use a tripod, so decided an outdoor location was the best option to give the required light. The public gardens of the Gulbenkian Foundation were within easy access for both of them and provided a range of possible backgrounds and props.

Composition

It's tempting to think you have to show the whole of a person's face in order to reveal their character but sometimes, with very careful framing, it can be more revealing to be selective. That approach worked particularly well for this shot where the leaf guides the viewer's eye to the subject's eye. Manuel tried several shots at different angles but found this had the most impact. 'I really wanted a close-up but also wanted to include the big leaf near Carolina, so decided to frame only part of her beautiful face,' he says.

Lighting and technique

'The sun was very hot and the light very harsh,' recalls Manuel. 'To avoid a contorted face due to the strong light, I decided to go amongst the undergrowth where there was some shade. I pushed the film by one stop to allow a faster shutter speed and avoid camera shake. I also used the maximum aperture of f/2.8 to give me narrow depth of field and focused on Carolina's eye. Only part of the big leaf would also be in focus, which I felt would be interesting. An orange filter on the lens turned Carolina's face even paler. I knew the leaves could be a little too dark being in the shadow, but I knew my faithful "Viragem LAB" in Lisbon could take care of that!'

'For the last two years I have only used lenses of 21mm up to 50mm. Like Robert Capa, I like to be very close.'

Frédéric Pascual

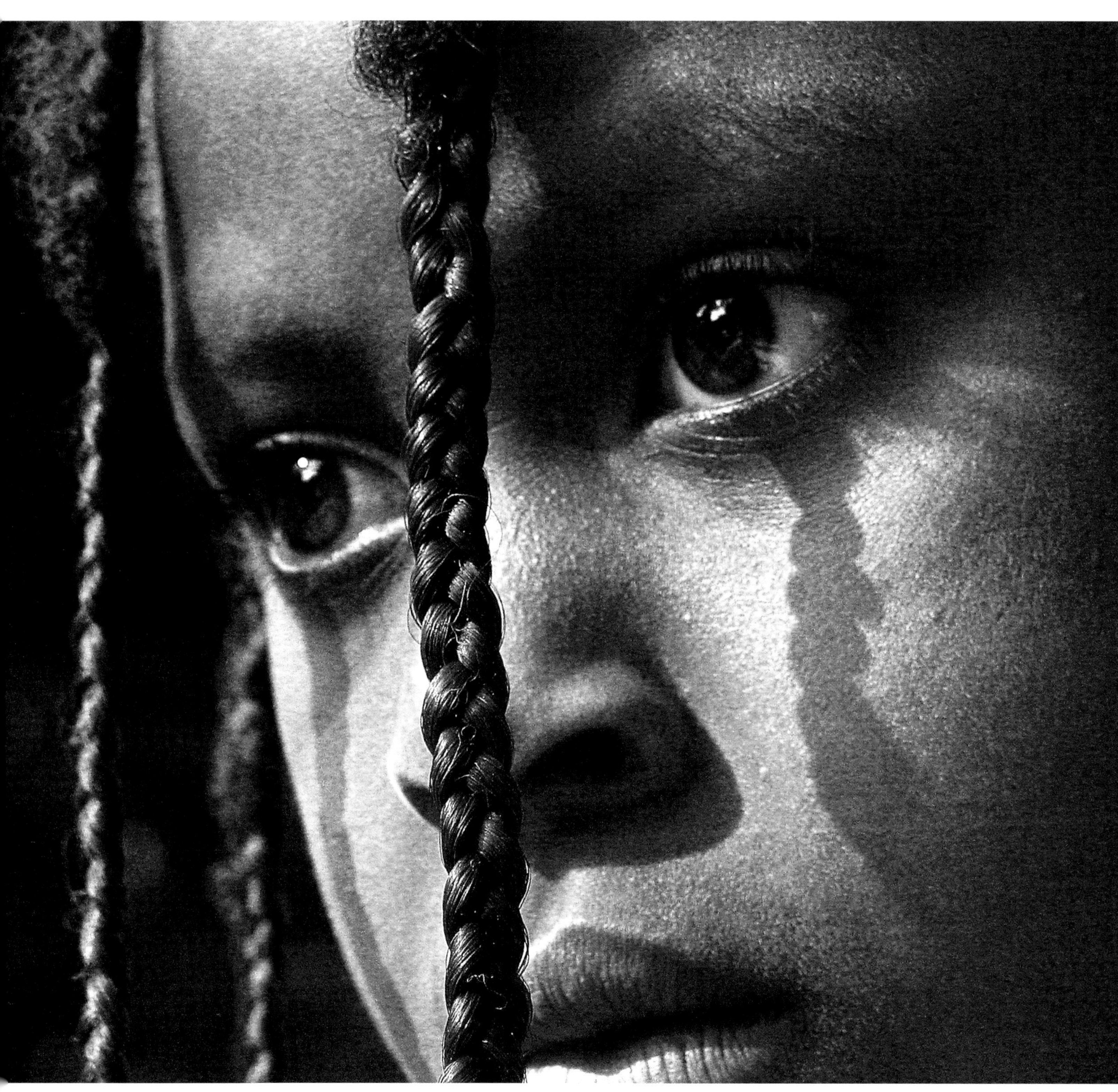

The concept

This was a candid portrait, taken in the street while the little girl in the picture was playing with Frédéric's own daughter and some other children. 'I often take my camera out with me. Depending on the weather and my personal mood, I feel I need it with me,' he says. 'Sometimes, like this, a moment just comes when you sense a photo, so I prepared my camera to shoot quickly.'

Fact file

Photographer: Frédéric Pascual
Location: Paris, France
Time of day: 4pm, May

Technical details

Camera: Canon G5 (digital)
Lens: 28.8mm
Film: n/a
Exposure: 1/1250sec at f/4

The location

The girl's surroundings in the street were nothing special and were, in any case, irrelevant for the type of shot Frédéric was after.

Composition

Frédéric favours tight portraits and in this case tried to capture the juxtaposition between the bright light from the sun, with its connotations of good weather and uplifting mood, and the melancholy look in the girl's eyes. He feels the hair adds weight to the image, and it also creates strong vertical lines, contrasting with the diagonal of the eyes.

Lighting and technique

The sun was very strong and still high in the sky, which, as Frédéric says, can be a difficult time to take portraits because of the resulting strong shadows. Here, though, they help to make the picture. 'The shadows under the eyes remind me of tears,' he says. Using a short lens, Frédéric was very close to his subject, but she was too preoccupied to notice him or his camera.

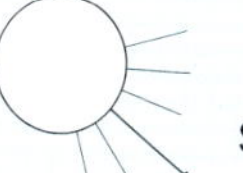

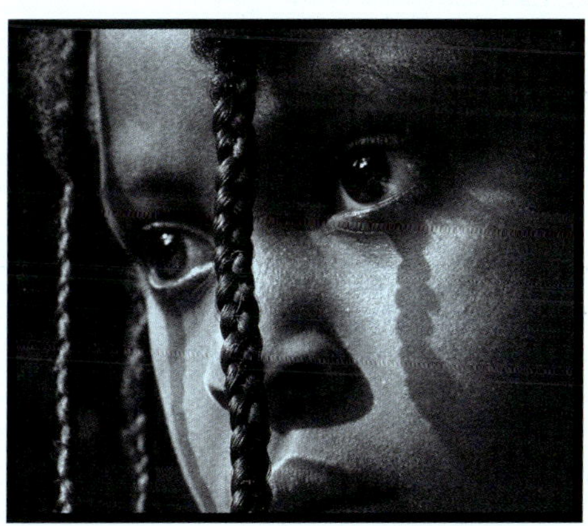

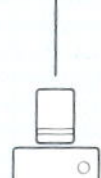

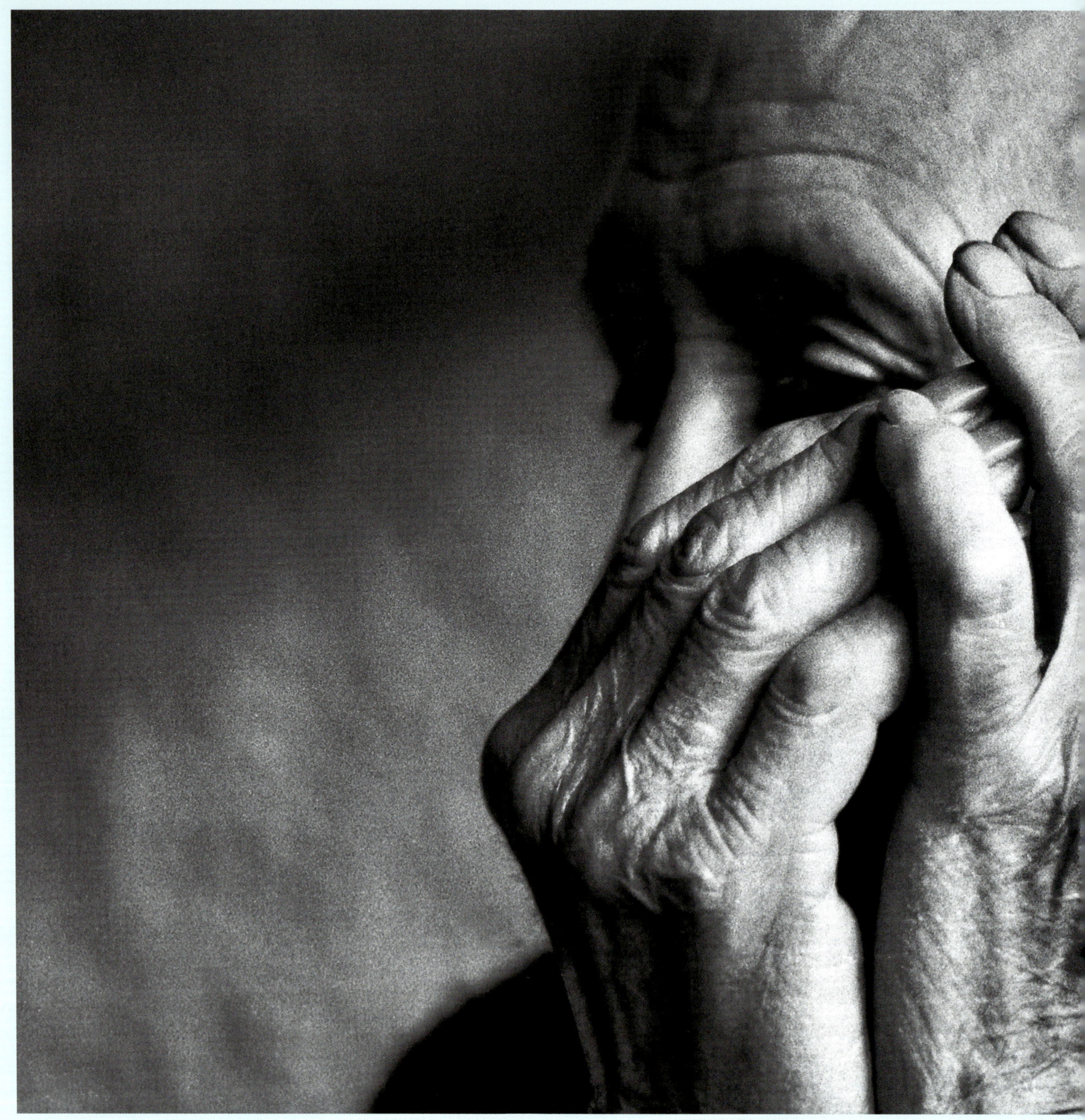

‘My grandfather used to put his hands like this when he was thinking, or taking a rest. It was common to see him like that.’

Frédéric Pascual

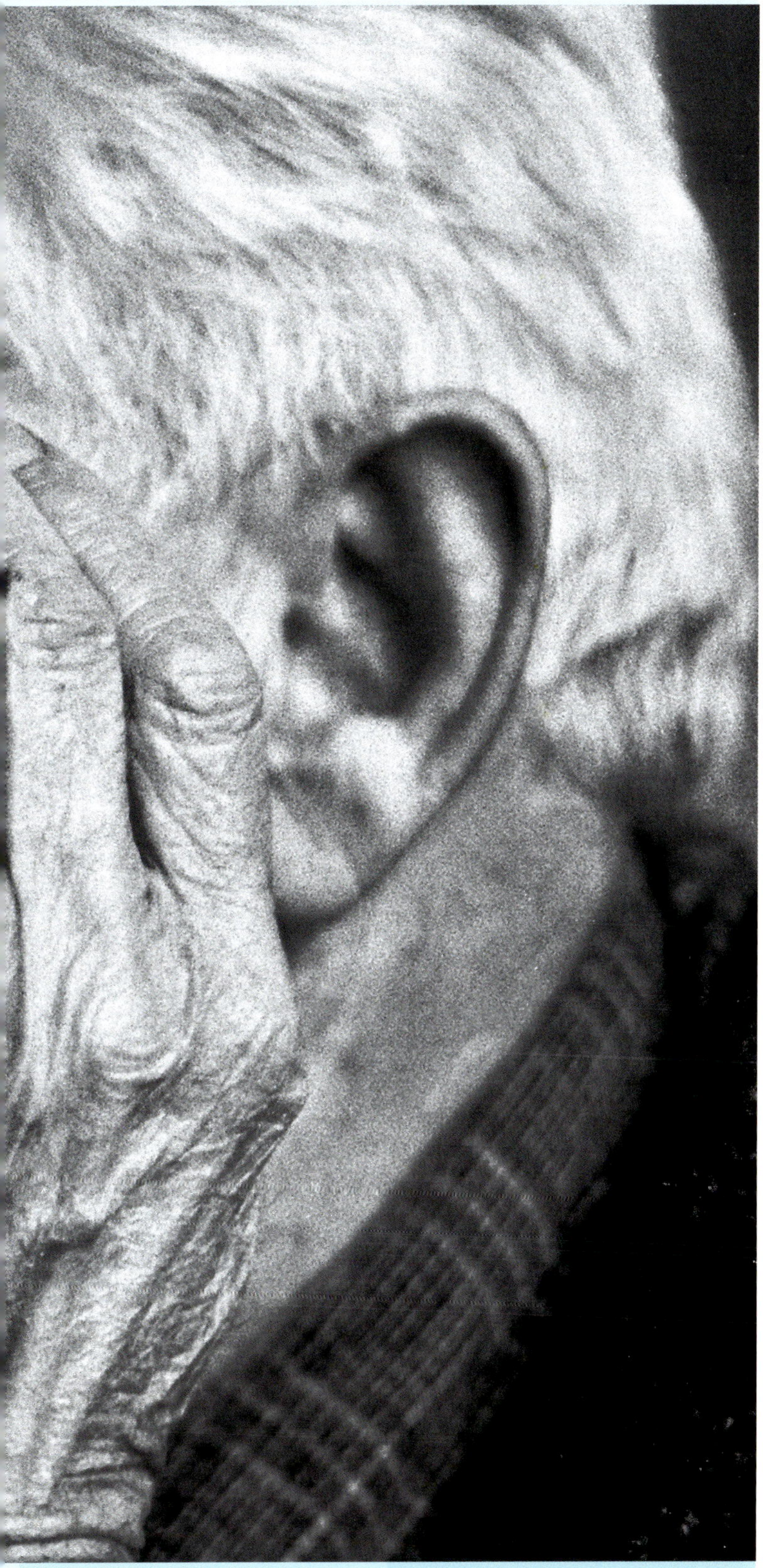

The concept

This was not a posed portrait but a personal photograph of Frédéric's elderly grandfather taken after a family lunch gathering. 'He had the death penalty hanging over him since after the Spanish Civil War because he was a member of anarchy organisations,' says Frédéric. 'As a political refugee he fled to south west France to live as a quiet farmer, leaving his wife and children behind in Spain.'

The location

The gathering took place at the grandfather's farm and he was sitting at a table in a large outbuilding, open at the front but partially covered by a roof.

Composition

Frédéric used a 200mm lens and moved in close enough to his subject to frame tightly without the need for cropping afterwards. Sometimes a person's hands – particularly those of the elderly – can say almost as much about them as their face. This was especially true of this gentleman as he regularly placed them close to his face like this, giving the portrait a special meaning to those who knew him.

Lighting and technique

The summer sun was quite bright, coming from the right, but the subject was shaded from its harshest rays by the roof of the building. This softening of the light meant that the all-important detail and texture of the skin was not lost. The background is a white stone wall, rendered out of focus by a shallow depth of field.

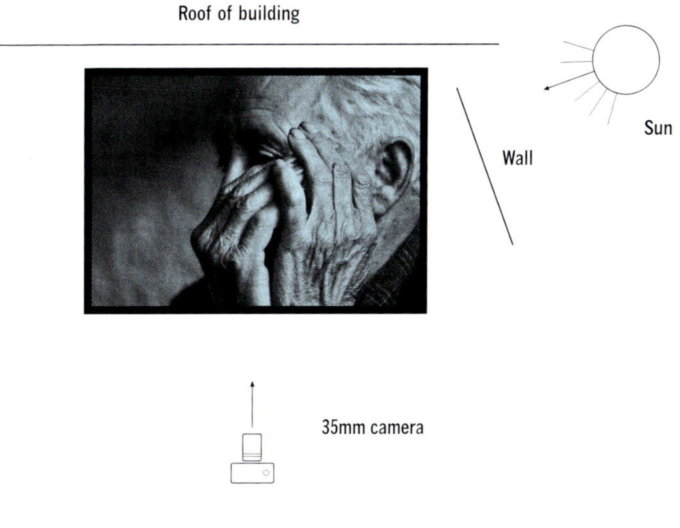

Fact file

Photographer:	Frédéric Pascual
Location:	Narthoux, Tarn, France
Time of day:	Mid-afternoon, July

Technical details

Camera:	Contax 139Q
Lens:	200mm
Film:	Ilford HP5
Exposure:	Not recorded

‘This was just a spot in the park where the light was right and 5–10 shots later I had what I was looking for. The windy day provided just the right touch to make it work.’

Alan Smilie

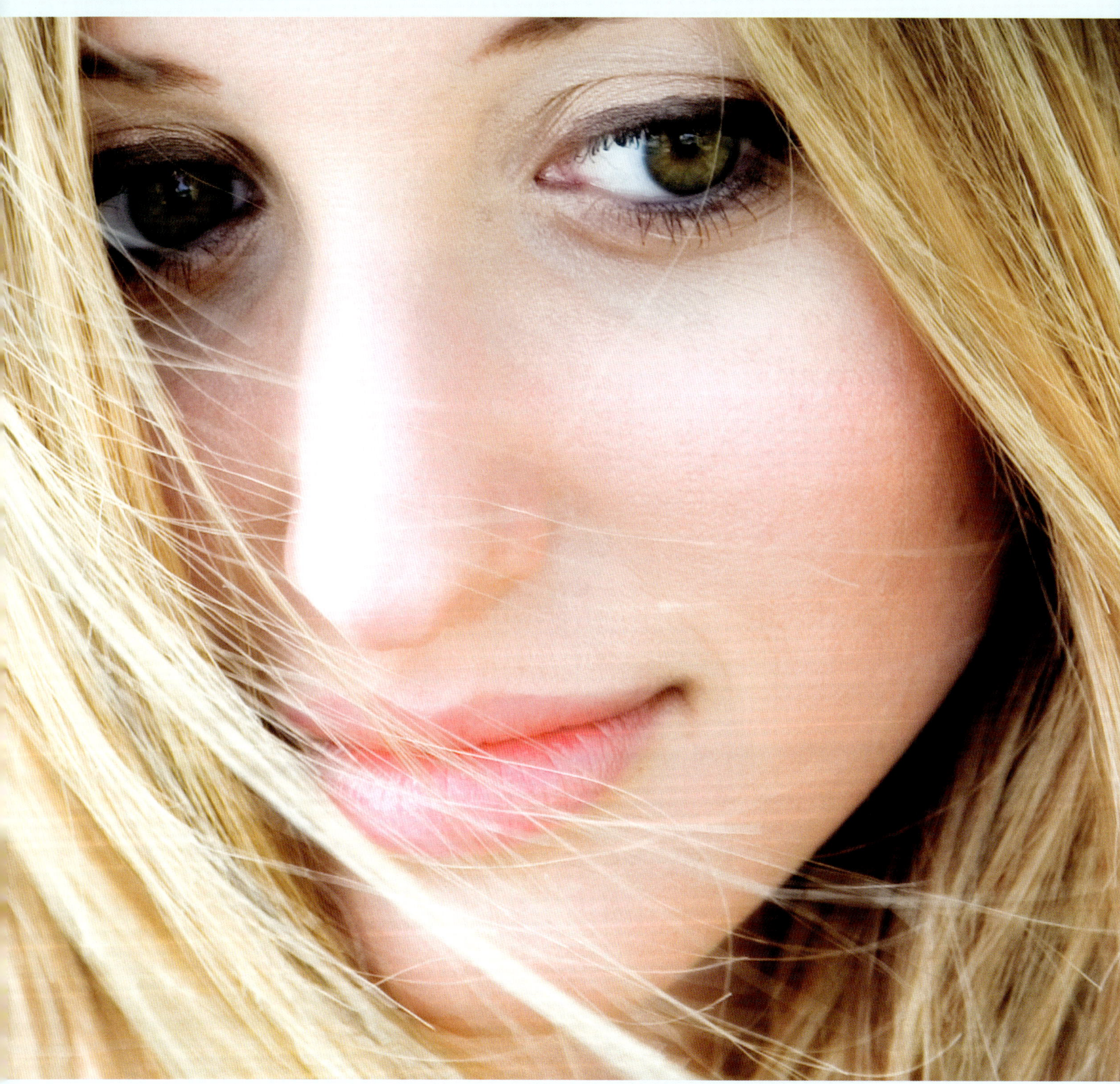

Fact file

Photographer: Alan Smilie
Location: Orlando, Florida, USA
Time of day: 9.20am, March

Technical details

Camera: Nikon D100 (digital)
Lens: 24–85mm
Film: n/a
Exposure: 1/100sec at f/5

Sun diffused by trees

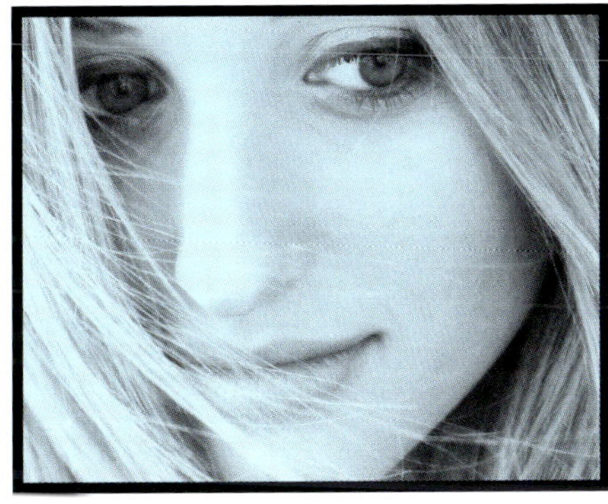

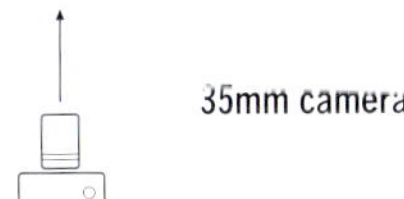

35mm camera

The concept

'I was doing some test shots for the model, aiming for a trendy, fashion look,' says Alan. 'The wind provided an unexpected look that made the image.'

The location

Alan chose a public park in downtown Orlando because the attractive scenery would give him plenty of scope for a variety of pictures. Also the sun was fairly bright and he knew the trees would provide plenty of cover to diffuse the light.

Composition

Alan took shots of the model from a number of different angles to show her versatility, which is important in putting together a portfolio. Here, though, the extreme close-up works superbly, not least because of the beauty of the model – other subjects may not take so kindly to such an approach! Using a medium-range telephoto, there was little distance between the lens and the model, and Alan cropped the image further in Photoshop, also enhancing the colour and sharpness. It's the hair that really makes the image stand out, though, as it frames the face perfectly, leaving a little hidden, which adds a touch of mystique.

Lighting and technique

Alan would have had to work hard in the studio to achieve such a look but, outdoors, all the elements came together quite naturally. 'The great thing about this shot is the simplicity of it,' he says. 'The light was partially diffused by the trees and there was no need for any other equipment or props.'

‘As she wasn’t 100 percent well that day, my daughter stayed very calm.’

Nina Andersen

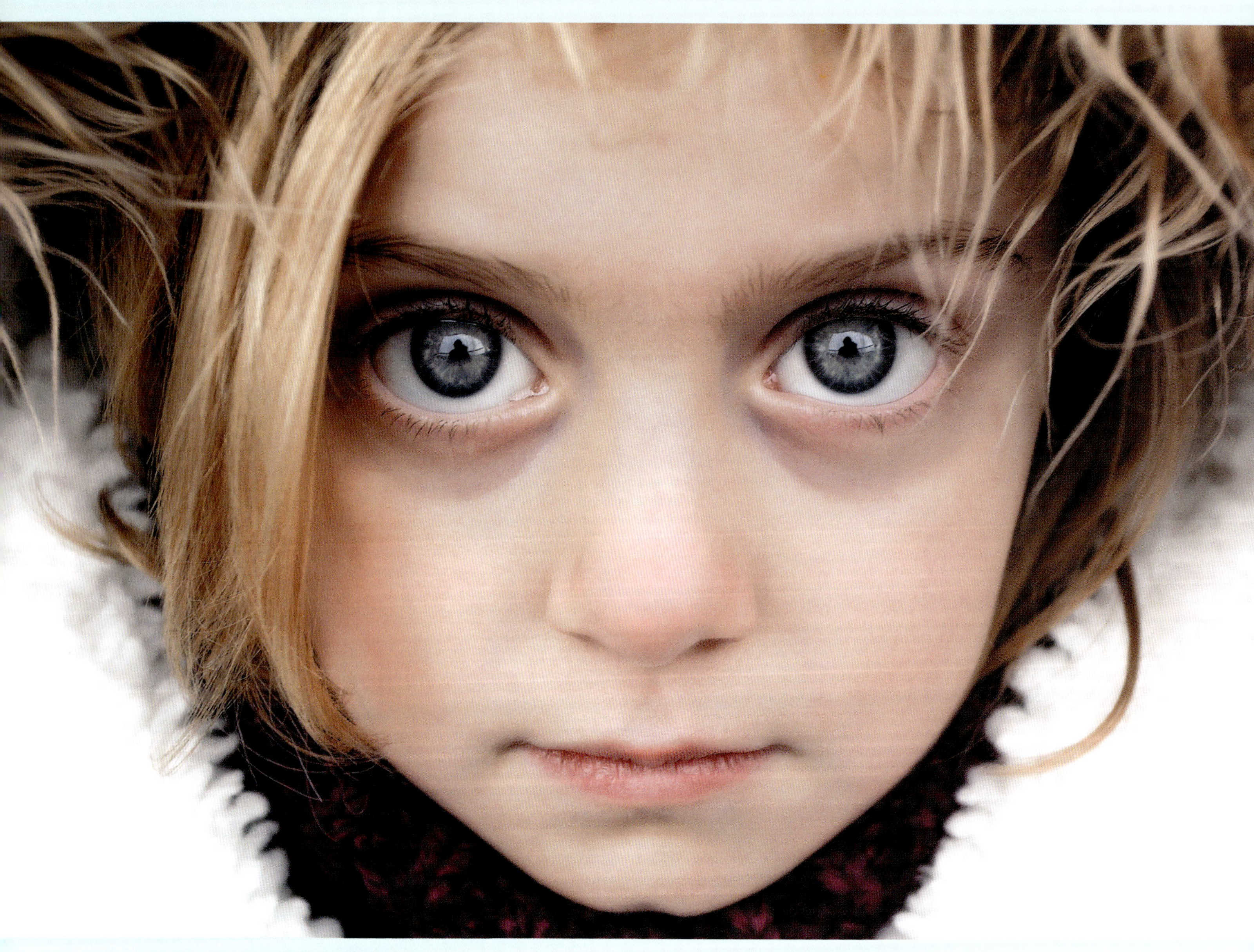

Fact file

Photographer: Nina Andersen
Location: Oslo, Norway
Time of day: Noon, February

Technical details

Camera: Canon EOS 10D (digital)
Lens: 17–40mm
Film: n/a
Exposure: 1/30sec at f/5.6

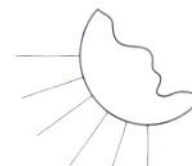
Light diffused through cloud

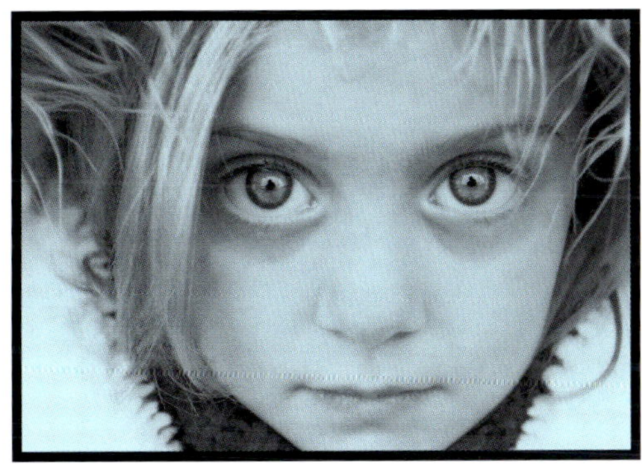

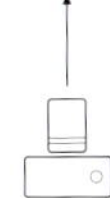
35mm camera

White walls reflect some light

The concept

'This is a picture of my daughter, taken out on our veranda one day,' recalls Nina. 'I had stayed at home with her because she wasn't feeling very well. After a while she got a bit better and we decided to go outside and take some shots of her in one of my jackets. As she wasn't 100 per cent well that day, she stayed very calm and this shot is one of the last I took.'

The location

Nina prefers taking portraits in natural light and, since her daughter was unwell, the veranda was the closest place she could get it. For close ups such as this, there is no need to go further than the back door, so long as the quality of the light is suitable for your purposes.

Composition

Nina wanted to fill most of the frame with her daughter's face to capture those big, emotional eyes. The angle of the head is pointing down slightly and the foreshortening effect of this makes the eyes seem even larger. Placing the head centrally in the frame creates a symmetry that is very effective here, reinforced by the white fur of the collar on either side, with the contrasting colour of the scarf making the skin tones stand out.

Lighting and technique

'This was photographed on a cloudy day so there was no direct sun,' says Nina. 'Our veranda has our neighbour's one above it, which also takes away some light but there are white walls which reflect a little back. I knew from previous experience that I could get some great shots out there on cloudy days as the light is very soft but with a little bit of modelling.'

Fact file

Photographer:	Trine Sirnes Thorne
Location:	Boat trip near Fredrikstad, Norway
Time of day:	Noon, April

Technical details

Camera:	Nikon Coolpix 880 (digital compact)
Lens:	Built-in
Film:	n/a
Exposure:	1/248 sec at f/4

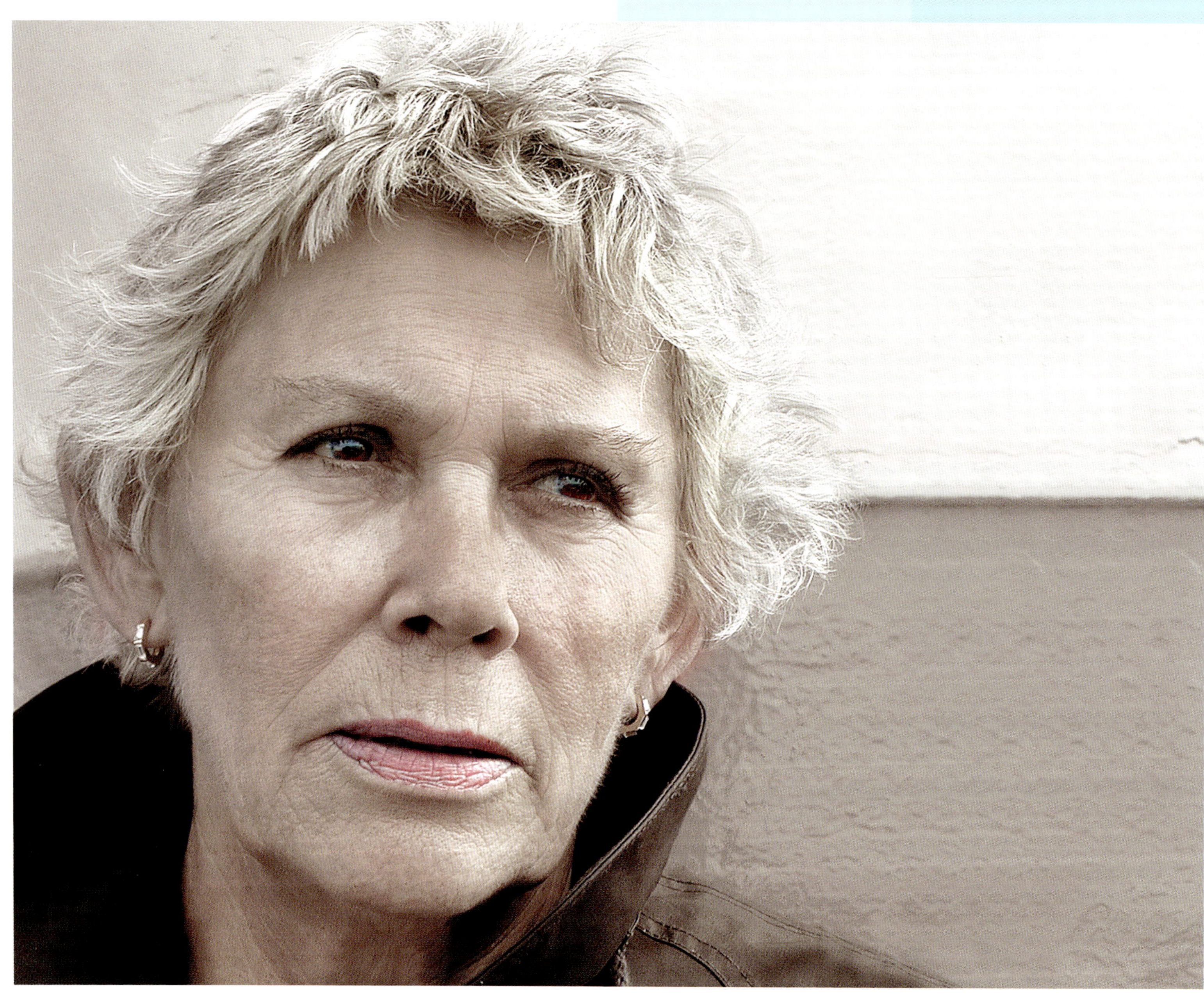

'The feedback from people who have seen this photo, but never met my mother, suggests that I did succeed in capturing her personality.'

Trine Sirnes Thorne

The concept

'This is a photograph of my mother,' says Trine. 'She and I are not the most photogenic of people. We tend to put on a "face" when someone points a camera at us. My intention here was to get a good photo of her that would reveal her personality and show who she really is.'

The location

Trine was with her whole family on a boat trip in the Swedish/Norwegian Archipelago. 'We were on deck, having a good time and I felt the mood was right for trying this.'

Composition

Composing with digital compact cameras can present a couple of problems. Like film compacts, the viewfinder doesn't give a completely accurate presentation of how the picture will turn out – unlike SLRs where what you see is what you get. Also, there can be a slight delay between pressing the shutter and the image actually recording, so if the subject moves a touch during this time you can miss the shot you thought you had in the bag. As this was a posed portrait, and the subject was briefed to keep still, that wasn't a problem here. Trine used the built-in zoom lens to frame in tightly on her subject, but allowed more space around her mother's head than you can see here, allowing for exact cropping and framing in Photoshop. The large amount of space on the right of the frame allows an area for the subject to look into, with the line of the paintwork behind, following the line of her gaze. The tones of the background and the subject are also complementary, giving a peaceful and harmonious feel to the portrait.

Lighting and technique

'It was a bright, sunny day with lots of reflections from the sea, so the light was pretty harsh,' says Trine. 'I took many shots, trying to ensure my mother didn't close her eyes to keep out the sun. She sat with her back to the large "pipe" of the boat, with the sun coming in on her left side. The water on both sides acted as reflectors, preventing too many shadows.'

Fact file

Photographer: Frantisek Staud
Location: Kyoto, Japan
Time of day: Early afternoon

Technical details

Camera: Nikon FM2n
Lens: 105mm macro
Film: Fuji Astia
Exposure: 1/100sec at f/2.8

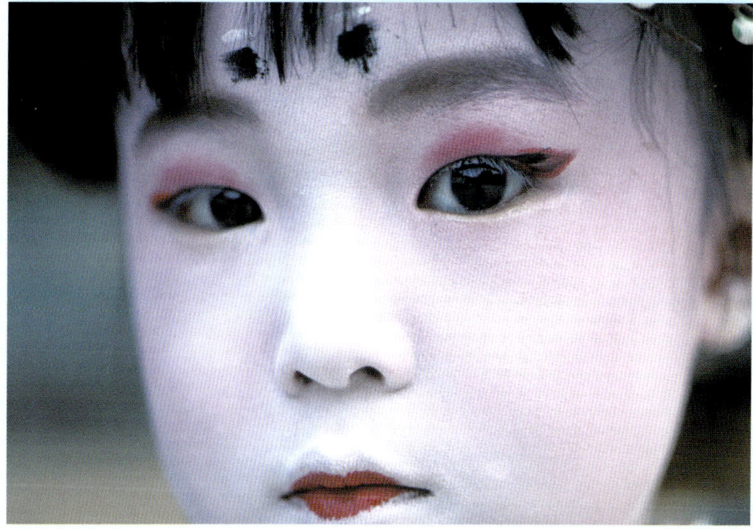

Taken at a small festival in Kyoto, this is a bold crop, cutting off the child's face just below her mouth, but it is all the more eye-catching in the way only the important details are included. 'I wanted a direct look at the camera and also liked the effect of one eye in focus and the other blurred,' Frantisek says. 'I took both horizontal and vertical pictures, but for this tight crop, taken with a macro lens, I believed horizontal orientation would work best. Thanks to that, this picture has been published several times as a double-page spread.'

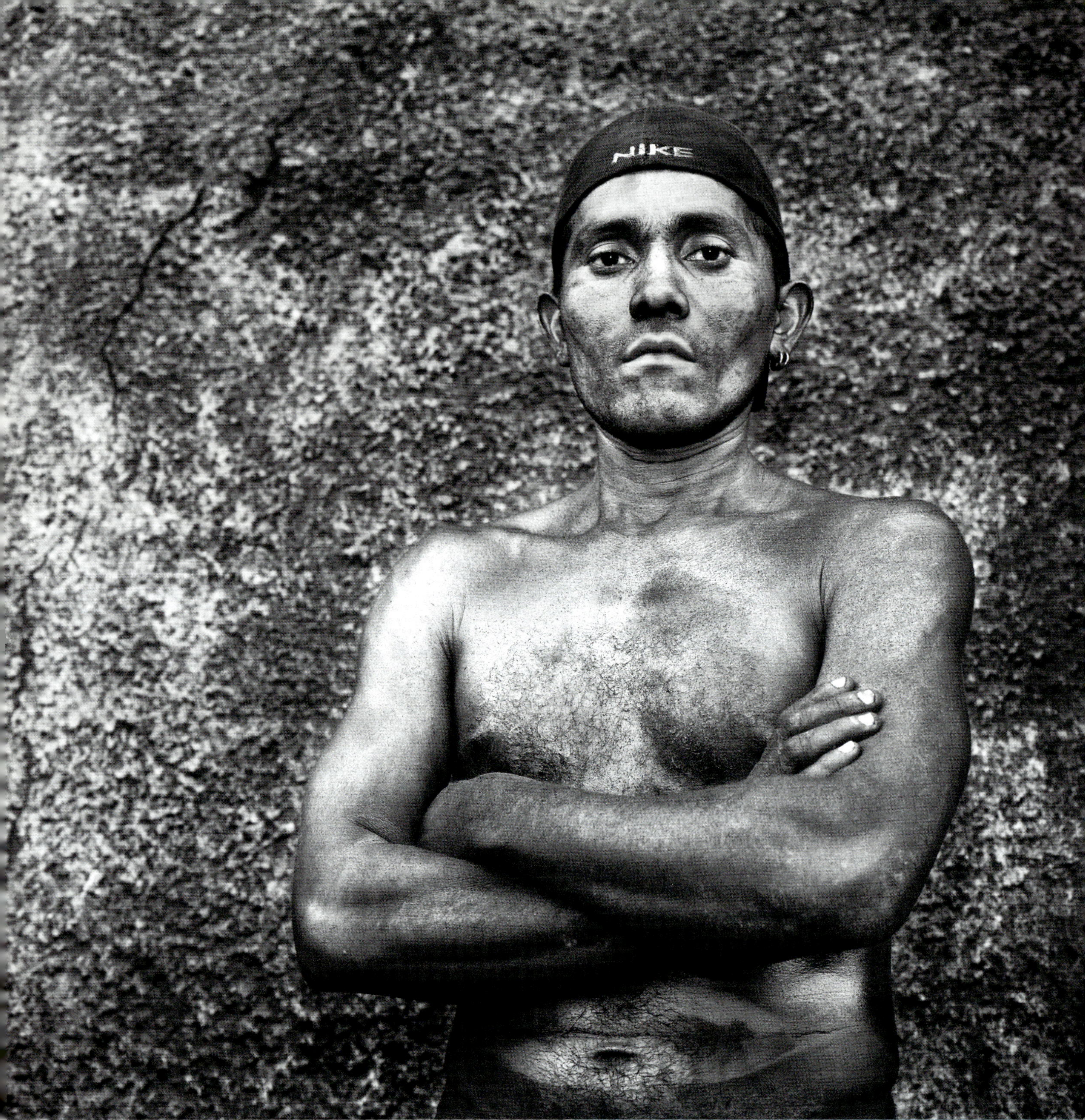

Fact file

Photographer:	Roumen Koynov
Location:	Manaus, Brazil
Time of day:	2pm, February

Technical details

Camera:	Mamiya 6
Lens:	75mm
Film:	Kodak Tri-X 400
Exposure:	1/60sec at f/8

The concept

Roumen's portrait of a coal seller is part of a larger project on people and life in the Amazon region of Brazil, which he is hoping to publish as a book.

The location

'This place is next to a bridge, which is almost in the town centre and one can always find people selling barbecue coal there,' he explains. 'Everything is covered in a film of black dust, including the people who work there. The wall behind them makes a superb natural background.'

Composition

Roumen likes composing portraits within the square format of his Mamiya medium format camera. He chose a low viewpoint to accentuate the severe expression and posture of the subject and placed him slightly off-centre in the frame to create a feeling of unbalance. The gritty texture of the wall is picked up in the patches of coal dust on the man's face and body.

Lighting and technique

'Along the equator, where the picture was taken, the sun hardly changes its position all year round,' explains Roumen. 'All the people selling coal are in front of a high wall that provides shade. After I made some observations, I decided to take the picture in the early afternoon, when the sun is still high and intense, but diffused in the shaded area where the workers are. The street across from the people is lined with white houses, which partially reflect and improve the light. I went for a slightly cloudy day so the light is even softer. This was all done with the intention of making the portraits dark in tone, without any part of them standing out. I used fill-in flash in auto mode, two or three stops underexposed, to give a very slight sparkle to the eyes of the coal seller.'

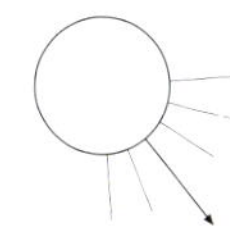

Light from sun is partly blocked by wall

Wall

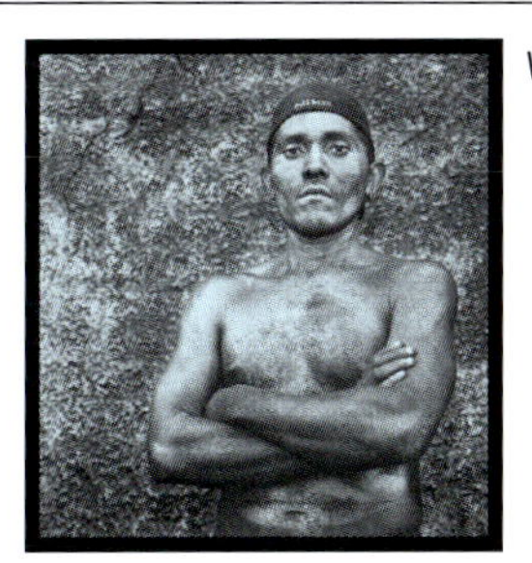

Medium format camera with fill-in flash

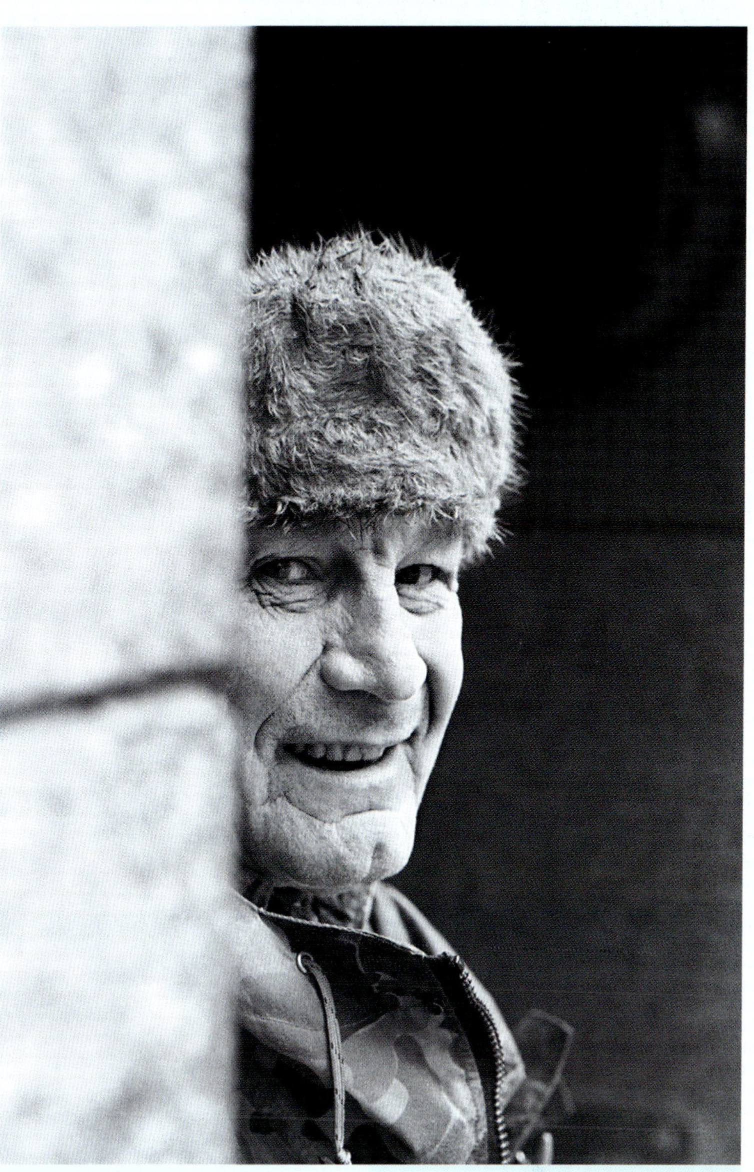

Fact file

Photographer:	Craig Biertempfel
Location:	Pittsburgh, USA
Time of day:	Noon, November

Technical details

Camera:	Nikon FM2
Lens:	80–200mm
Film:	Kodak T-Max 400 rated at 800 ISO
Exposure:	1/260sec at f/5.6

There is plenty of texture revealed in this characterful portrait – in the subject's hat, his face and the concrete wall on the left – counter-balanced by the plain black tone behind him. The horizontal line on the side wall also helps to draw the viewer's eyes straight to those of the subject. He is a homeless man in downtown Pittsburgh, photographed by Craig as part of a six-month project about people who live on the streets in that area. 'Most of those I met in the alleys were hardened individuals whose faces revealed far more stories and detail than I expected to uncover,' he says.

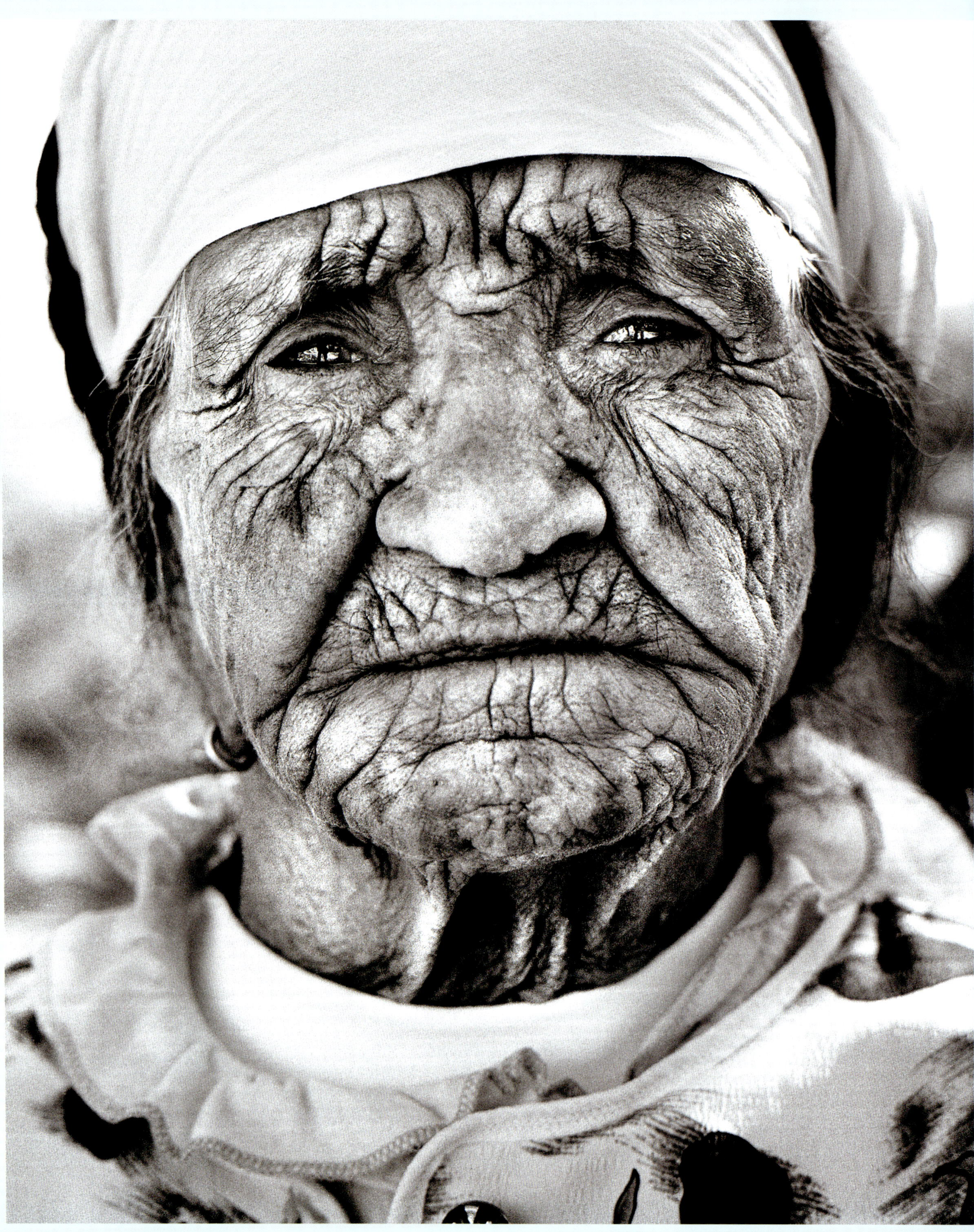

The concept

'My mother and I went to visit my auntie Fatima at her home in Had Jbarna, a few months before she died. She was 93 and disabled,' explains Nour Eddine. 'In the country we get up very early to gather wood and water from far away. The sun was shining and I had all my cameras ready for taking some pictures. I started taking some pictures of my cousins and then asked my aunt if she could pose for me. She was not too sure but did let me take some pictures before we had breakfast.'

Fact file

Photographer: Nour Eddine El Ghoumari
Location: Taza, Morocco
Time of day: 6am, August

Technical details

Camera: Mamiya C330
Lens: 80mm
Film: Ilford FP4
Exposure: 1/125sec at f/8

The location

The picture was taken in a small village near the ancient town of Taza in the north east of Morocco. 'I didn't want to move my aunt from where she was sitting. The side wall, which was situated on the left, kept the sun away from us, which was perfect,' explains Nour Eddine.

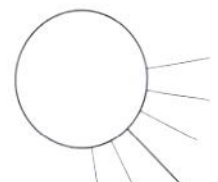

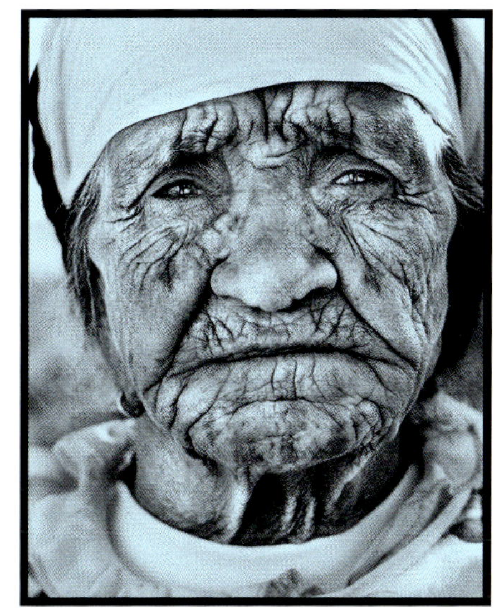

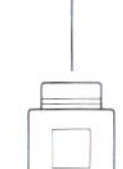

Composition

'My aunt's face is a very striking one. The first thing that you notice is the intensity of her wrinkles. The rigid texture of her skin looks unreal – more like the covering of a tree or an animal. This is due to the harsh sun in her environment and the fact that she never felt thirsty and didn't drink much water,' says Nour Eddine. 'I didn't want her fragile health to be visible in her eyes, but the mouth gives it away. I could have lifted it up in Photoshop, but I decided against it in the end. I wanted to capture her as she is known to us in the family.'

Lighting and technique

Nour Eddine was pleased he took the picture so early in the morning, with shade provided by the wall. 'Any later and the sun would have covered the whole area, making the light too harsh and crude for taking pleasing outdoor portraits,' he says. The dodging and burning tools in Photoshop were used to work on the shadows and highlights in the face, emphasising the texture further and finally, a slight sepia tone was added to give some warmth to the image.

'I really wanted a picture of a proud old lady with more wrinkles than the windy sand dunes of the Arabian Desert. Here, each wrinkle tells the story of her courageous life.'

Nour Eddine El Ghoumari

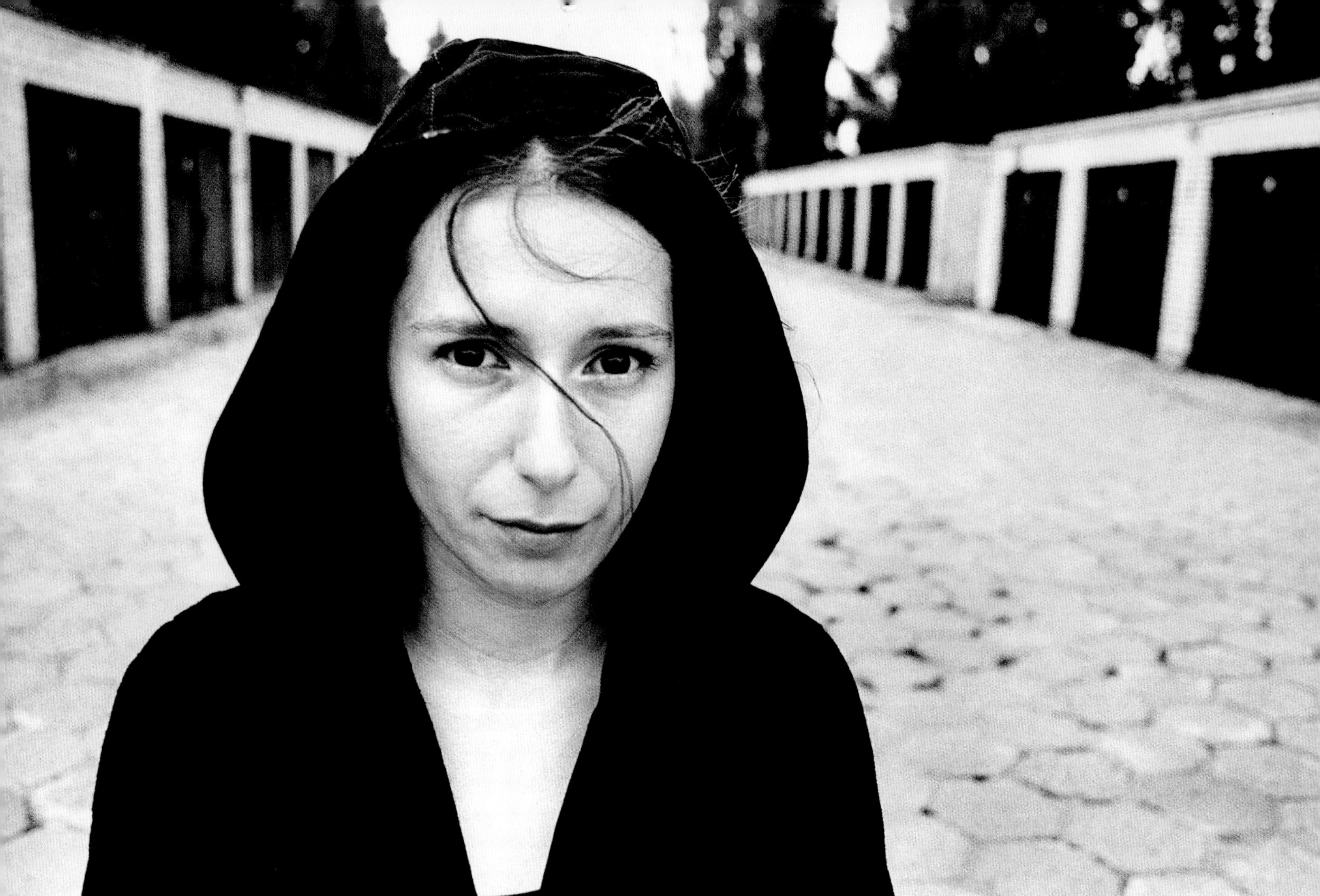

The concept

This is a personal portrait of Tomek's wife. He usually carries his camera with him and takes pictures whenever the circumstances strike him as being right for a good shot.

The location

This shot wasn't planned for in advance, but as soon as he spotted the perspective of the double line of garages, they immediately struck Tomek as a good background for a portrait.

Composition

The sense of formality about this portrait comes from a number of different aspects. The background immediately sets the tone, with its symmetry and graphic horizontal lines, and Tomek has placed his subject centrally in the frame to maximise this effect. The cropping of her at chest height means that only the shapes of her coat around the hood and shoulders are shown – again symmetrical – and any fussy details are left out. Finally, the direct eye contact and serious expression add weight to the image.

Lighting and technique

In overcast light, Tomek took a meter reading from the light on the subject's face and used an aperture of f/5.6 to ensure that the garages were clearly visible, but not so sharp as to distract attention away from her. The image was scanned into a computer and sharpness, brightness and contrast adjusted in Photoshop.

Fact file

Photographer: Tomek Paczkowski
Location: Warsaw, Poland
Time of day: Noon, January

Technical details

Camera: Olympus OM2n
Lens: 28mm
Film: Kodak Academy 200
Exposure: 1/60sec at f/5.6

'I framed the picture so that the garages pull the viewer's eyes into it, making the subject's eyes stand out.'

Tomek Paczkowski

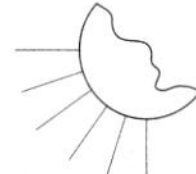

Sun behind clouds

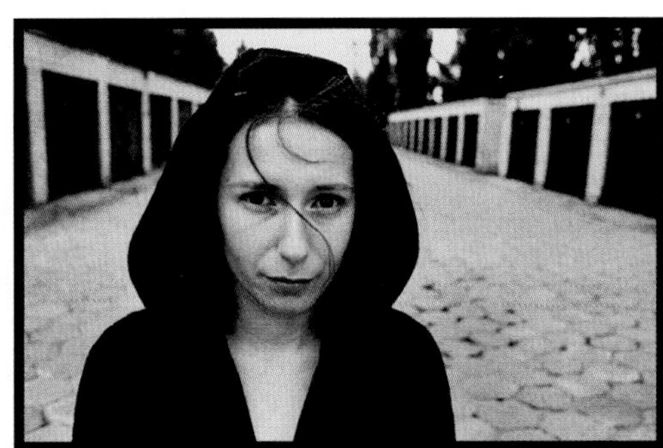

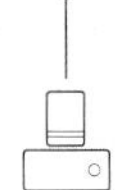

35mm camera

Fact file

Photographer: Tomek Paczkowski
Location: Warsaw, Poland
Time of day: Noon, January

Technical details

Camera: Olympus OM2n
Lens: 50mm
Film: Fuji Superia 200
Exposure: 1/60sec at f/4

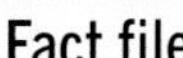

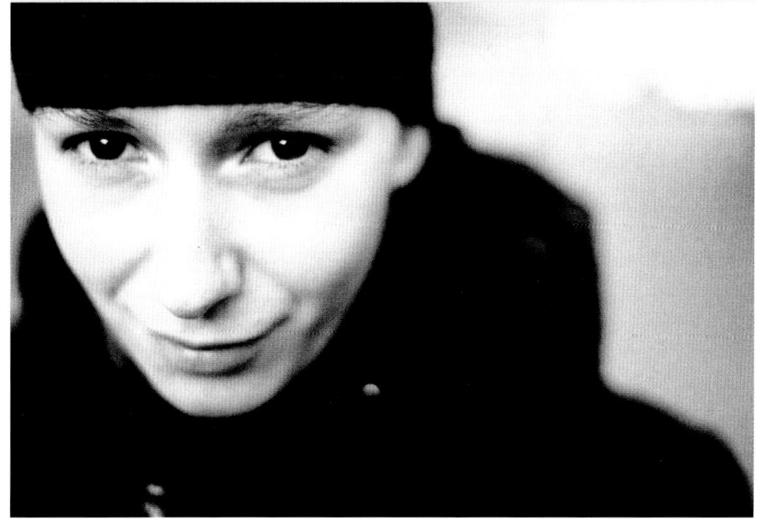

This is the same subject as the main image, Tomek's wife Ania, but the tone of it is altogether different. Placing her off-centre in the frame with quite a tight crop gives a much more informal feel to it. The expression is also more relaxed, as though she has just looked up to see her photograph being taken. ⏶

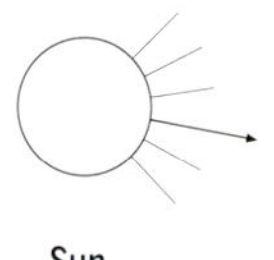

Sun

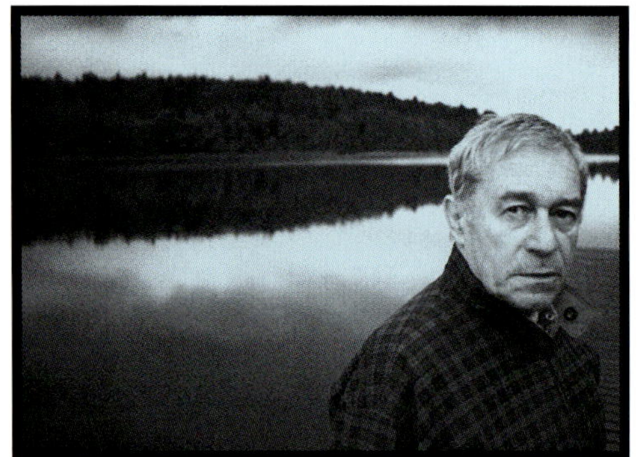

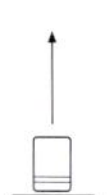

35mm camera

Fact file

Photographer: Tomek Paczkowski
Location: Tucholskie Forest, Poland
Time of day: 7pm, summer

Technical details

Camera: Olympus OM2n
Lens: 28mm
Film: Ilford HP5 Plus
Exposure: 1/30sec at f/4

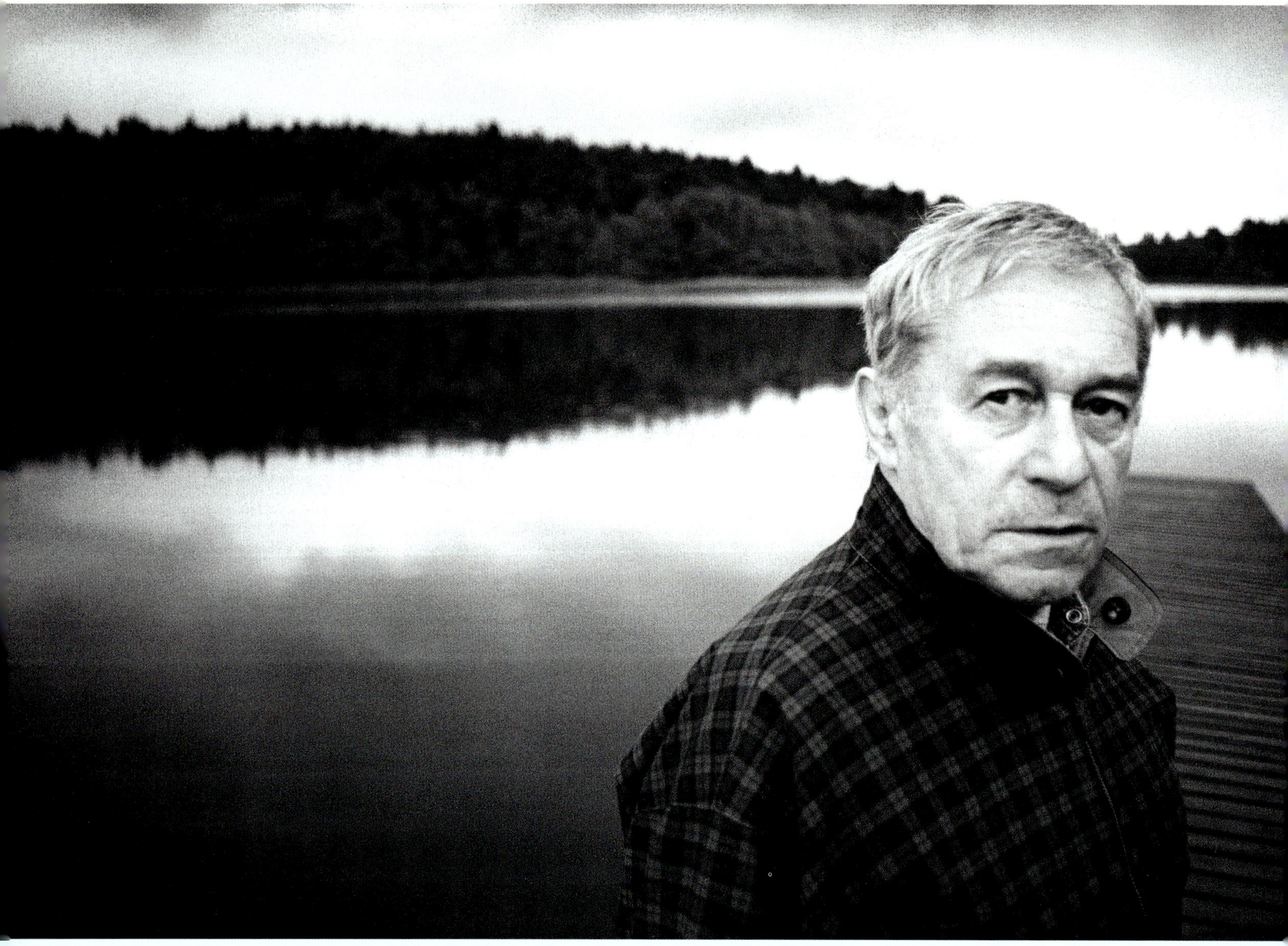

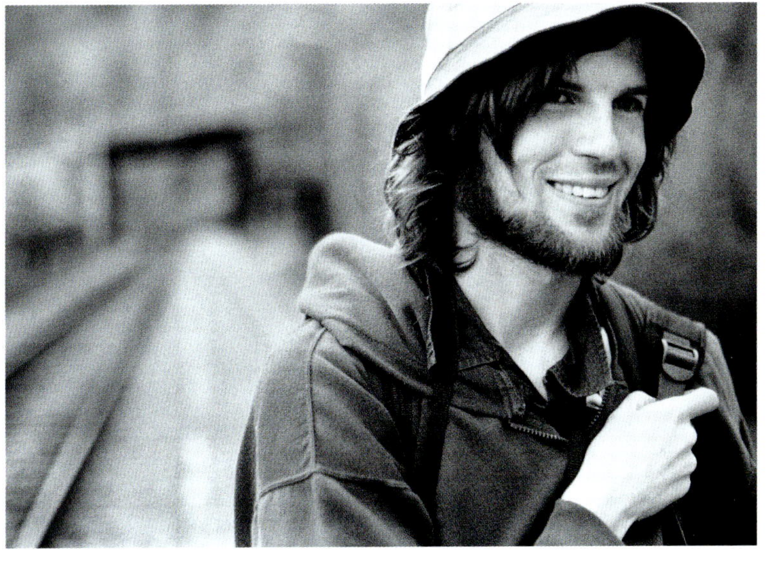

Fact file

Photographer: Tomek Paczkowski
Location: Zegiestow, Beskidy Mountains, Poland
Time of day: 5pm, summer

Technical details

Camera: Olympus OM2n
Lens: 50mm
Film: Ilford HP5 Plus
Exposure: 1/60sec at f/1.4

This subject, a friend of Tomek's, is framed in a very similar way to his father-in-law, but it is a much more casual image. That's partly due to his appearance and expression, but also in the way he looks as though he is about to move out of the frame. The blurred railway track leading to a tunnel also gives the impression of movement. ◀◀

The concept

This personal shot of Tomek's father-in-law came about while they were walking together in a beautiful forested area of the country. He was inspired by the light and the location to take the portrait. 'I just wanted to capture the moment,' he says.

The location

'It was a very special place at that time, especially the way the clouds and trees were reflected in the water.'

Composition

This would have been a very different picture in colour but in black and white it has a certain starkness and intensity to it. It isn't always easy to take a serious portrait of people who are well known to you and the subject can find it difficult to play it straight as well. These two have managed it very successfully – there seems nothing fake about the direct expression of Tomek's father-in-law.

Lighting and technique

It was partly the quality of the evening light that drew Tomek to take the shot. There was still plenty of brightness but it was softened by cloud cover, so there were no shadows on the face. He used aperture priority at f/4 to give some, but not too much, depth of field and a red filter to increase contrast, especially in the clouds.

'There was a special atmosphere about this – something a little "final" about a man coming towards the end of his life.'

Tomek Paczkowski

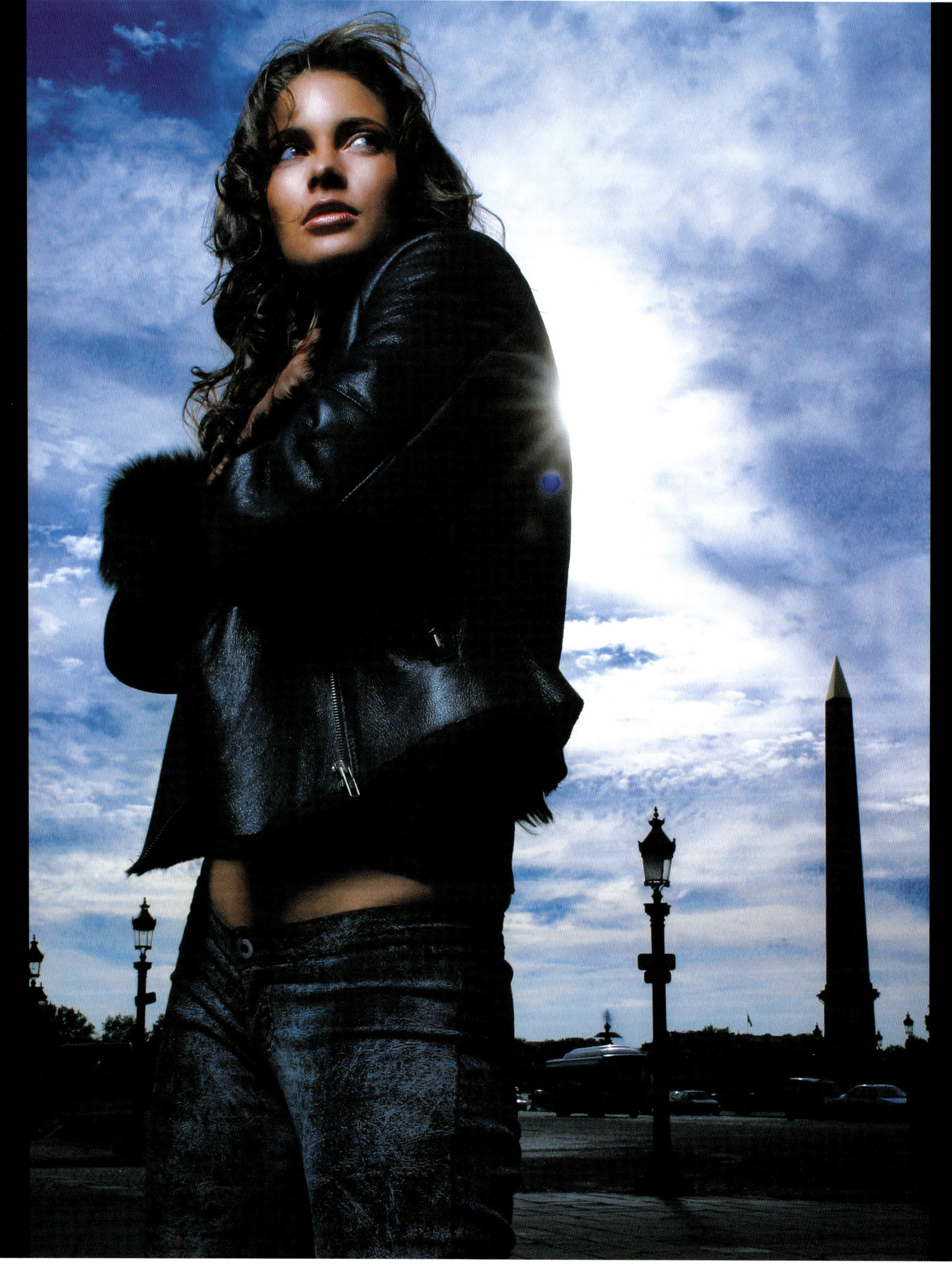

Stéphane Bourson

Chapter 4: **Image**

It isn't always the photographer who calls the shots over a portrait. Sometimes the subject will have their own agenda – an image of themselves that they want to convey to the outside world. Or he or she may be a model, with both of you having a client to please. This is usually the case with commercial photography – advertising, fashion and entertainment, for example – but personal pictures can also fall into this category.

There may be a brief to follow, but even if there isn't, it is up to you to read what is required from the portrait and use your skills to deliver it.

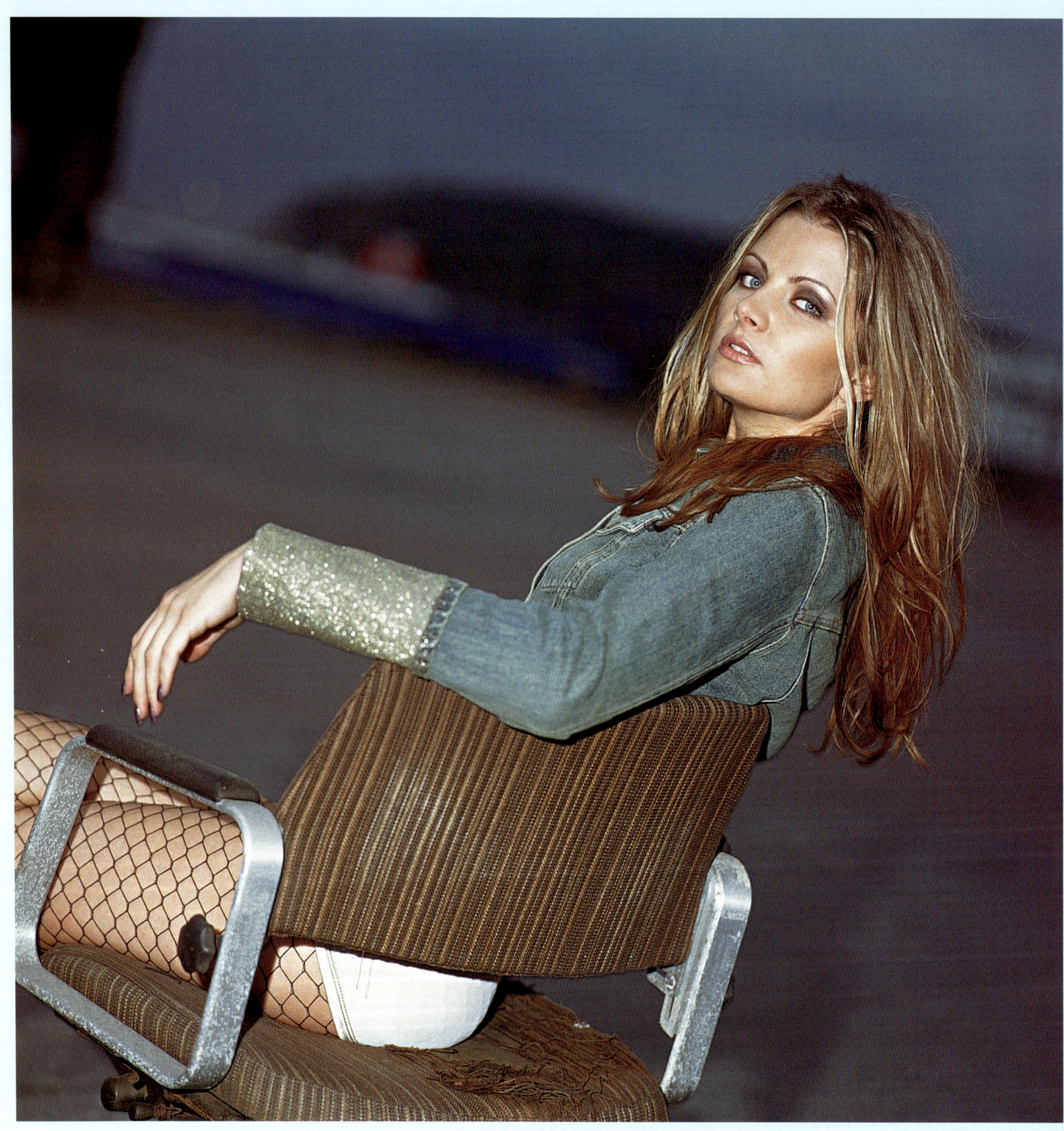

The concept

'This picture was commissioned by Avenue Modeller model agency in Gothenburg for Eleanor, a model,' recalls Christel. 'I was asked to take images that differed from her existing pictures. She already had smiling shots in her portfolio, so I had to create a moody look.'

Fact file

Photographer: Christel Sundebäck
Location: Gothenburg, Sweden
Time of day: Mid-afternoon, July

Technical details

Camera: Hasselblad 500CM
Lens: 150mm
Film: Kodak Ektachrome VS100
Exposure: 1/60sec at f/4

The location

Christel chose to shoot in an old industrial shipping area in Gothenburg. She didn't want the image to look too prettified and the bleakness of this setting provided a good contrast to the glamour of the model.

Composition

Christel chose the model's clothing and worked with the stylist to arrange her roughed-up hair and make-up, which gives a sexy, urban feel to the shot. The camera was tilted to unbalance the horizon and give the impression of movement. Again the idea was to achieve something different and more eye-catching than a straight beauty portrait.

Lighting and technique

'I took an ambient light reading with my Minolta Auto 4 meter, then decided to darken my background by underexposing one stop with the shutter speed,' Christel explains. 'I then used fill-in flash, overexposed by half a stop.' Although it was actually a bright, sunny day, the effect of this was to make it look like it was taken at dusk. 'The choice of the background and the styling of the model was to show a strong contrast between beautiful and ugly.'

'The background and the styling of the model were chosen to show a strong contrast between beautiful and ugly.'

Christel Sundebäck

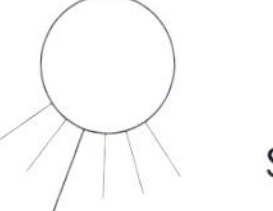

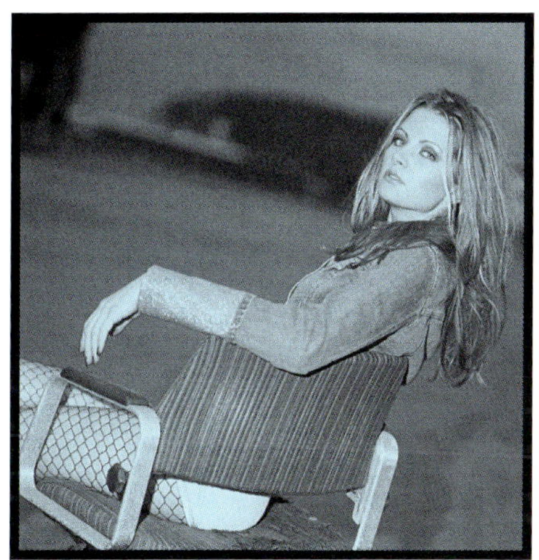

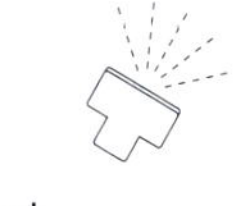

Fact file

Photographer: Trevor Brady
Location: Gastown, Vancouver, Canada
Time of day: 6pm, May

Technical details

Camera: Hasselblad 500CM
Lens: 80mm
Film: Agfa APX 400
Exposure: 1/125sec at f/5.6

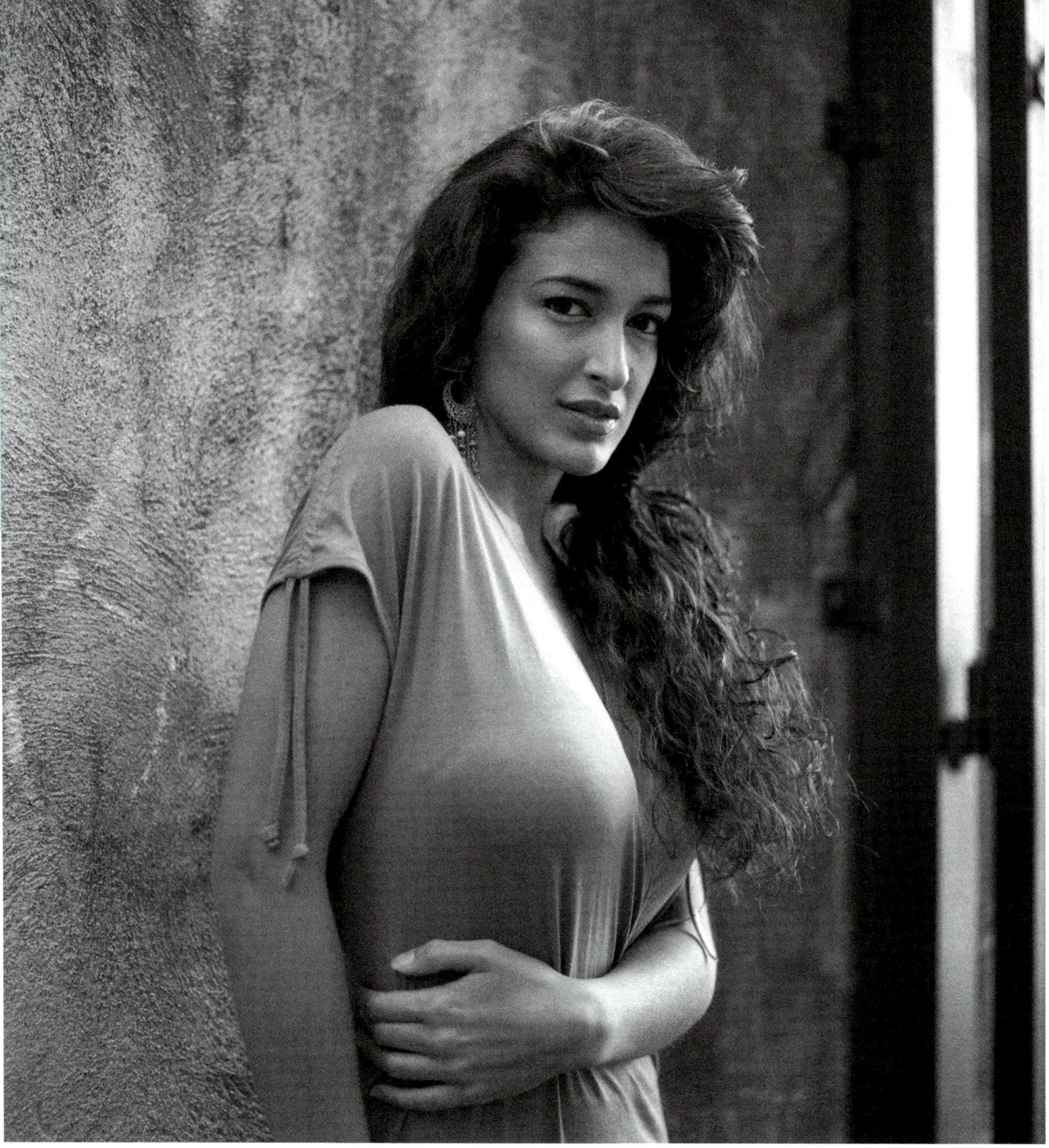

The concept

'This shoot was to develop new images for the model's portfolio,' says Trevor. 'I had seen the other stuff she already had in her book and it was mostly sexy, edgy, highly-styled work. I wanted to produce a simple and timeless photograph.'

The location

Trevor wanted a simple background that would not detract attention away from the model. A narrow alley provided this, but was also ideal for channelling and diffusing the direct sunlight, lighting her with a soft side-light that was flattering.

Composition

Trevor wanted a timeless portrait and the model's pose and look here have something of the 1950s about them – glamorous and alluring. The inclusion of the doorway gives the impression she is about to leave the scene and is turning to see if the viewer will follow.

Lighting and technique

Only natural light was used. The sun was reflected off the wall on the right to bounce on to the right side of the subject, providing enough highlights to produce some modelling without harsh shadows. Trevor metered for the light coming from the left side to make sure this darker area was correctly exposed.

‘The composition and pose helped to give the feeling that she is leaving and it was important to include a little of the gate and frame to give a reason for this.’

Trevor Brady

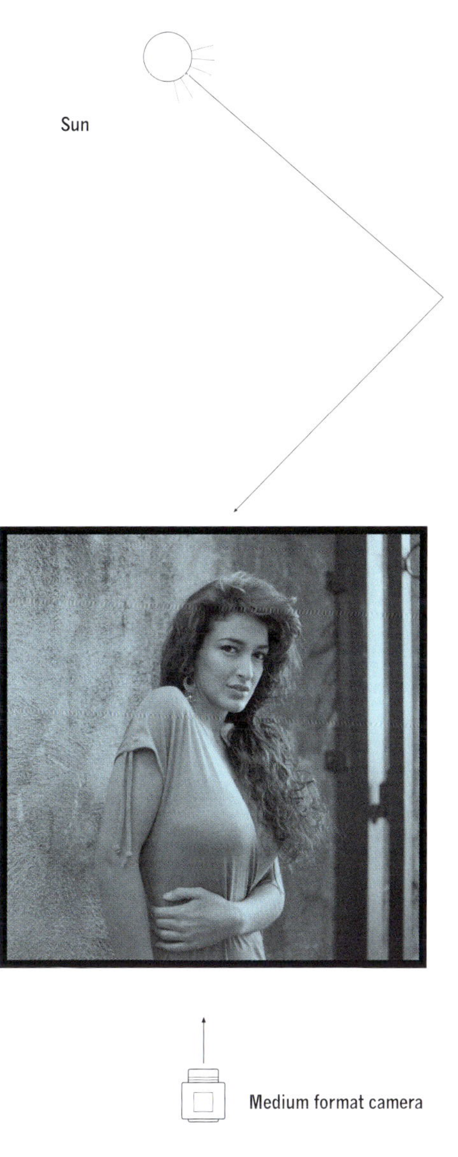

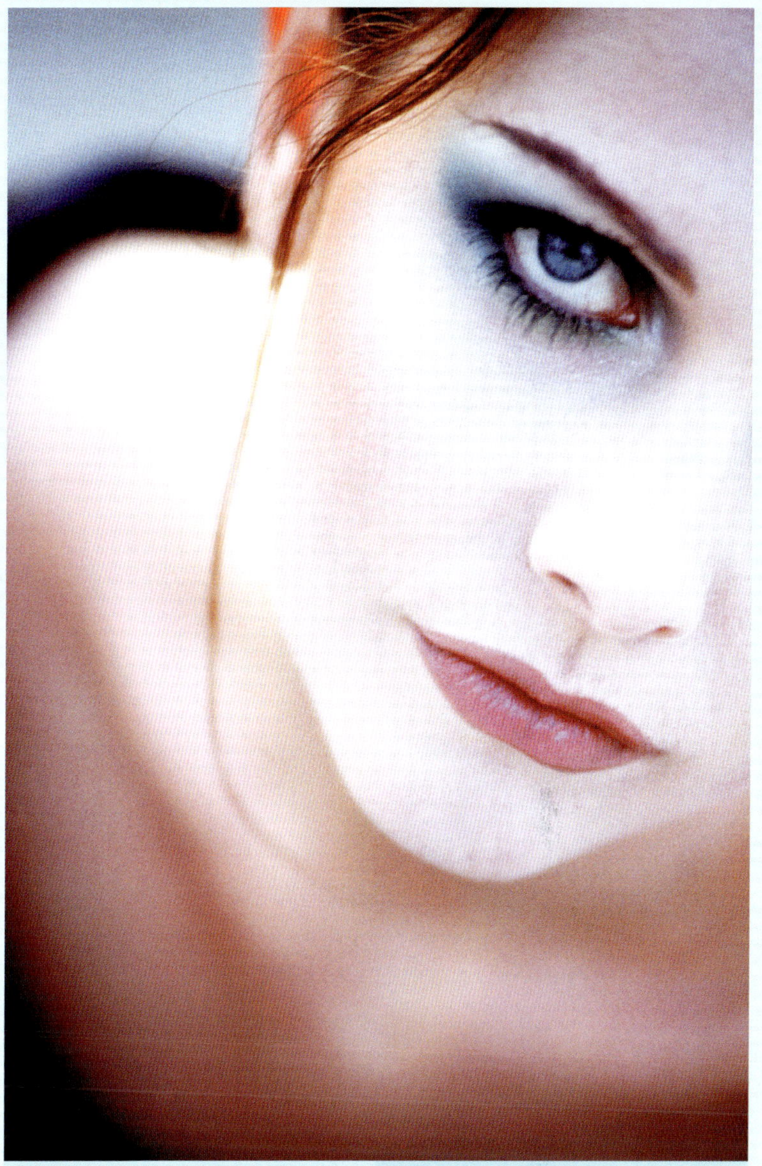

Fact file

Photographer: Marco Tenaglia
Location: Italy
Time of day: 6pm, June

Technical details

Camera: Nikon F90X
Lens: 200mm
Film: Fuji Astia
Exposure: 1/125sec at f/2.8

This was a test shoot for the model, commissioned by her agency, and Marco wanted some more unusual shots that would really make her stand out. This extreme close up and bold crop does the job, mainly because the model has the looks to carry it off. Marco was ready to filter the sunlight through a transparent white panel, but white clouds appeared, creating a better effect naturally.

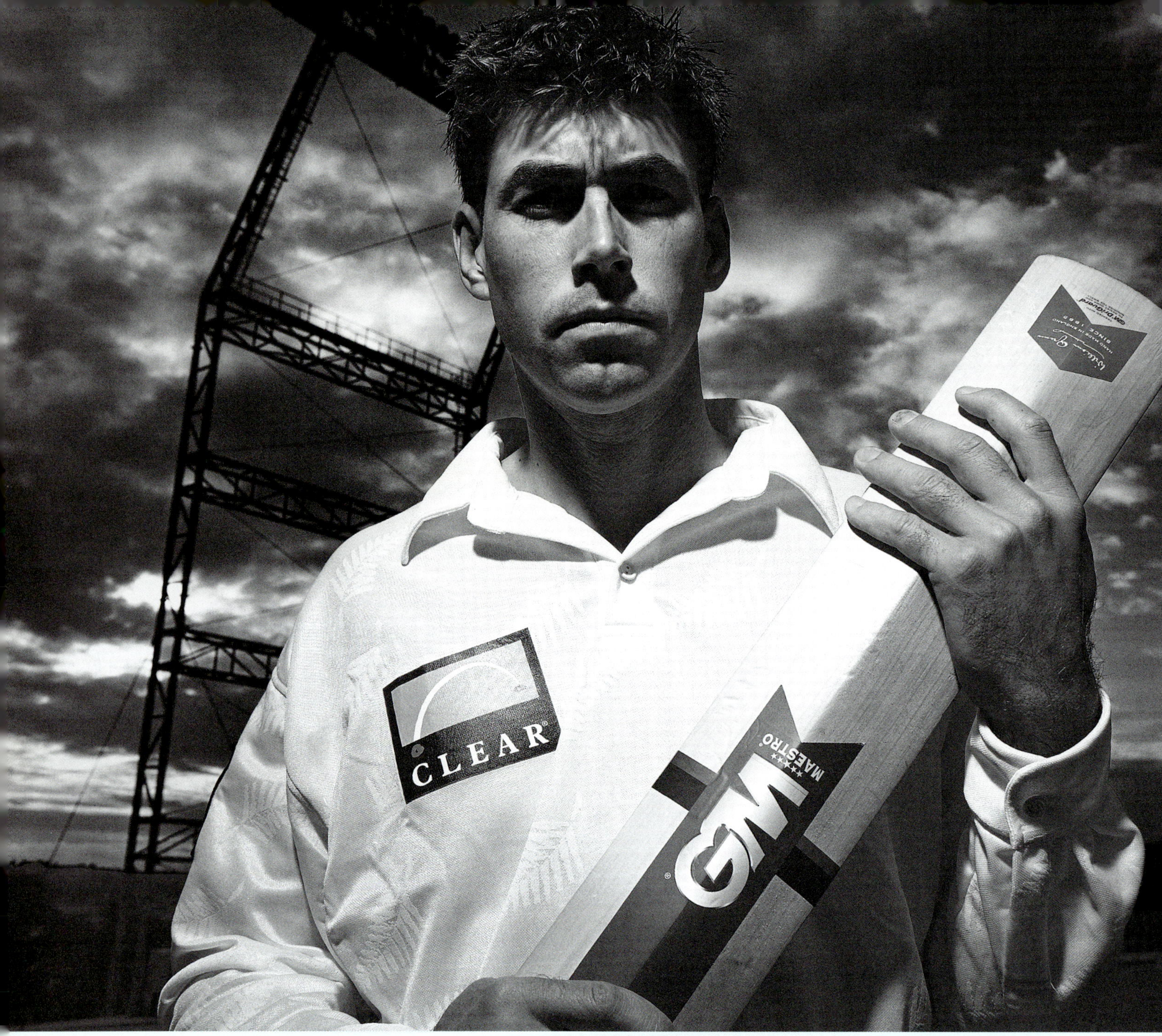

'I had Stephen Flemming place the bat prominently to the camera, not only because he is a great batsman, but also to show his fabulous hands.'

Michael Hall

Fact file

Photographer: Michael Hall
Location: Christchurch, New Zealand
Time of day: Sunrise, late winter

Technical details

Camera: Hasselblad 503 SW
Lens: 50mm
Film: Agfa APX 100
Exposure: 1/500sec at f/5.6

The concept

'This commission came from the picture editor of Panorama, the Air New Zealand in-flight magazine,' explains Michael. 'Stephen Flemming is the captain of the New Zealand cricket team, which was about to embark on a tour of Australia. The brief was to portray Stephen as a gladiator and this was used as a cover shot.'

The location

Since the portrait was for a profile of the cricketer in connection with his sport and his team, the setting of the cricket stadium in Christchurch was a natural choice.

Composition

The image that Michael was asked to portray of his subject was that of a fighter, about to go into battle and win. The low camera angle, causing the subject to look down slightly at the viewer, increases the sense of his dominating presence, his expression is strong and determined and even the bat looks as much like a weapon as the tool of his trade. The towering structure in the background and the brooding sky also give a sense of power.

Lighting and technique

Mixing flash with daylight can be a good method of hardening the image of a subject. Often the two are balanced so the flash is barely noticeable, but here Michael wanted definite contrast between the subject and background. 'I lit him with a fairly hard light above and to the left of the camera and dropped the early morning sky and stadium lighting two stops darker to bring some mood to an otherwise dull day,' he explains.

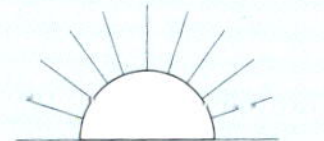

Sunrise

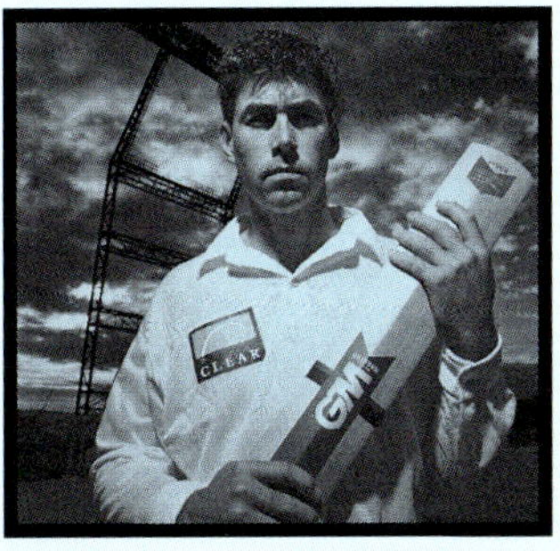

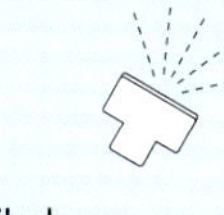

Flash

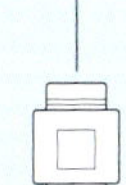

Medium format camera

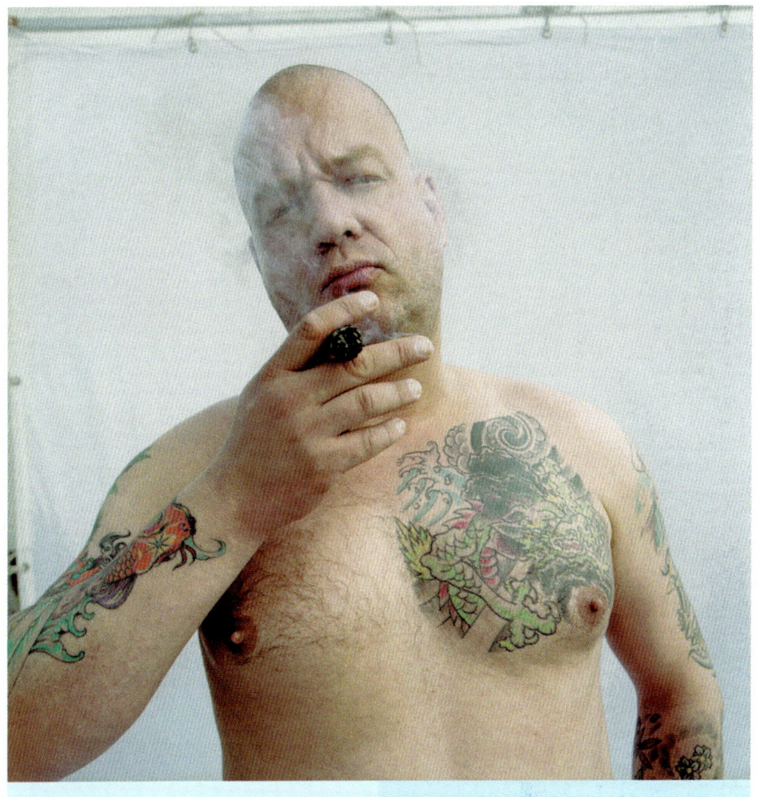

Fact file

Photographer: Michael Hall
Location: Vancouver, Canada
Time of day: Mid-afternoon, July

Technical details

Camera: Hasselblad 503 SW
Lens: 50mm
Film: Kodak 160 VC
Exposure: 1/125sec at f/8

'Andreas is one of my clients, a creative director. We were shooting at a film set in Vancouver and I had erected a white background in order to capture some portraits of the actors as they came off set. I had an umbrella and flash head to camera right slightly above lens height.' The archetypal hard-man image was tongue-in-cheek here, portrayed through the slightly aggressive stance of the subject, complete with shaven head and tattoos, with fat cigar as a finishing touch.

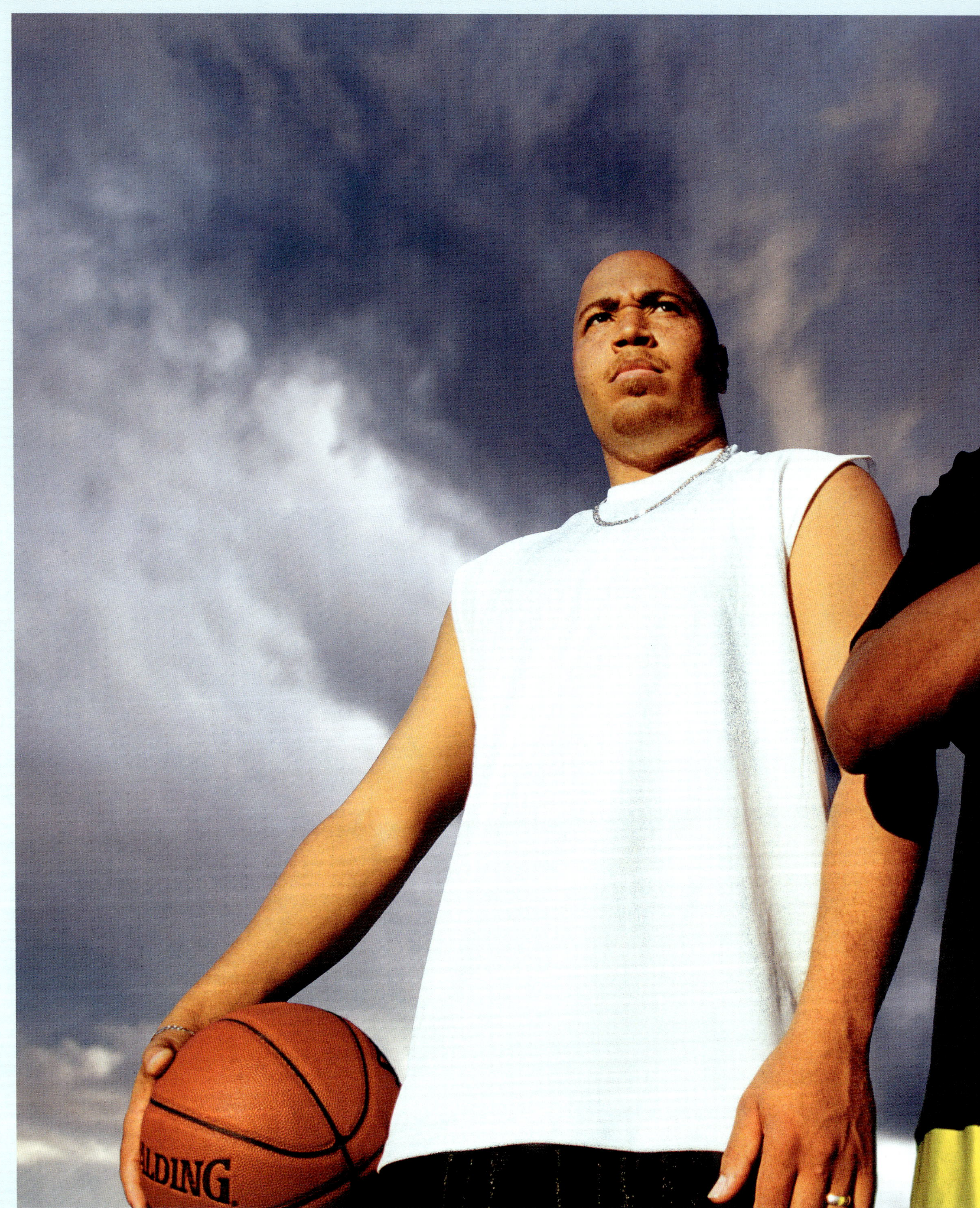
LDING

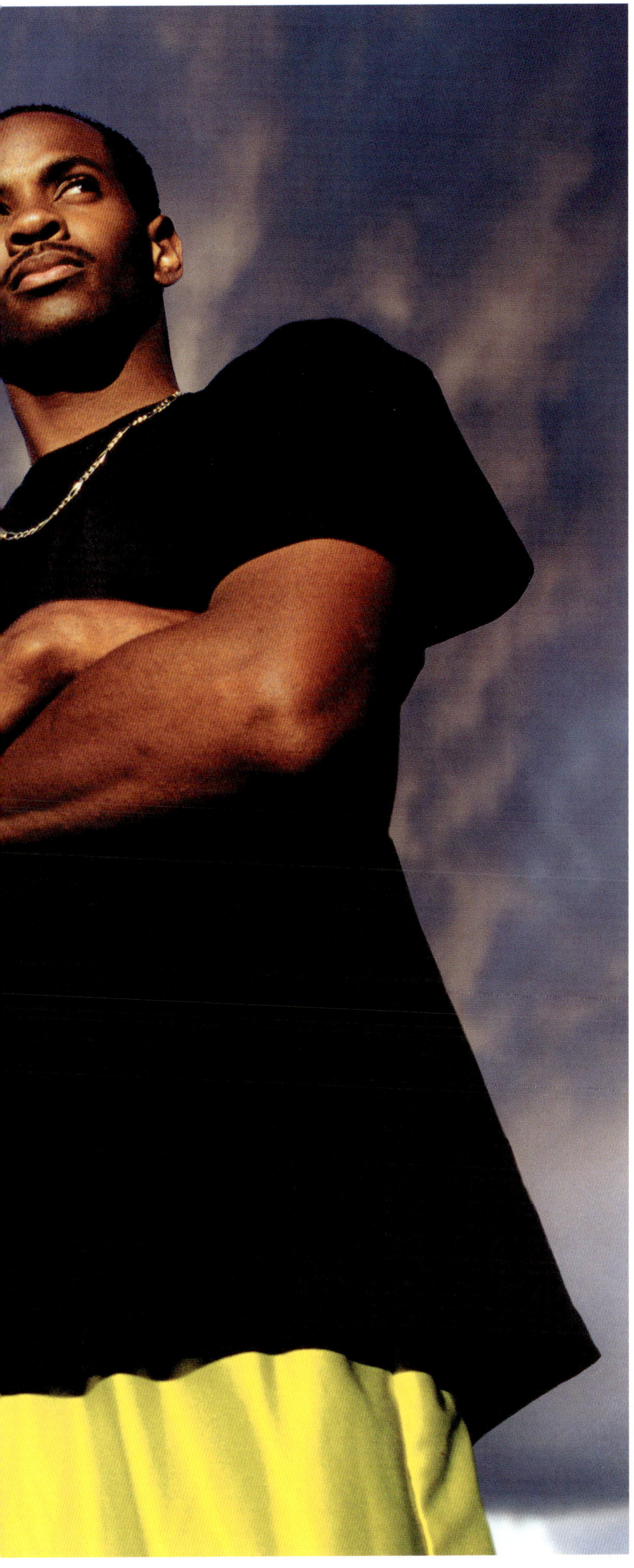

Fact file	
Photographer:	Guy Crittenden
Location:	Richmond, Virginia, USA
Time of day:	Late afternoon, October

Technical details	
Camera:	Canon 1DS (digital)
Lens:	28–70mm
Film:	n/a
Exposure:	1/300sec at f/11

The concept

Guy was commissioned for this by a sportswear company to use as part of a promotional advertorial. There was no art director or stylist involved so he had the freedom to plan and direct the shoot himself.

The location

Guy had decided in advance to shoot from this angle, so the location simply had to be anywhere outdoors. He used the basketball court in a public park.

Composition

Fashion photographs need to sell the image and lifestyle that goes with the clothes and here it is unmistakably cool and tough. The pose and expressions are part of this and the low camera angle makes these two seem like people you would look up to. The foreboding sky also adds to the hard image and helps the subjects, and the clothes, stand out.

Lighting and technique

Only natural light was used here – the warm sunlight of late afternoon that gives a golden glow to the skin and the clothing. 'The dramatic cloudy background was added from a shot later that same day,' says Guy. 'When outdoor conditions don't co-operate, we take artistic license to create the drama without making the shot unbelievable.'

> 'I used street talent – not paid models – and asked them to give me some "attitude". They did a great job and looked very natural doing it.'

Guy Crittenden

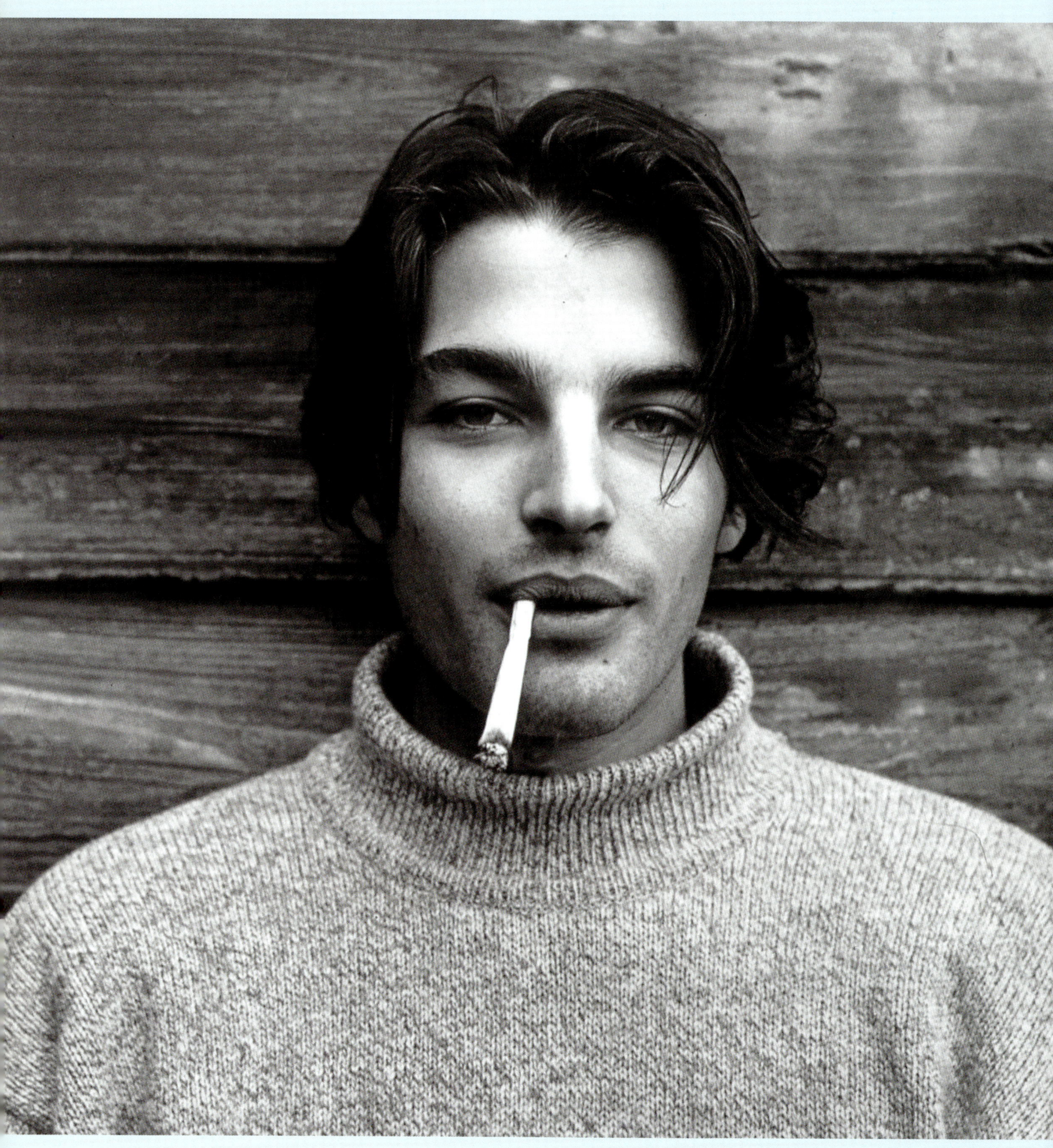

The concept

This was taken some years ago when Roderick had recently bought a medium format camera and was experimenting with the square format by taking portraits of actors and people he knew 'with interesting faces'. This is someone he knew from childhood, the son of actor Dave Prowse – Darth Vader in the first Star Wars film.

Fact file

Photographer: Roderick Field, Trevillion Picture Library
Location: Brighton, UK
Time of day: Mid-afternoon, October

Technical details

Camera: Mamiya C220
Lens: 105mm
Film: Kodak Tri-X
Exposure: 1/125sec at f/4

The location

Roderick always shoots portraits using only natural light, although he usually prefers window light indoors, finding it more controllable. This shot was taken outside the subject's own house, however, as the light conditions were favourable at the time.

Composition

This head and shoulders composition, with the subject making direct eye contact, was a theme Roderick was working to at the time. 'They are almost like mug shots,' he says. This 'look' came directly from the subject with no influence from Roderick. 'That's just the kind of person he is, a bit of a peacock! I always let the people I am photographing do what they like.'

Lighting and technique

Roderick finds natural light outdoors can be too harsh and unflattering in Britain, making eyes disappear into their sockets. Flat light is no good, in his view, either. 'There needs to be direction to the light to give modelling,' he says. On this occasion direct sunlight was slightly diffused through clouds, providing the required modelling on the left side of the subject's face and neck.

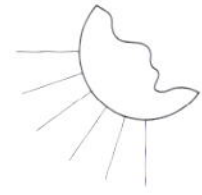

Sun diffused by cloud

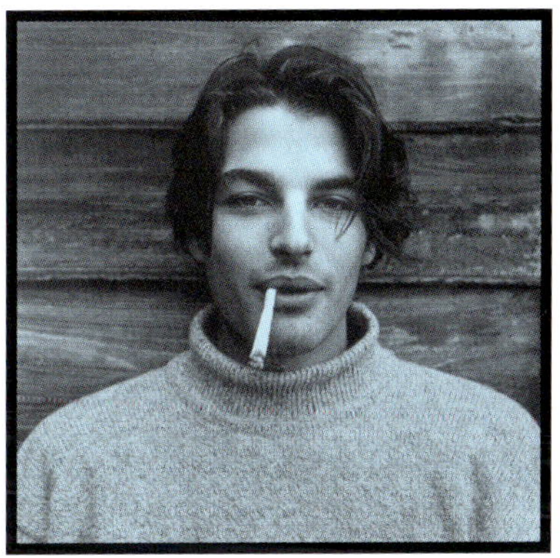

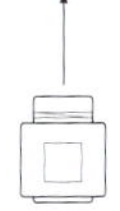

Medium format camera

'Taking portraits is about developing a relationship with the subject so they can be themselves – the photography side is almost incidental. If they feel uncomfortable, it will always show.'

Roderick Field

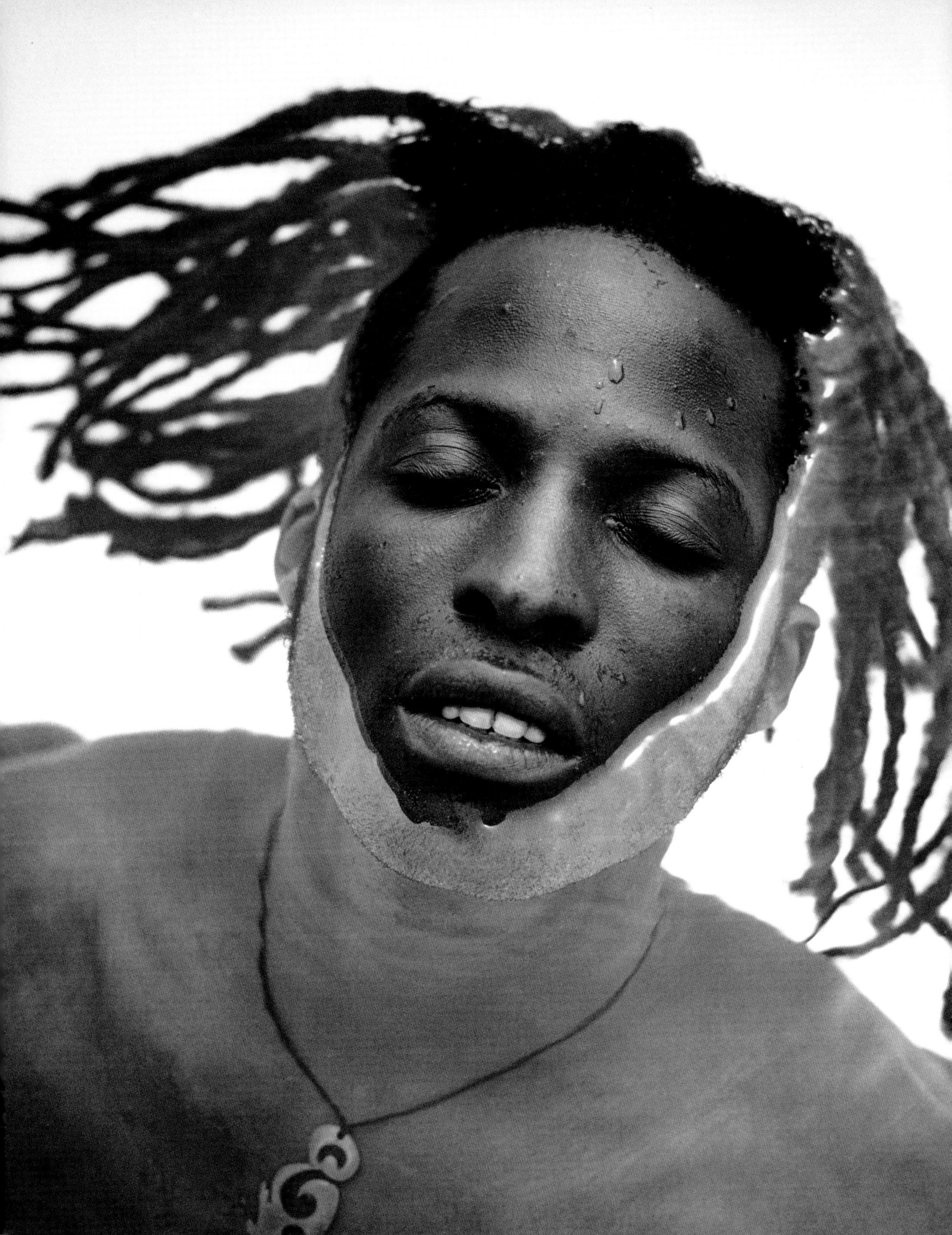

Fact file

Photographer: Michael Hall
Location: Wellington, New Zealand
Time of day: Noon, summer

Technical details

Camera: Hasselblad 501C
Lens: 80mm
Film: Agfa APX 100
Exposure: 1/125sec at f/8

'One of the aspects I so love about photography is that you can do extraordinary things with such minimal equipment.'

Michael Hall

The concept

You can imagine this image used on an album cover, but it was actually a personal shot, taken just for the fun of it but used as self-promotion in Michael's portfolio. 'I'd been wanting to take my friend Colin's portrait for some time and had been trying to formulate an idea,' Michael explains. 'I finally decided his black skin would work well in water on a bright sunny day.'

The location

Michael used the local outdoor swimming pool in his home city of Wellington.

Composition

It takes a while to work this shot out, as Michael says, 'it's a very confusing situation,' but in fact it was photographed in a straightforward way. He asked Colin to recline in the shallow end of the pool, so just part of his face was above the water. This was in full sun, which has added to the strangeness of the image. 'I like its incongruous nature; the fact you have definitive shades of black, white and mid-tone grey with very little in between. I love the specular highlight running along the left of his face and the weird outline the water has created, emphasised by the full sun.'

Lighting and technique

Taken simply with a hand-held Hasselblad camera and standard 80mm lens, you might think that this has been heavily retouched. In fact it is a straight print on grade 3 paper with just a little dodging and burning for effect.

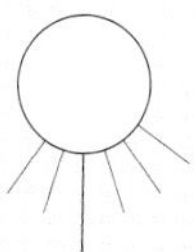

Strong, overhead sun

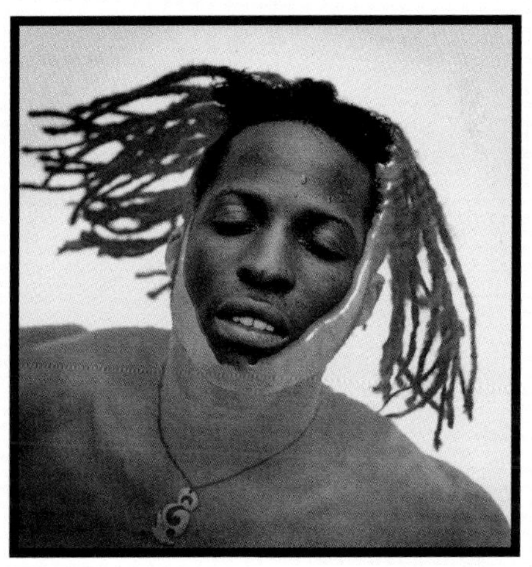

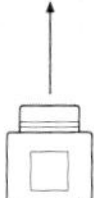

Medium format camera above the subject

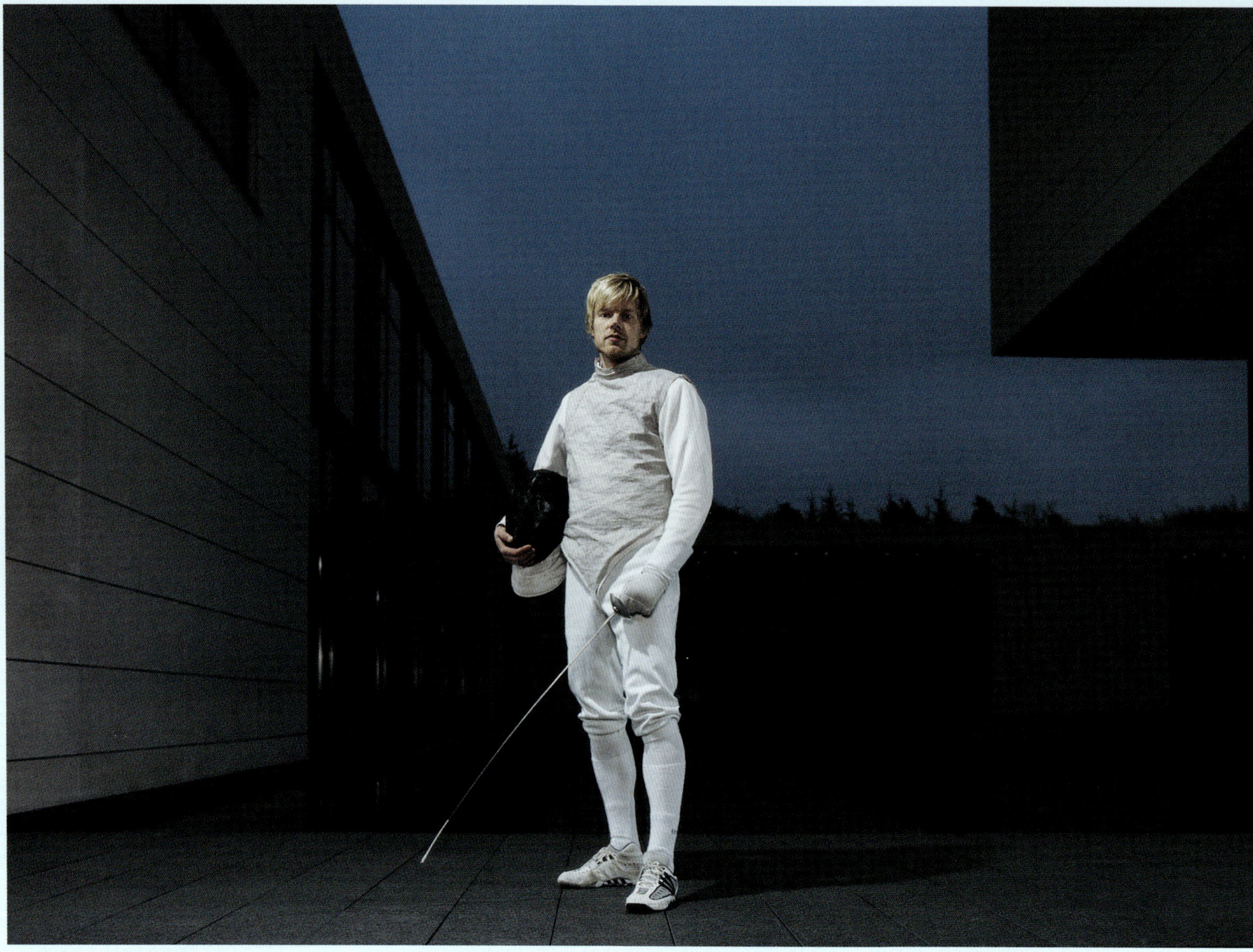

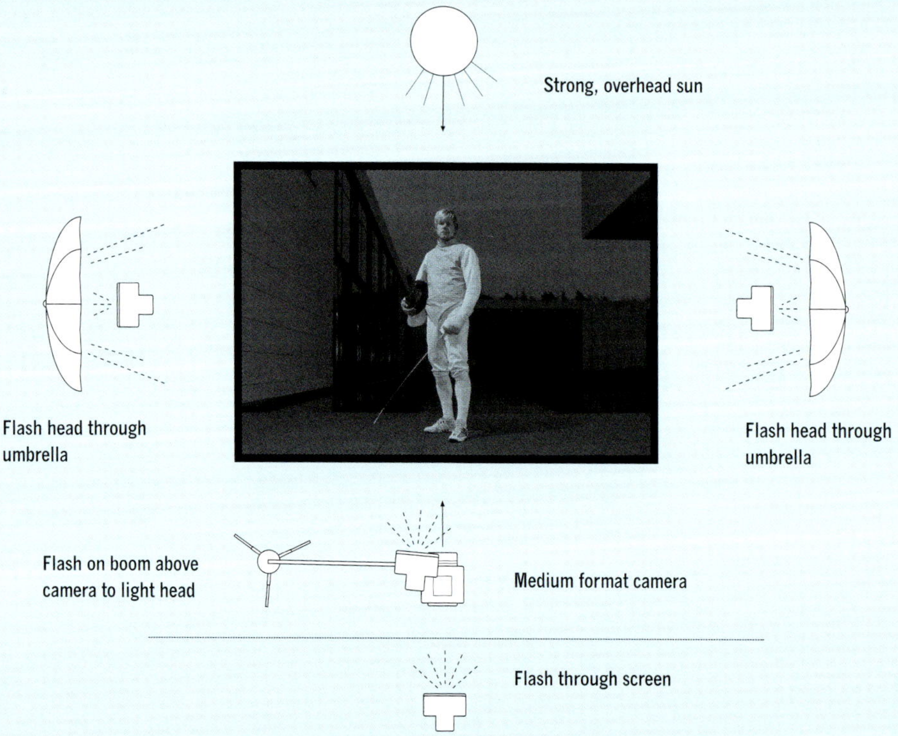

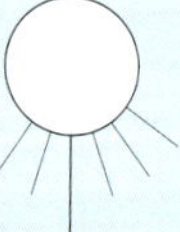

Strong, overhead sun

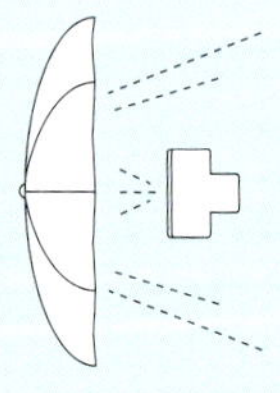

Flash head through umbrella

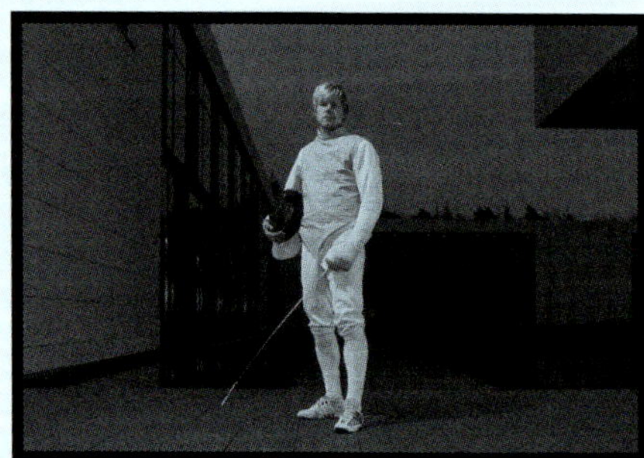

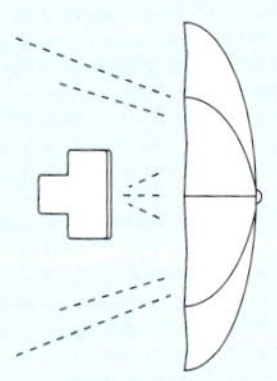

Flash head through umbrella

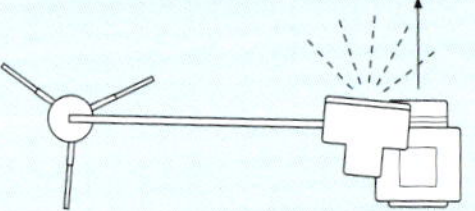

Flash on boom above camera to light head

Medium format camera

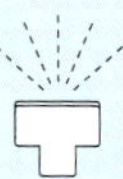

Flash through screen

Fact file

Photographer: Fredrik Clement
Location: Bjeringbro, Denmark
Time of day: Early morning, December

Technical details

Camera: Hasselblad 500CM
Lens: 50mm
Film: Kodak GX 100
Exposure: 1/250sec at f/5.6

The concept

This was part of a worldwide advertising campaign that Fredrik shot for Grundfos, a large Danish company and sponsor of the 2004 Danish Olympics team.

The location

'The brief from the agency was to shoot sportsmen and women at the premises of Grundfos,' Fredrik explains. 'I visited the place weeks before I took this shot, and planned the exact location and decided how I would light it.'

Composition

This image was designed for use as a poster-sized advertisement to go on the various premises of Grundfos worldwide and so it had to be bold, eye-catching and uncluttered with room for text to be added. Fredrik kept the pose and the composition simple, using the lighting to make the subject leap out from the background.

Lighting and technique

Early in the morning on a grey, winter's day, Frederik supplemented the natural light with four flash heads. Next to the camera was a 4x4 foot silk screen to diffuse a Broncolor A4 head, providing a large, soft light source. A telescopic boom with a ProFoto B7 head was angled to light the subject's head specifically, while two more ProFoto B7 heads with umbrellas were placed on either side of him to provide fill-in.

'I use flash on a telescopic boom quite a lot in my pictures. I find that it helps to give shape to the face.'

Fredrik Clement

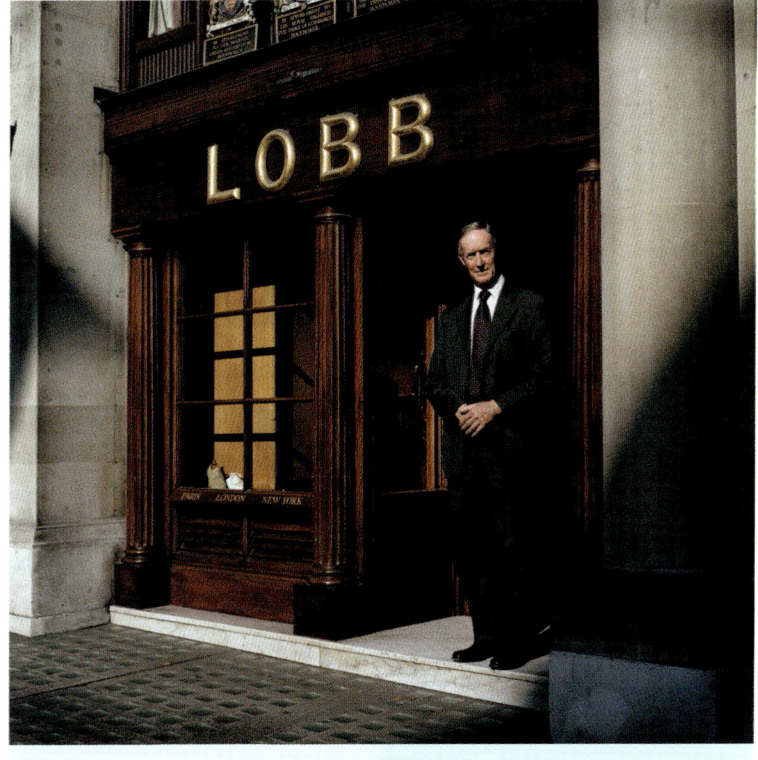

Fact file

Photographer: Fredrik Clement
Location: London, UK
Time of day: 3pm, September

Technical details

Camera: Hasselblad 500CM
Lens: 80mm
Film: Kodak 160
Exposure: 1/125sec at f/8

Fredrik was commissioned for this portrait by Provenu, a magazine published by Danske Bank, a large Danish bank. 'The assignment was for a story about one of the finest shoe shops in the world. The price for a pair of Lobb shoes starts at £2,000,' he explains. 'Arriving at the location, the light was perfect so I got the journalist to ask Mr Lobb to come outside right away. Three minutes after I had finished the second roll of film the light was gone and I knew I had the shot.'

Fact file

Photographer:	Rene de Haan
Location:	Amsterdam, Holland
Time of day:	3pm, May

Technical details

Camera:	Hasselblad 500CM
Lens:	80mm
Film:	Kodak Tri-X 400
Exposure:	1/125sec at f/5.6

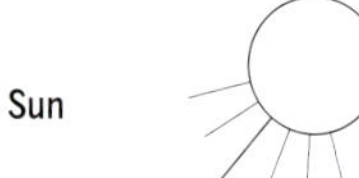

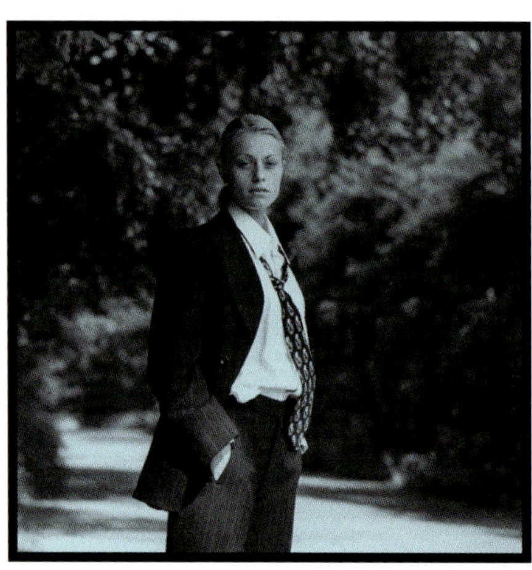

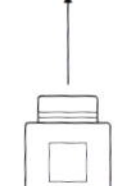

The concept

'I've photographed this model many times, but they have been mostly nudes and I wondered how she would look in my suit,' says Rene. 'I didn't want just another studio shoot, and as it was a nice spring day we went to the woods and took a series of pictures.'

The location

Based in Amsterdam, Rene went to a small forest just outside the city to do the shoot. It was chosen as a deliberately unlikely location in which to find a woman dressed in this way.

Composition

There are plenty of contradictions in this portrait that add to its mystery and appeal. The model is dressed in an ill-fitting man's suit with her hair drawn back, but despite the masculine attire, confident pose and slightly sneering expression, her feminine beauty shines through. The incongruous woodland setting also helps soften the formality of the shot.

Lighting and technique

The direct sunlight was very strong that afternoon, so Rene placed the model in the shade of trees. 'It was much better for her face, without harsh shadows, but also for the white shirt she's wearing, which would look like just a white patch in direct sun,' he says.

'The contrast between the natural look of the forest and the businesslike look of the model appealed to me.'

Rene de Haan

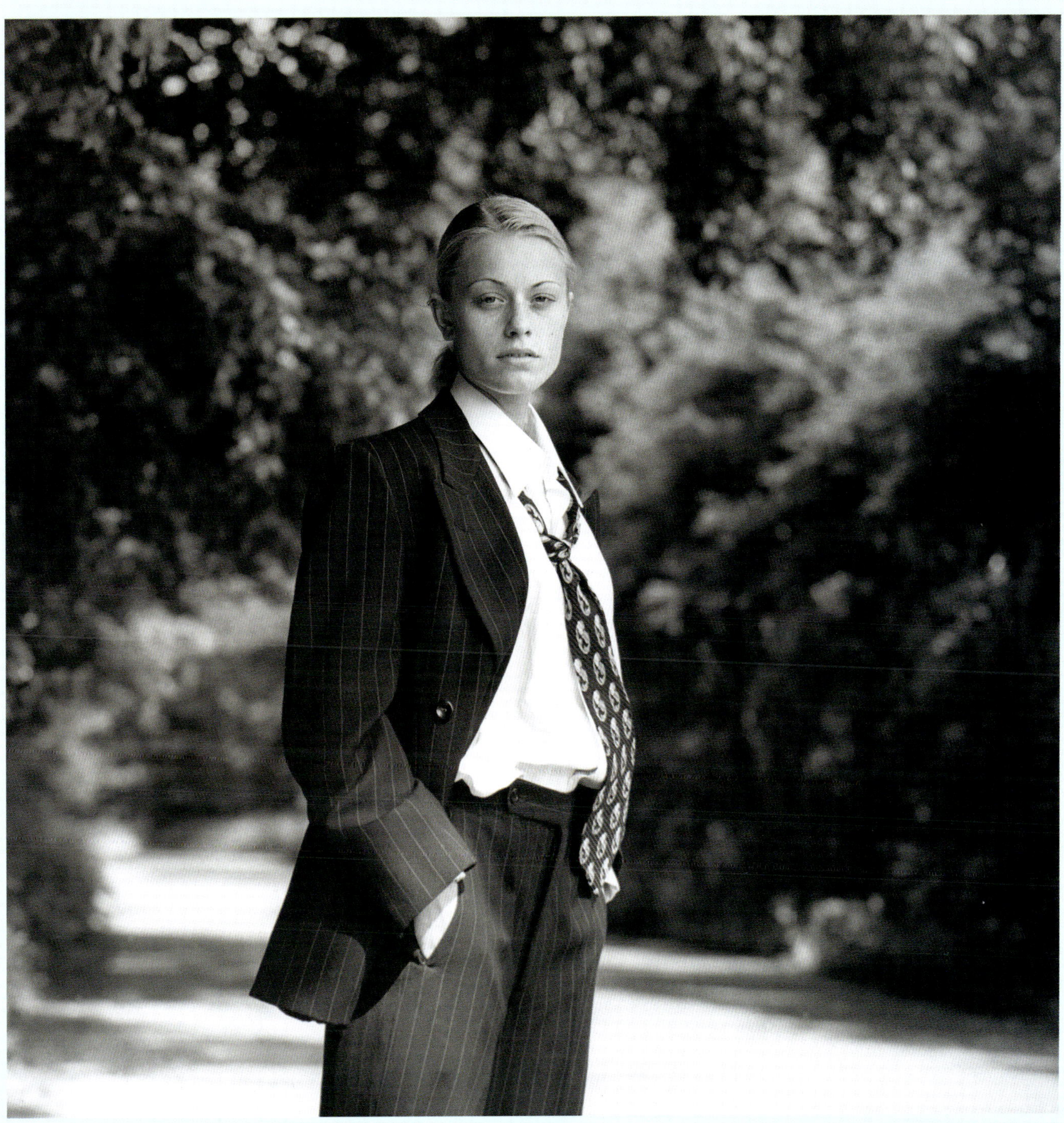

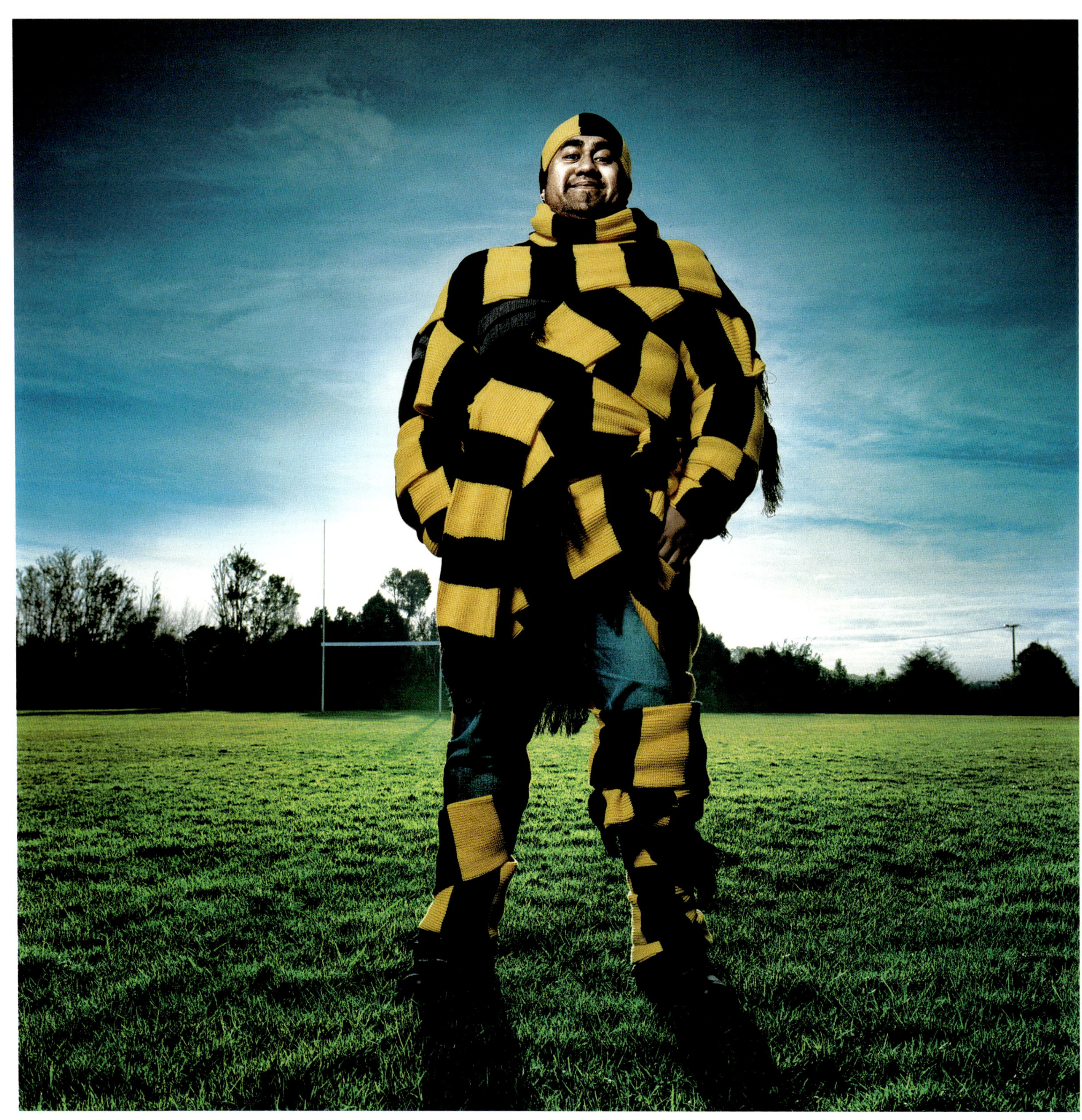

Fact file

Photographer: Michael Hall
Location: Auckland, New Zealand
Time of day: Mid-afternoon, winter

Technical details

Camera: Hasselblad 503SW
Lens: 50mm
Film: Kodak 160 VC
Exposure: 1/125sec at f/11

The concept

Michael was commissioned for this shot by the electricity company, Genesis Energy who sponsor Taranaki Rugby. 'Genesis supply a rig at the games which provides hot drinks and gas heating to keep the punters warm on those cold wintry days.' He explains: 'The art director, Jeremy Gleeson from Lowe Worldwide, wanted to portray this theme in a comical light. The copy reads "There are better ways to keep warm at the rugby".'

The location

'It was imperative we shot this scene to make it look cold and, although we didn't get the nasty wet weather we had hoped for on the day, there's a certain magic to the backlit dew on the grass, the low angle of the sun and the cirrostratus clouds in the steal blue sky. It all gives the sense that it is indeed winter and "cold" as I can assure you it was!'

Composition

Michael decided to use a low camera angle with a wide-angle lens to make the subject loom larger and provide visual impact. 'We were very lucky with the dew,' he adds, 'as this was the second shoot of the day and it was late afternoon by this time. The morning was taken up by a portrait at the local stadium, part of the same job.'

Lighting and technique

Michael used a single flash head on his ProFoto B7 with a scrimmed beauty dish to the left of the camera. 'This light gives a beautiful quality when placed away from the subject. It has a slightly hard edge but still remains soft enough to be kind to the subject. When metering for a situation like this, one must determine the ambient background light and set the flash accordingly. I knew I had to effectively underexpose the background to emphasise the colour and "coldness", but not so much that I lost the subtle hues in the sky and on the grass. I balanced the flash accordingly so that I didn't overemphasise the subject.'

'The light was aimed directly at the subject's head, falling off as it gets down to his legs and the ground. My intention was for the viewer to go straight to his face, as his expression gives a visual cue to the humour of the situation.'

Michael Hall

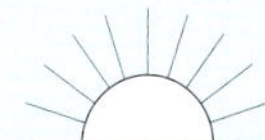

Low, late afternoon sun

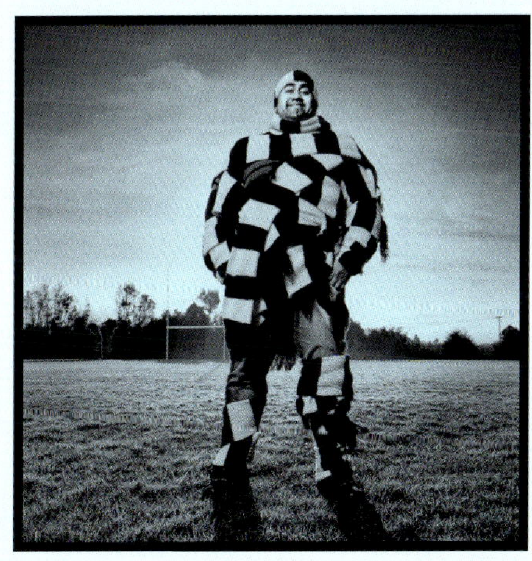

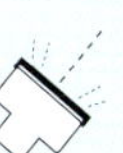

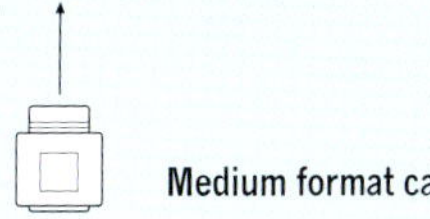

Medium format camera

Flash head with beauty dish

Fact file

Photographer: Sam Devine Tischler
Location: Tornillo, Texas
Time of day: 2.30pm, June

Technical details

Camera: Nikon F3
Lens: 28mm
Film: Kodak Tri-X 400
Exposure: 1/125sec at f/8

The concept

This is an American band called Ministry at the Sonic Ranch. Sam was commissioned to take a group shot of them by Home Recording Magazine, to accompany a feature but was given total creative freedom over the shoot.

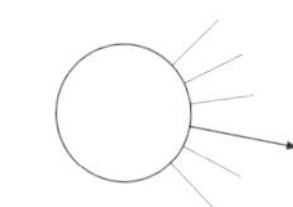

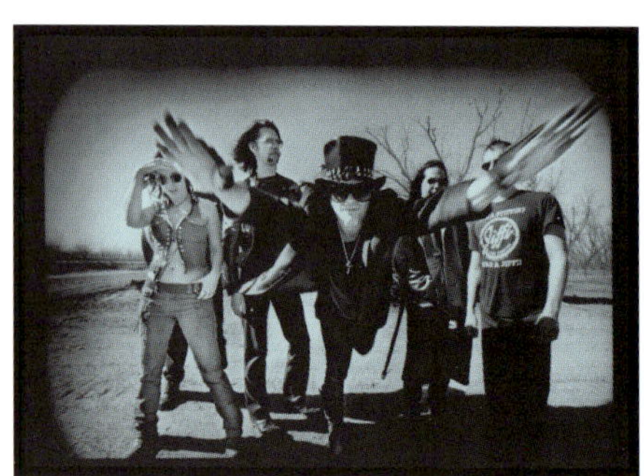

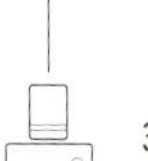

The location

Sam chose a rural location that also had a slight industrial feel to it and would also give him and the band members plenty of space to move in. 'Behind me was a ditch where workers were burning some old branches and things,' he recalls. 'I wanted to get some of the smoke in the shot, but what I got instead was the wind, which still worked out well.'

Composition

Photographing musicians and other performers can be a minefield if you have to take into account their egos, the way their management would like them to be portrayed and your own ideas. It's useful to have some shots planned in advance so the session has some structure, but also be prepared to seize unexpected opportunities. That was exactly what happened with this shot, as Sam explains: 'While I was shooting just a basic group shot, the singer, Al, spontaneously jumped towards me in a flying leap. It worked great.'

Lighting and technique

'I shot this around 2.30 in the afternoon – probably the hardest light you can ask for, with very strong shadows,' he says. 'I metered off the shadows and opened up by one and a half stops. That way I overexposed enough to get detail in the shadows, but not so much that I blocked up the highlights. Then, when I printed the shot, I dodged the shadow areas enough to bring out the detail.'

‘I had a lot of fun on this shoot. The band was great to me and willing to do whatever I asked. They even fed me lunch…’

Sam Devine Tischler

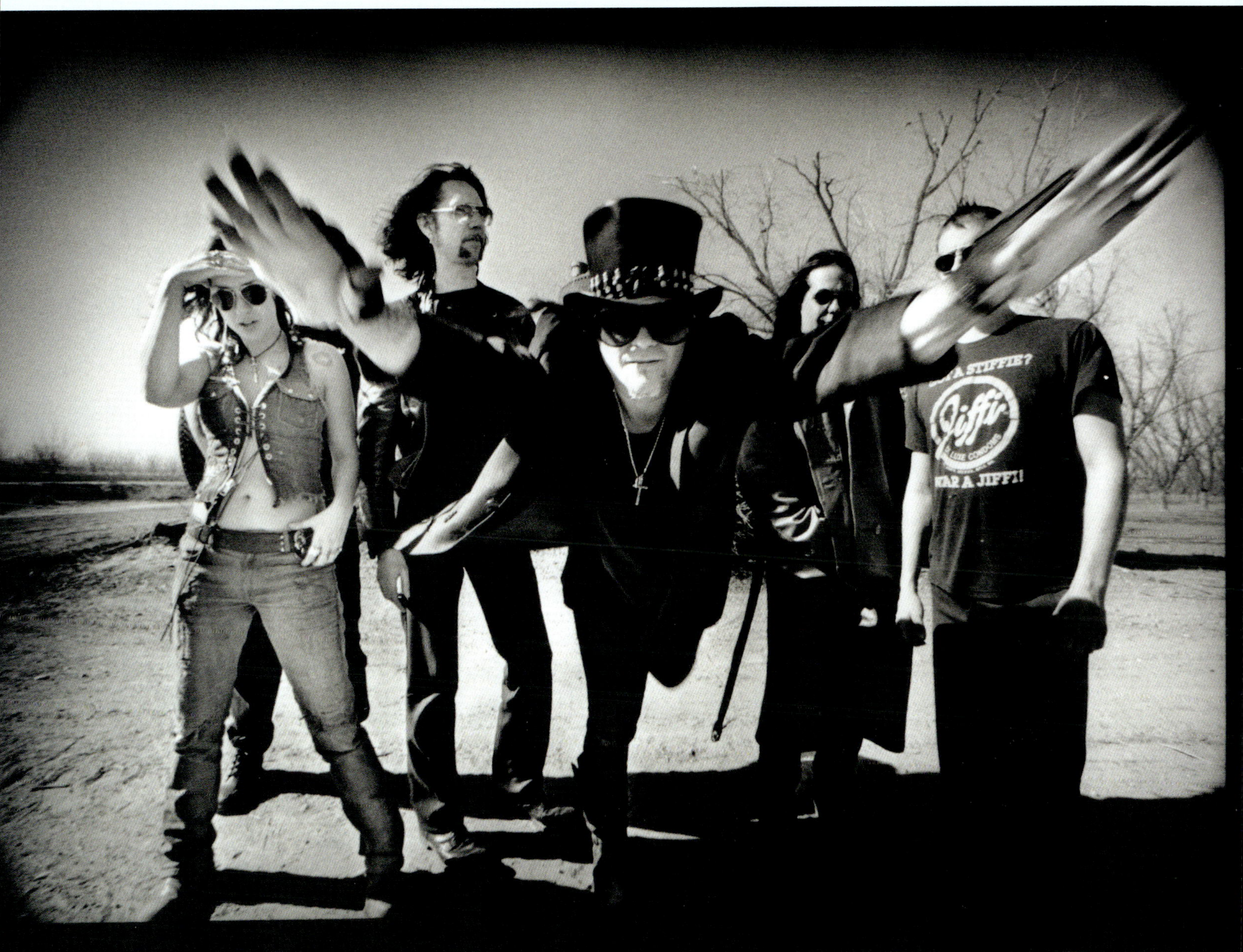

Matt Hoyle

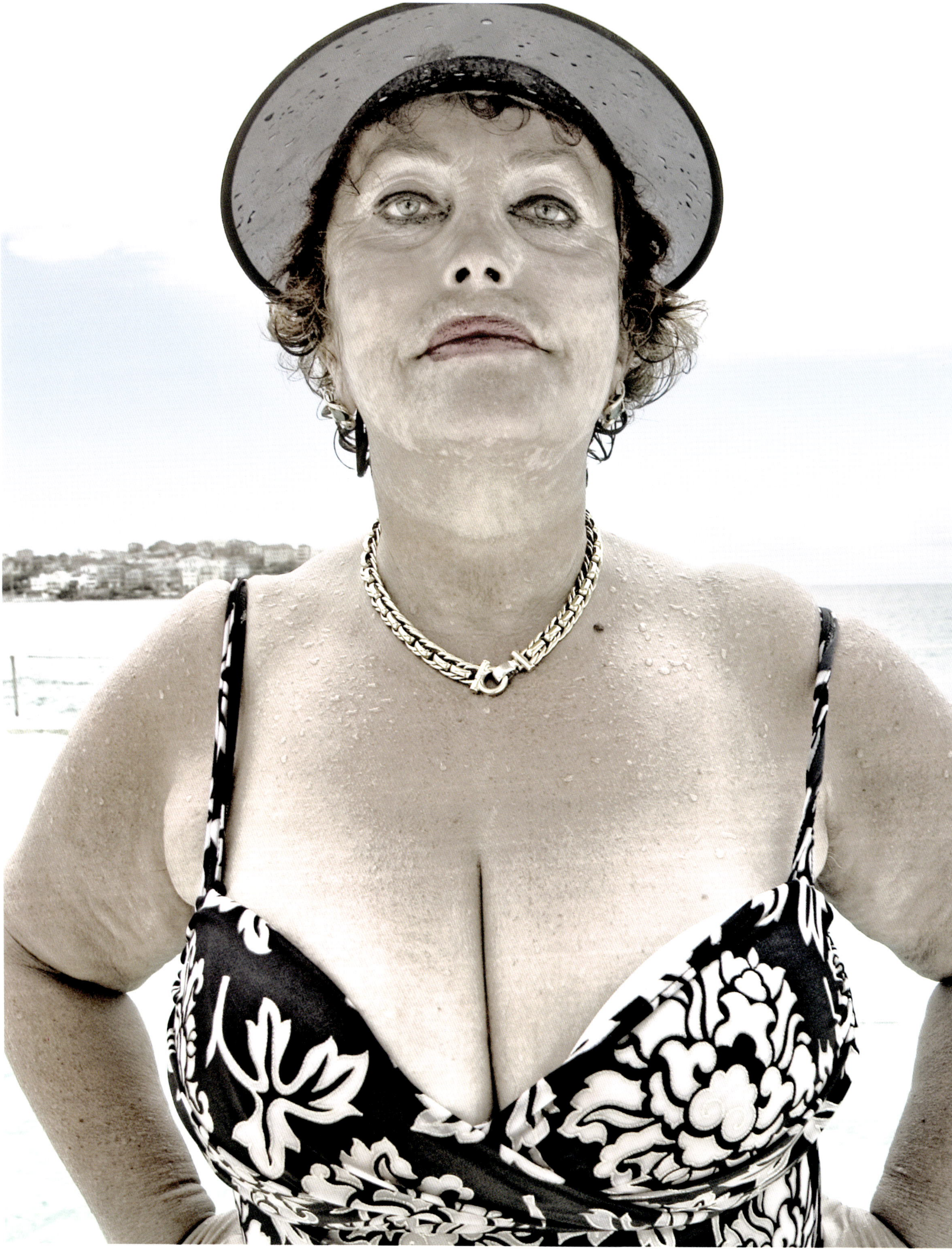

Chapter 5: **Themes and styles**

Like actors, photographers don't like to be typecast, but developing a personal style doesn't have to mean narrowing your options. Instead, it can be a way of concentrating on your particular qualities and preferences and putting an individual stamp on your portraits. Specific projects or themes are an ideal way to put this into practice.

Finding a subject that inspires you will offer the chance to pursue it in depth, producing a body of work that flows and knits together, which may have commercial value as a picture story as well as providing personal satisfaction. This chapter looks at two very different photographers who have taken simple themes and turned them into powerful and engaging sets of images.

The following photographs were taken by Lisbon-based photographer, Alberto Monteiro, who has spent two years visiting small fishing villages in Portugal and recording the lives of people who work in the trade. His style is that of a photojournalist, capturing people in their context and telling a story through the pictures. He explains his motivation and approach to the theme.

'Living in Portugal means living in contact with the sea. The seashores are a big part of the country and the work of the fisherman has always fascinated me. As I am mainly a street photographer, I spent a lot of time at each site, observing the movements and behaviour of the people around those locations. It enabled me to move into the right spots and find good angles to take pictures, without bothering people as they were working. This kind of approach needs some improvisation and also empathy with the people – I didn't want to harass them with close-up portraits. A smile and a chat about their work and their worries is always a good way of breaking the ice.'

'In this village, the seven-metre long boats that come in from the sea are pulled by an engine at the top of the cliff, with a 100-metre steel cable. Each boat's crew grabs the cable to hook it on to its boat and I wanted to capture this in action. I needed to take this shot quickly and I was lucky to capture such a good facial expression.'

'Taking advantage of a moment's rest while he was pulling the boat up with the steel cable, I approached this fisherman and asked him to pose for a portrait. My main preoccupation was getting all the elements – face, arms, ropes, boat – in the frame in a balanced way to give a complete idea of the environment.'

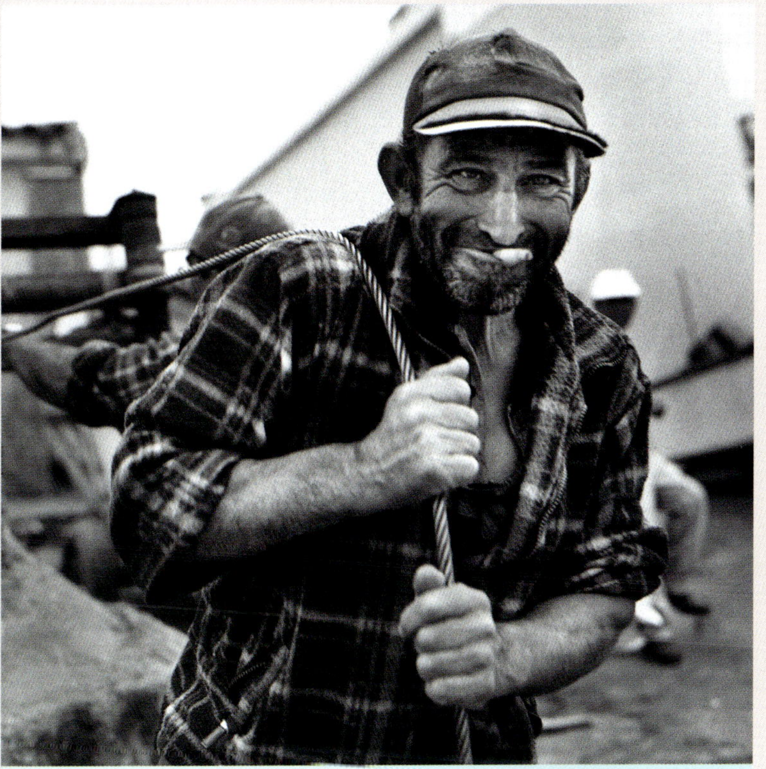

Fact file

Photographer: Alberto Monteiro
Location: Castelo de Neiva, Portugal
Time of day: 8am, June

Technical details

Camera: Bronica SQAi
Lens: 80mm
Film: Ilford FP4 Plus
Exposure: 1/30sec at f/4

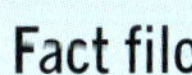

Fact file

Photographer: Alberto Monteiro
Location: Castelo de Neiva, Portugal
Time of day: 9am, June

Technical details

Camera: Bronica SQAi
Lens: 80mm
Film: Ilford FP4 Plus
Exposure: 1/30sec at f/4

'The equipment I carried on location was mainly lightweight and easy to manage so I was able to improvise in unplanned situations.'

Alberto Monteiro

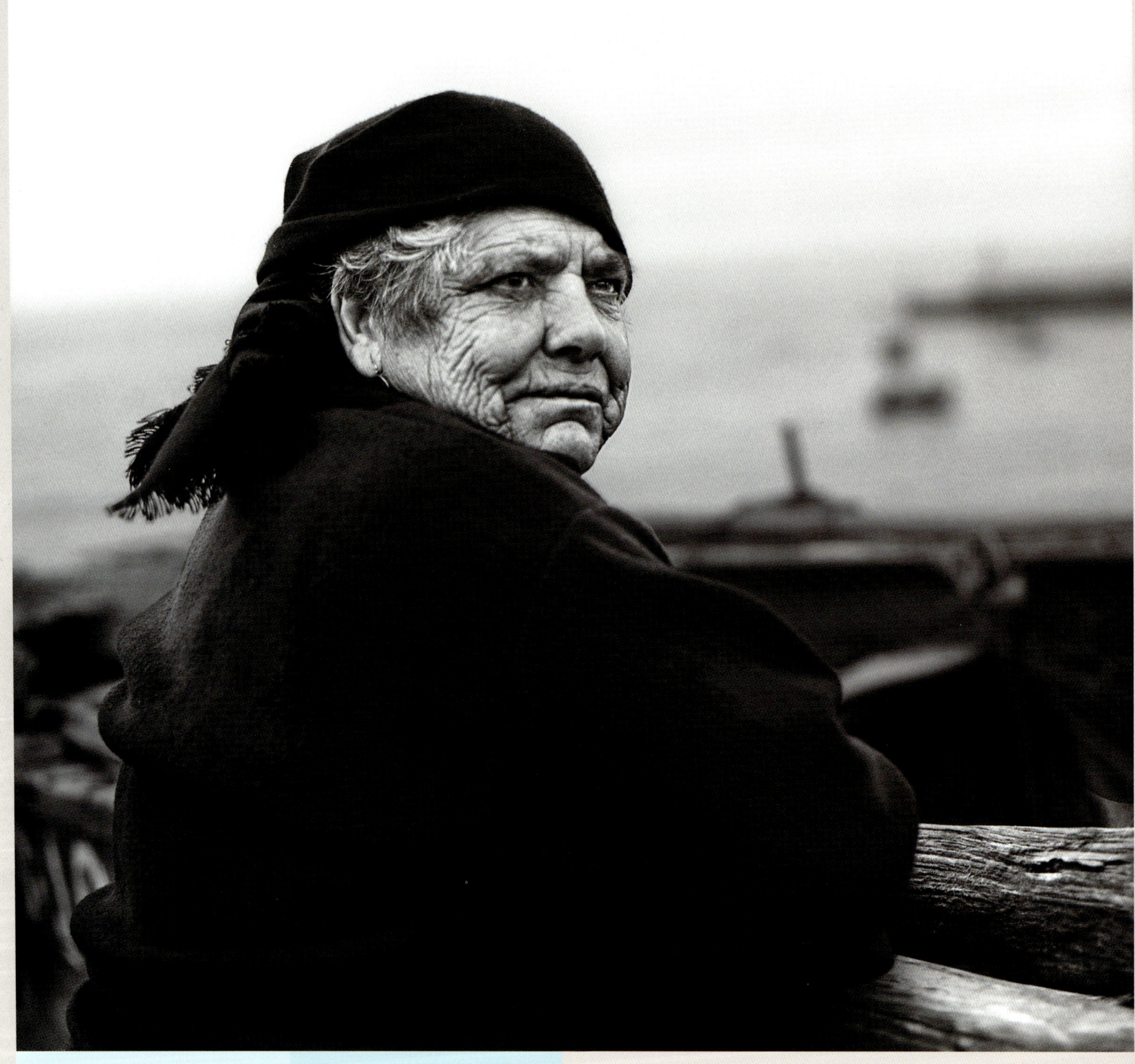

Fact file

Photographer: Alberto Monteiro
Location: Castelo de Neiva, Portugal
Time of day: 8.30am, June

Technical details

Camera: Bronica SQAi
Lens: 80mm
Film: Ilford FP4 Plus
Exposure: 1/30sec at f/2.8

'This village is one of the few that remain with a genuine character, unspoilt by tourism. This woman was waiting for a boat to come in and I wanted to capture her expression. This was a cloudy morning with the sun rising behind me. I had difficulty metering because the woman was wearing black and the background was almost white so, to avoid using flash, I had to meter the light with the camera pointing down and frame the picture without too large an area of sky.'

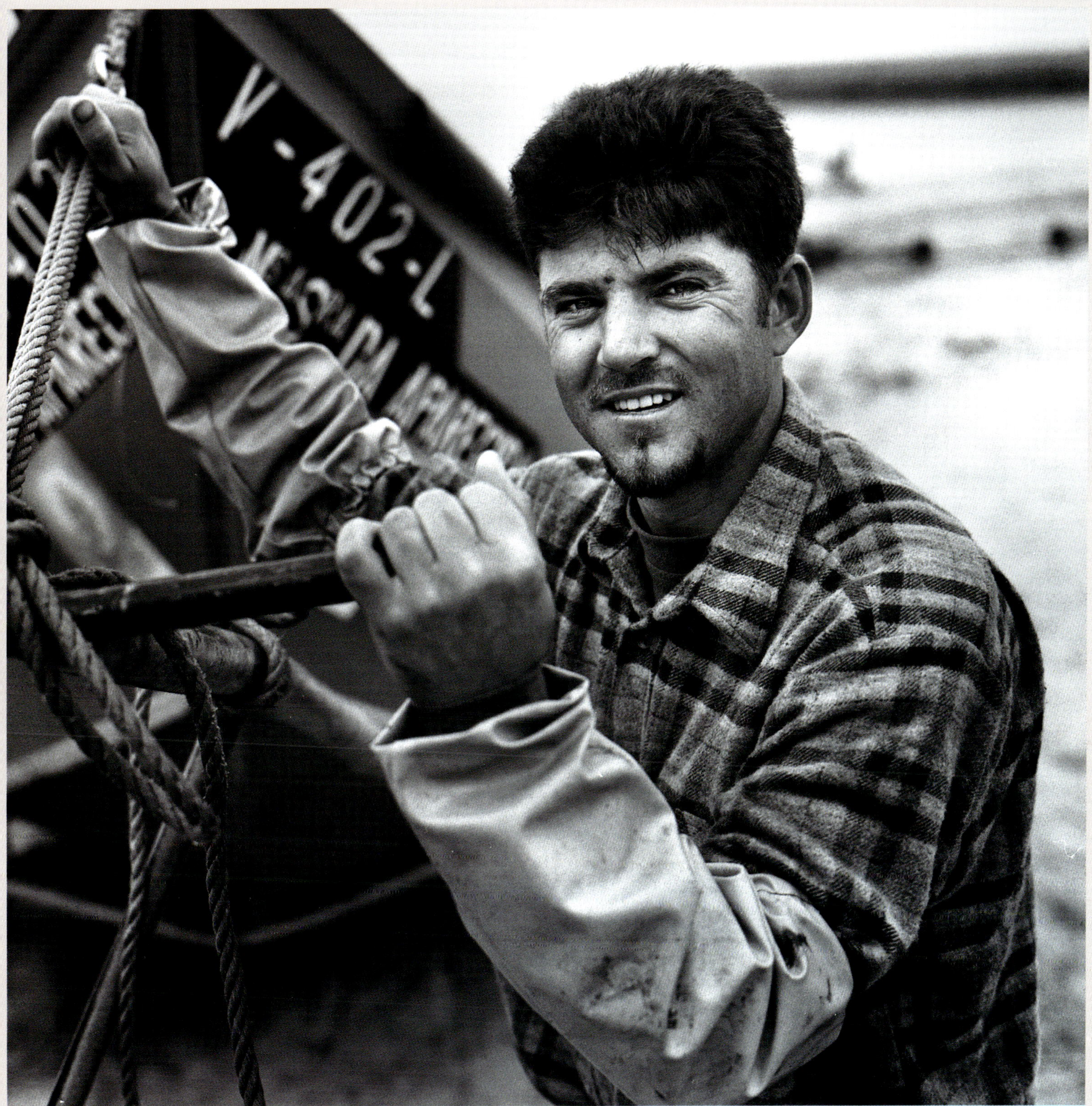

'This was a planned shot. I told the fisherman I wanted to take his picture and he replied that I could once he had finished his work. I waited and he finally posed for me with this proud expression. I prefer to shoot in cloudy weather to get smooth shadows, so I tried to arrive at the locations early in the morning. Even if it turns out sunny, you at least have better oblique light in the first hours. Here it was initially a little too dark to get a fast enough shutter speed to hand-hold the medium format camera, so I had to wait for a brighter cloud to give me 1/60sec. I had to make some compensation in Photoshop to the brighter areas of the background.' ⏶

Fact file

Photographer: Alberto Monteiro
Location: Castelo de Neiva, Portugal
Time of day: 9am, June

Technical details

Camera: Bronica SQAi
Lens: 80mm
Film: Ilford FP4 Plus
Exposure: 1/60sec at f/4

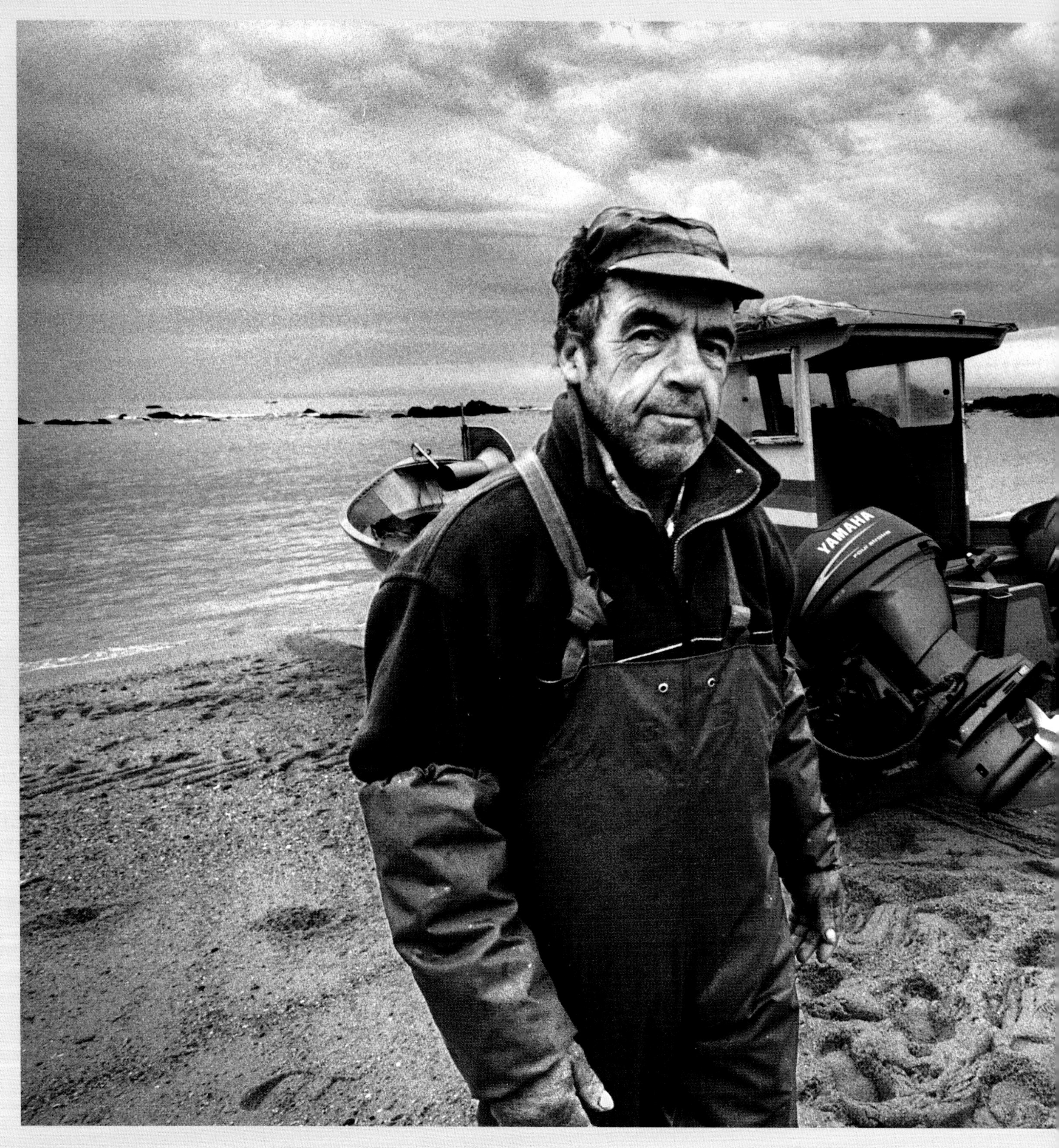
YAMAHA

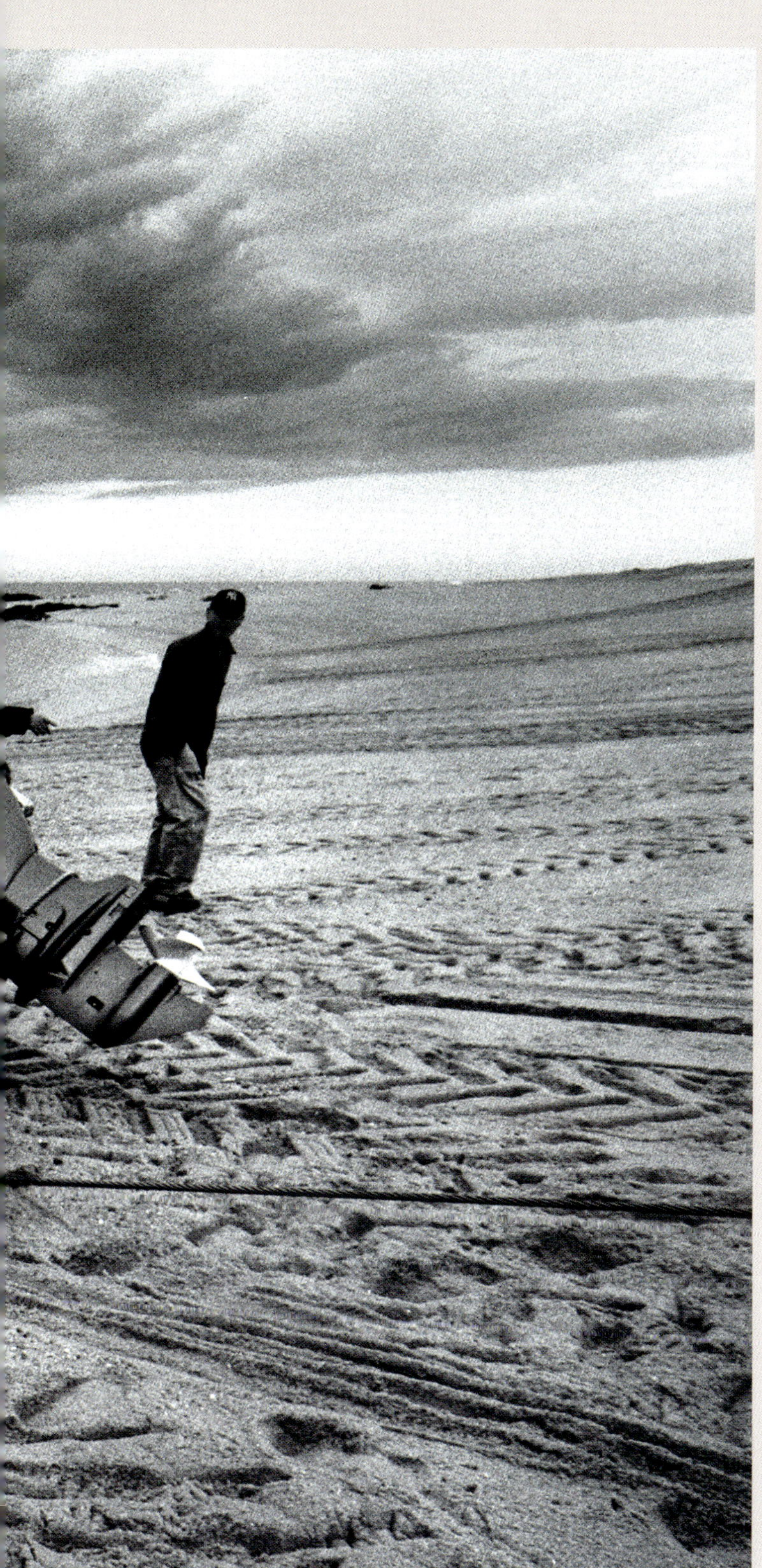

'For some of the portraits I wanted to show the wider environment so I used a 35mm SLR with a 24mm or 20mm wide-angle lens. This village, 15km north of Oporto, was a good place to take shots because, when the fishermen arrived from the sea, they launched their boats on to the sand without stopping. After arriving they would dump the fish in some boxes and begin an outdoor auction. A new indoor market has put a stop to this now.' ◀◀

'This wasn't a posed shot, so I took a light reading in advance, waited for him to look up at me and pressed the shutter as he did.'

Alberto Monteiro

Fact file

Photographer:	Alberto Monteiro
Location:	Angeiras, Portugal
Time of day:	8.30am, May

Technical details

Camera:	Nikon FM2
Lens:	20mm
Film:	Ilford Delta
Exposure:	1/125sec at f/11

Inspired by the thought of producing a book, Matt Hoyle spent a series of Sundays one Australian winter, rising early to visit a swimming pool. This wasn't any ordinary pool, but the famous Bondi Icebergs Club in Sydney, renowned for its spectacular views of Bondi Beach and its hardy members who relish the thought of outdoor swims during winter. Matt had his style for these portraits firmly in mind from the outset – honest, direct, facing the camera and cropped below the neck or above the waist. The resulting collection has been published in magazines and won several competitions, including first prize for portraiture in an international photographic competition.

'I wanted to create a series of portraits that depicted the swimming club in an original way,' he explains. 'Not the bronzed, beautiful people on the beach below, nor the postcard views, but to depict these dedicated people who came to swim, not pose. I shot the "Icebergs" extremely close, about three feet away most of the time, and used a wide-angle lens, which slightly over-exaggerated their faces. I see them as larger than life and, like icebergs, quite dominating in their water environment.'

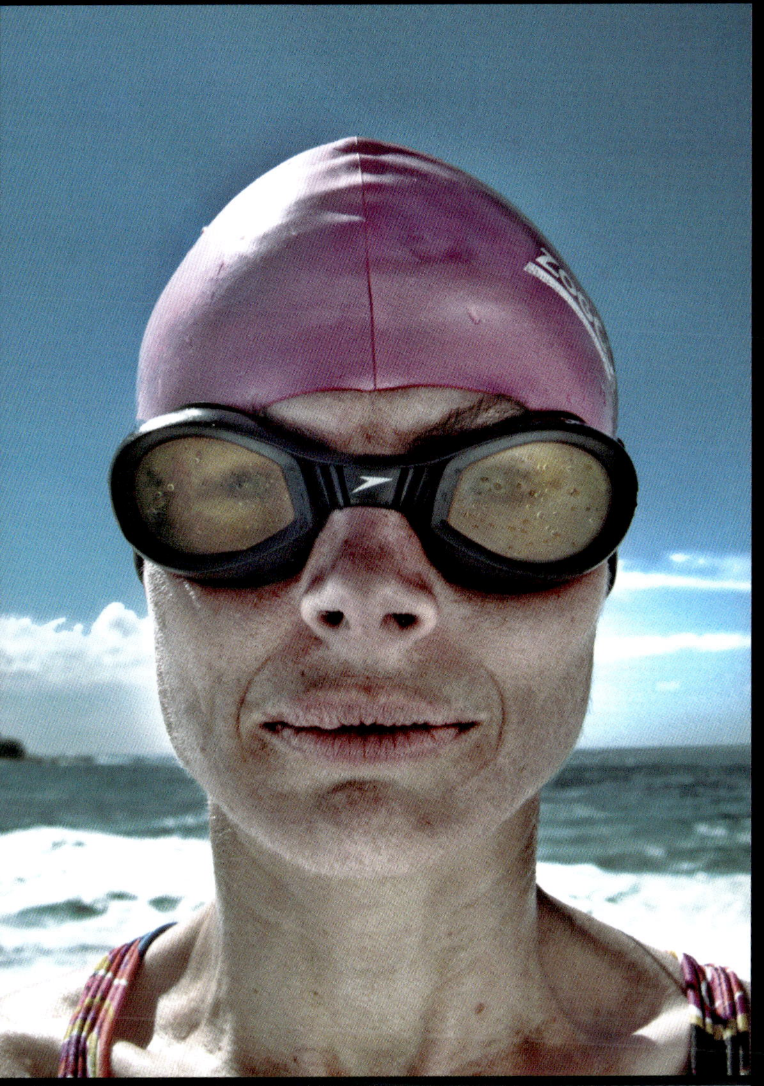

Fact file

Photographer:	Matt Hoyle
Location:	Bondi Icebergs Club, Sydney, Australia
Time of day:	7am, winter

Technical details

Camera:	Nikon D100 (digital)
Lens:	18–35mm
Film:	n/a
Exposure:	Not recorded

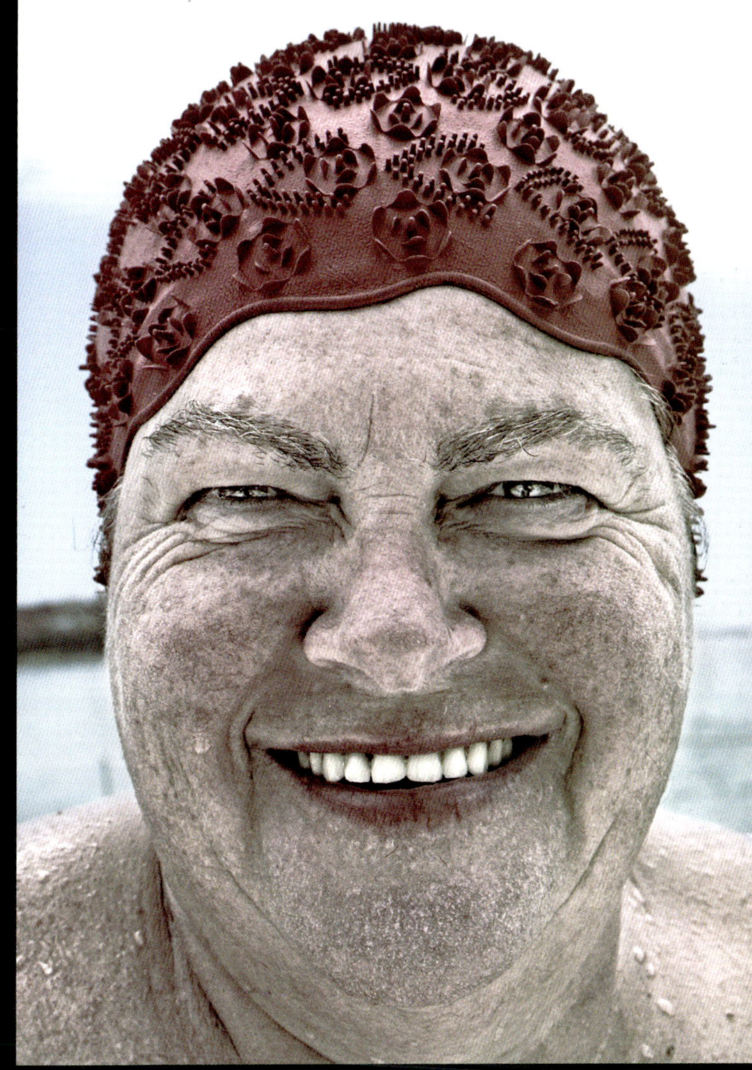

Fact file

Photographer:	Matt Hoyle
Location:	Bondi Icebergs Club, Sydney, Australia
Time of day:	7am, winter

Technical details

Camera:	Nikon D100 (digital)
Lens:	18–35mm
Film:	n/a
Exposure:	Not recorded

'I chose each and every subject because they stood out – Penelope for her out-of-this-world look with those goggles and cap. The club met at 7am every Sunday when the sun was in the far horizon of the ocean. I always placed the subject so that the sun was behind and to the left of the subject to give a softer key light to the right of the face. Then I used the pure white swimming pool as my fill light. The result looks quite surreal but was all quite natural. On overcast days I would add a gold reflector to enhance the fill from bottom right.' ⏶

'The Icebergs were a joy to shoot. Rosa's red cheeks matched perfectly with her swimming cap.'

Matt Hoyle

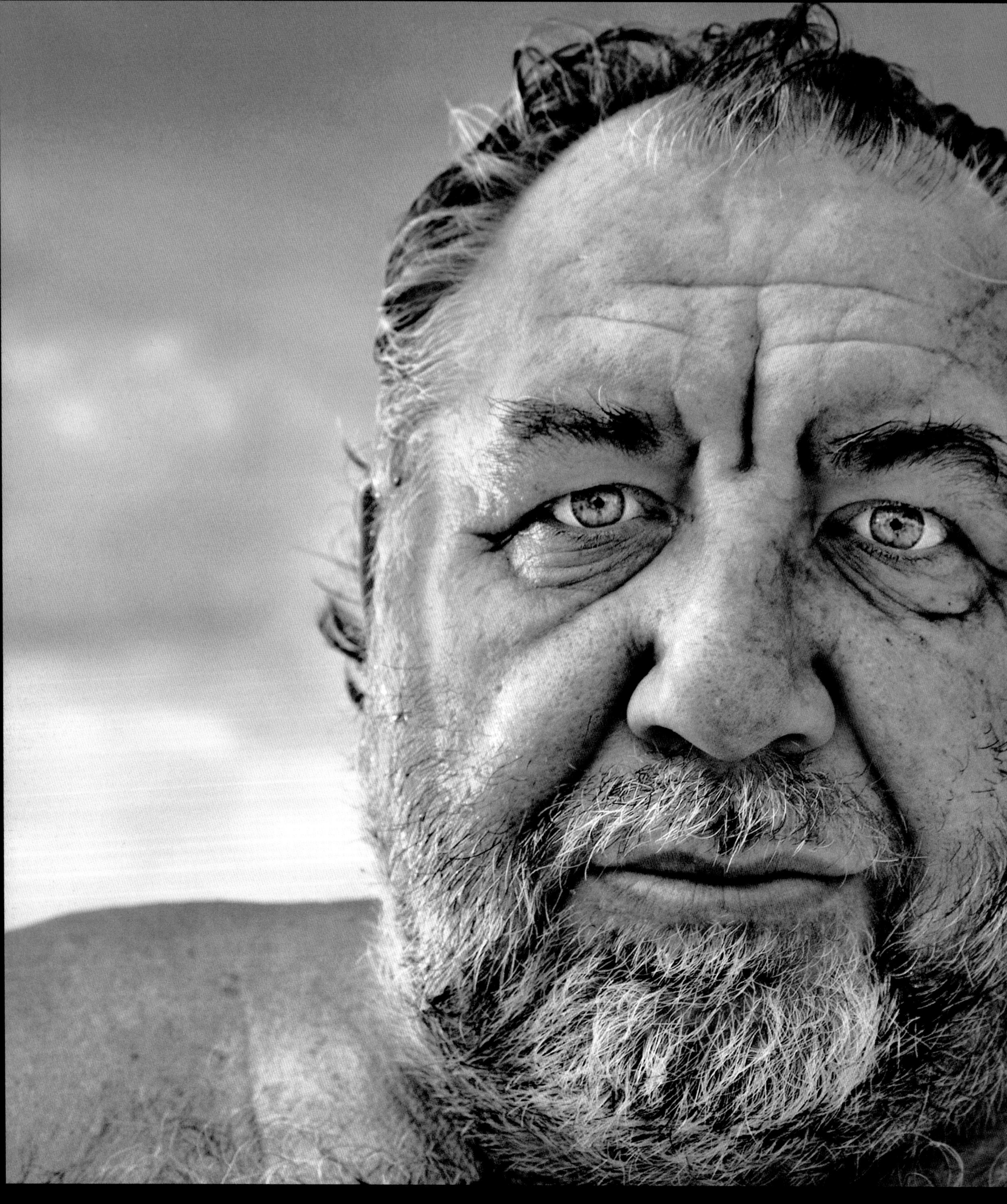

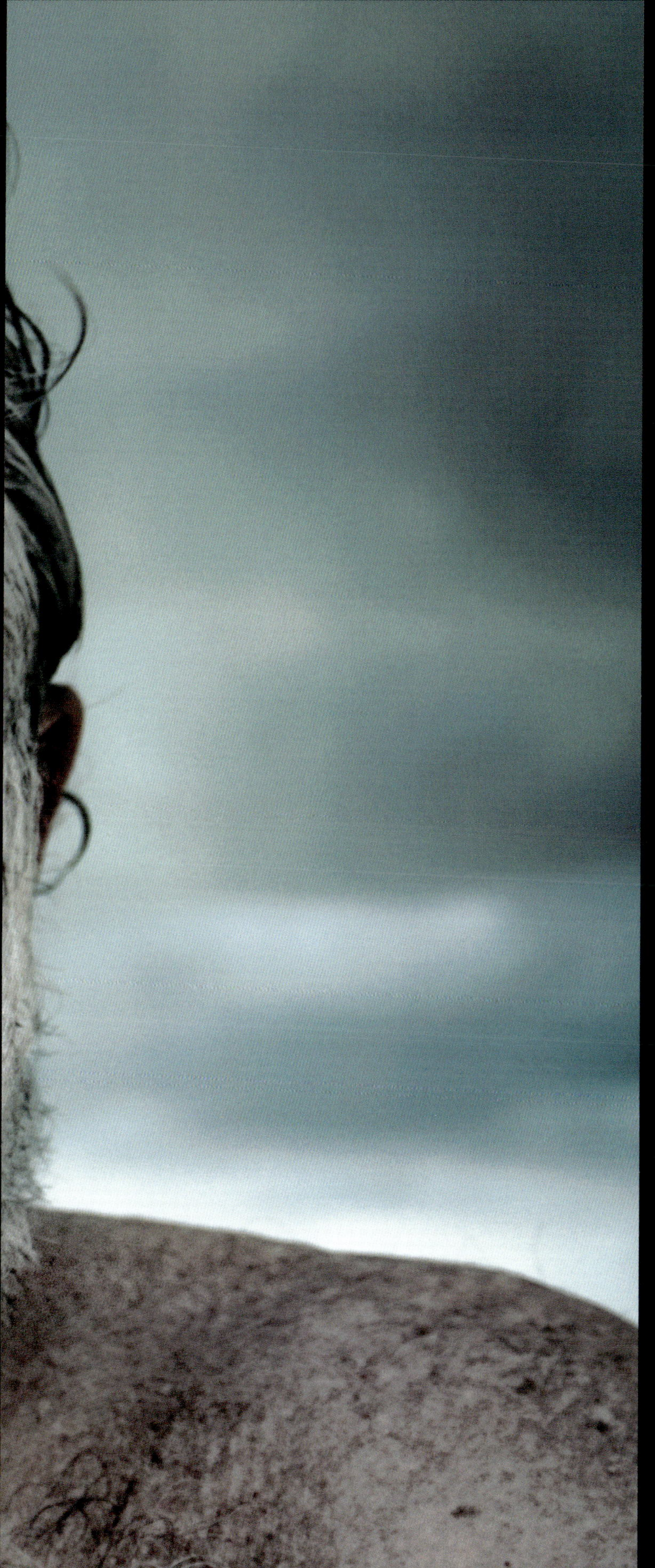

Fact file

Photographer: Matt Hoyle
Location: Bondi Icebergs Club, Sydney, Australia
Time of day: 7am, winter

Technical details

Camera: Nikon D100 (digital)
Lens: 18–35mm
Film: n/a
Exposure: Not recorded

'Lighting and technique are a bonus for me in photographs. Of course the better they are, the more aesthetically pleasing the picture, but the true heroes are the characters. Keeping things simple allows me to concentrate on the relationships between my subjects and myself. In that short period of time, trying to capture an original moment that both depicts them and their true character, you tend to get a little closer.' ◀◀

'People say that they can see in my photographs that I like my subjects, and it's true to a degree.'

Matt Hoyle

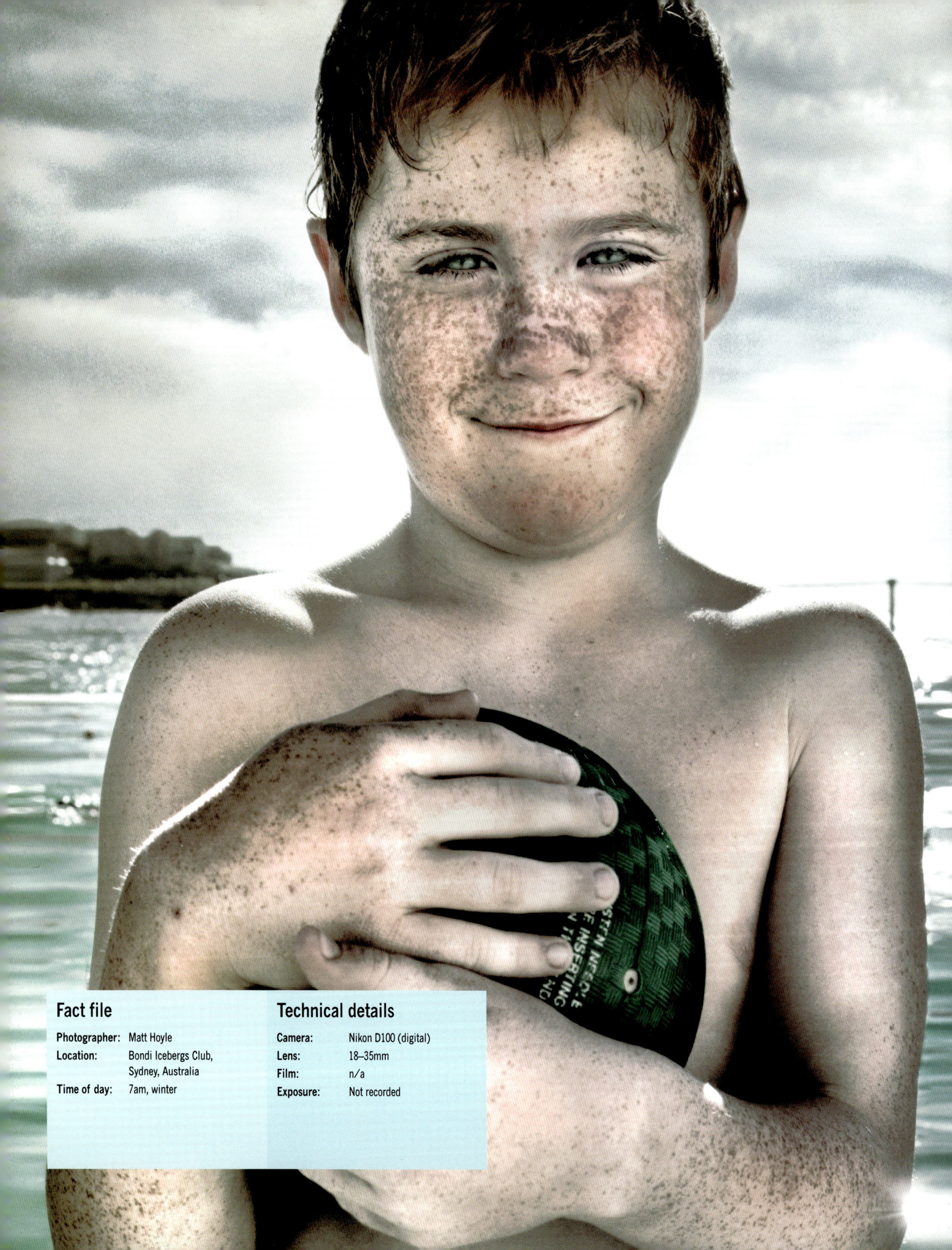

Fact file

Photographer: Matt Hoyle
Location: Bondi Icebergs Club, Sydney, Australia
Time of day: 7am, winter

Technical details

Camera: Nikon D100 (digital)
Lens: 18–35mm
Film: n/a
Exposure: Not recorded

'The members of the club all got to know me and I think they wanted to throw me in the pool by the end of it. But I think they were a little amazed that I found them interesting enough to do a book.'

Matt Hoyle

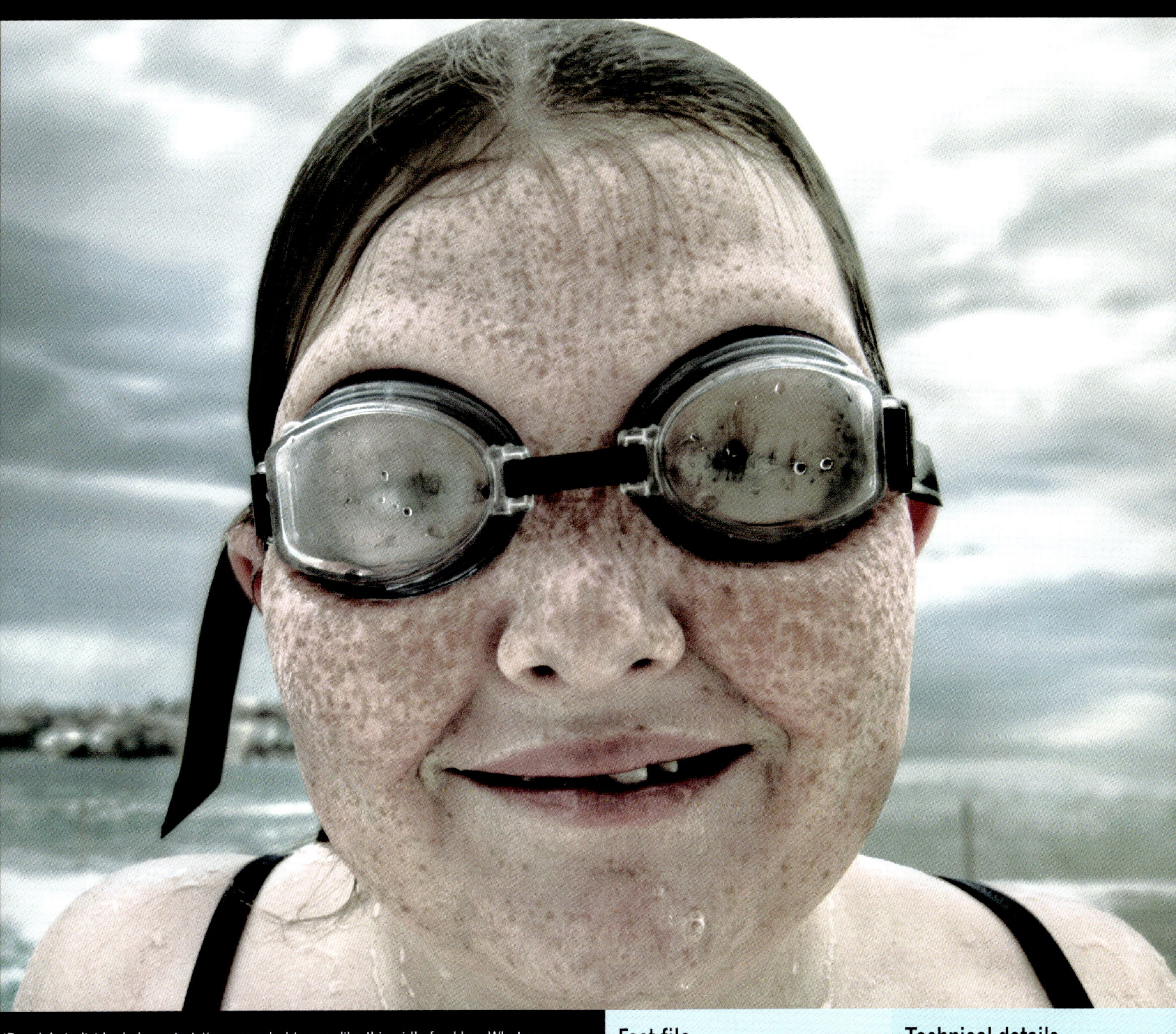

'People's individual characteristics appealed to me, like this girl's freckles. Whatever made these people a little different I was endeared to. I shot wide angle to enhance these features.' ⏶

'All the Iceberg pictures were shot with a digital camera and I do my styling in Photoshop. I try to keep the images true to what my vision was in the first place and for these it was to keep things cool, as this was a winter swimming club, so blue/green toning was added.' ⏴

Fact file

Photographer: Matt Hoyle
Location: Bondi Icebergs Club, Sydney, Australia
Time of day: 7am, winter

Technical details

Camera: Nikon D100 (digital)
Lens: 18–35mm
Film: n/a
Exposure: Not recorded

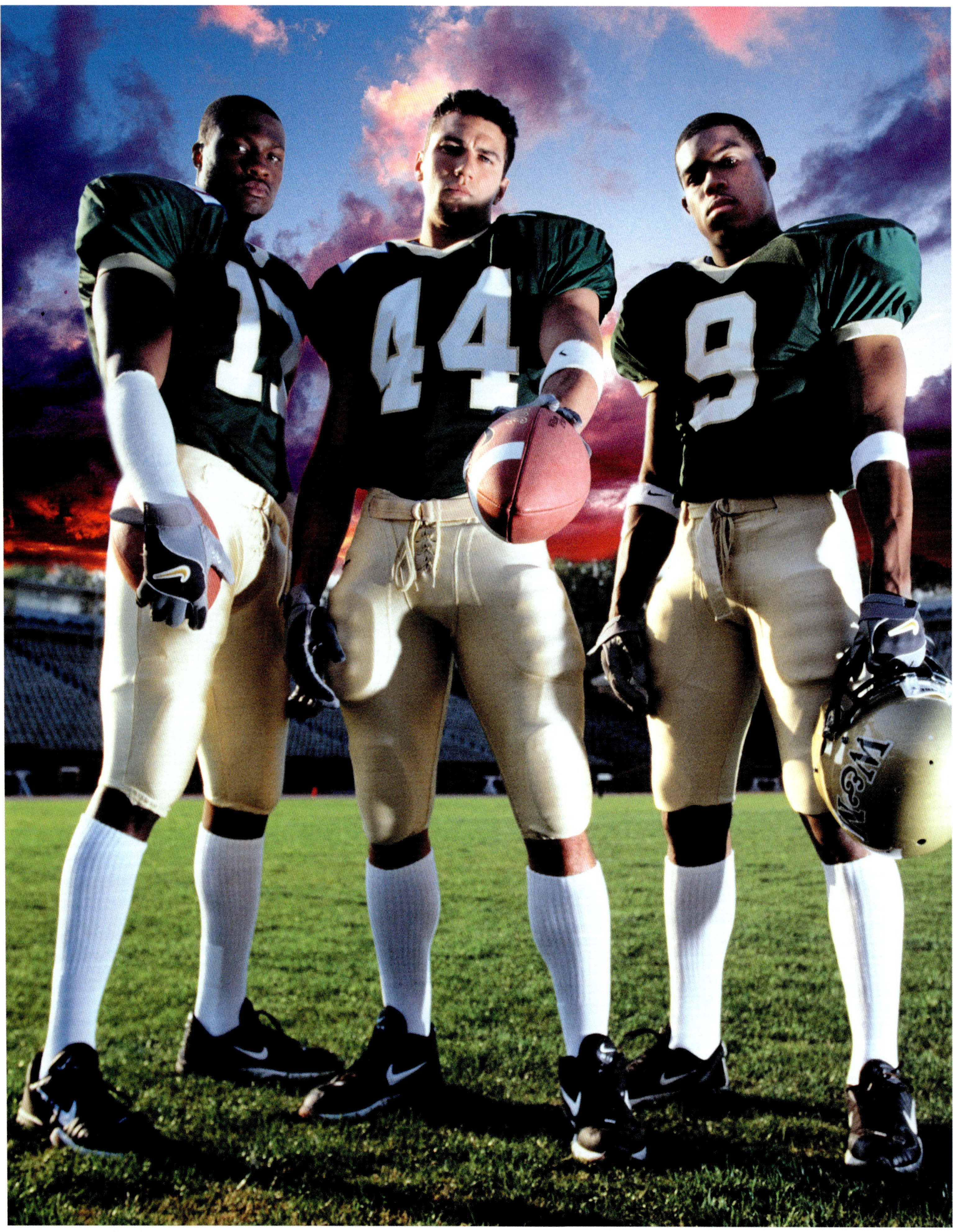

Guy Crittenden

Chapter 6: **Pairs and groups**

Taking a portrait of two or more people throws up more challenges than dealing with an individual. For posed shots to work well, the photographer needs to have an understanding and rapport with the subject and this is not so easy if you are confronted with very different personalities at the same time, not to mention several sets of eyes wandering all over the place.

Usually, the reason for photographing a pair or group is that there is some kind of relationship between them and if you can show them interacting naturally you are a long way there. Physical closeness in the pose helps keep the composition tight, but some people find it more comfortable to demonstrate than others, and it should never be forced. This chapter looks at different ways of approaching the task, some following a plan and others dealing with spontaneous situations.

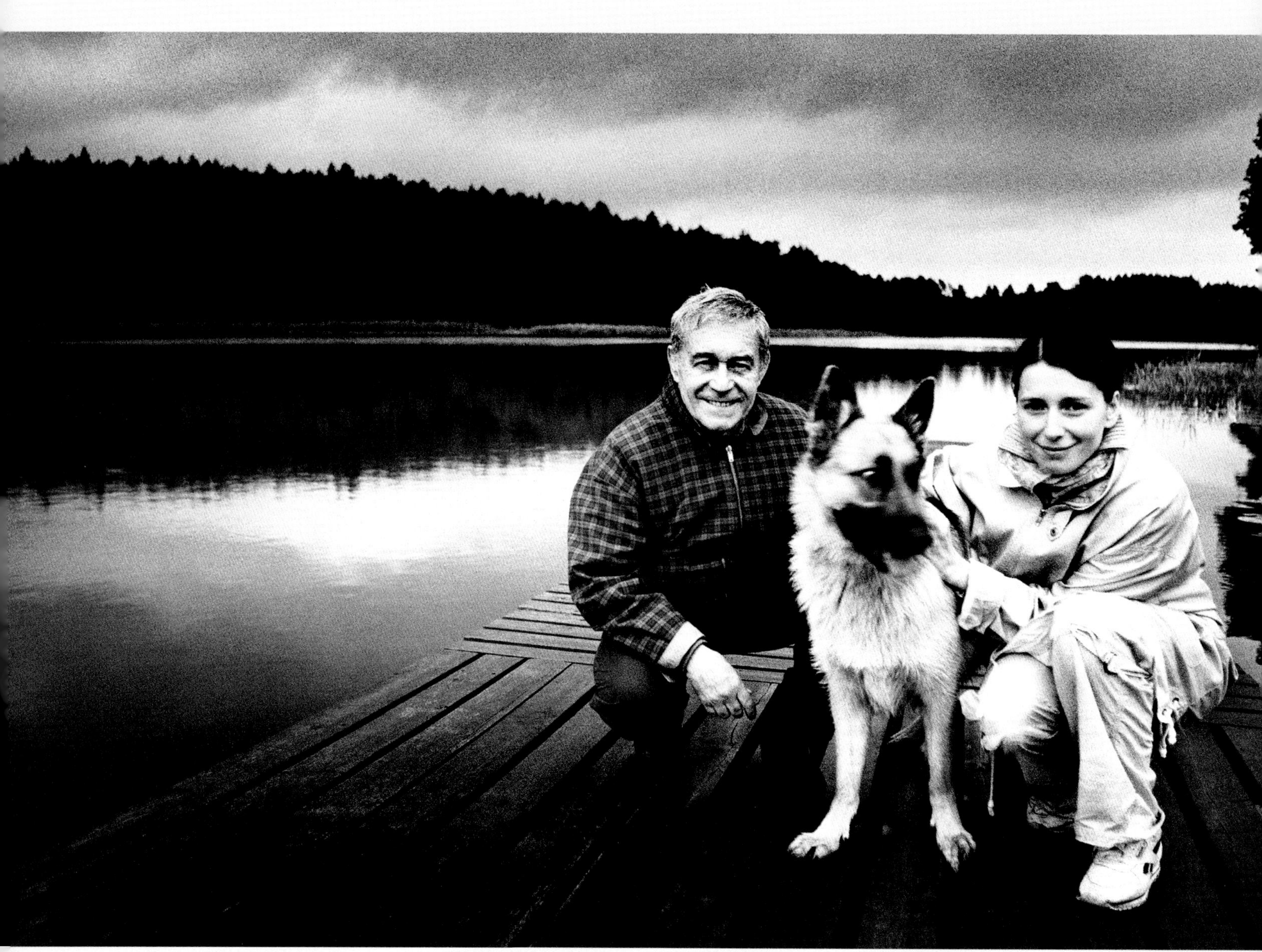

'I think this is the sort of photograph that is typical for a family album, but for me, it is also quite moving.'

Tomek Paczkowski

The concept

An unplanned photograph of Tomek's wife and her father, and Tomek's mother's dog, taken while they were walking in the countryside. Like most people, he often takes pictures of people close to him but they are always as carefully thought out as if they had been commissioned portraits of strangers.

The location

This beautiful spot in an unspoilt, forested area is a favourite of Tomek's and he has taken several portraits of family and friends there. In this shot, the setting is almost as important as the subjects.

Composition

Tomek positioned his wife and father-in-law on a jetty running into the lake and used a wide-angle lens to include the landscape and the reflections of the clouds in the water. The dog was included as a well-loved member of the family but it also serves a useful purpose in linking his wife and father-in-law. Having them crouch down to the dog's level allowed him to get a good angle on the background, with their heads just touching the top line of the trees.

Lighting and technique

The evening sun, diffused by cloud, was soft and even so there were no harsh shadows to contend with. Tomek used a red filter on the lens, as he often does with black-and-white film, to give the clouds a little more depth.

Fact file

Photographer: Tomek Paczkowski
Location: Tucholskie Forest, Poland
Time of day: 7pm, summer

Technical details

Camera: Olympus OM2n
Lens: 28mm
Film: Ilford HP5 Plus
Exposure: 1/30sec at f/4

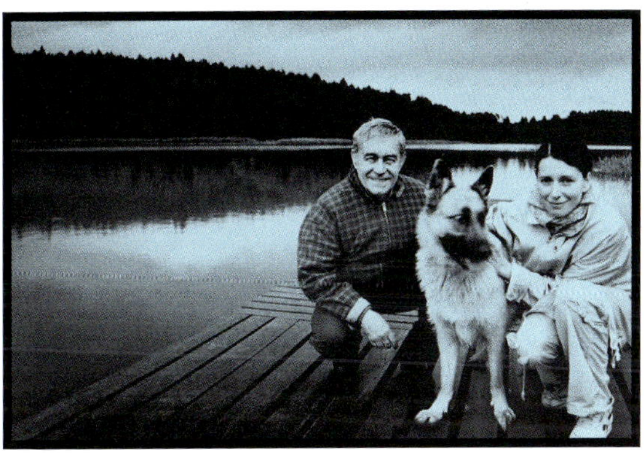

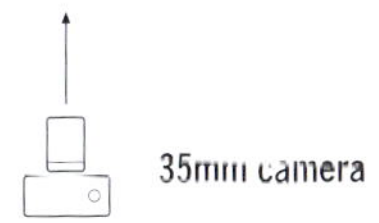

35mm camera

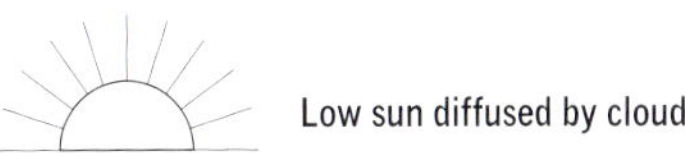

Low sun diffused by clouds

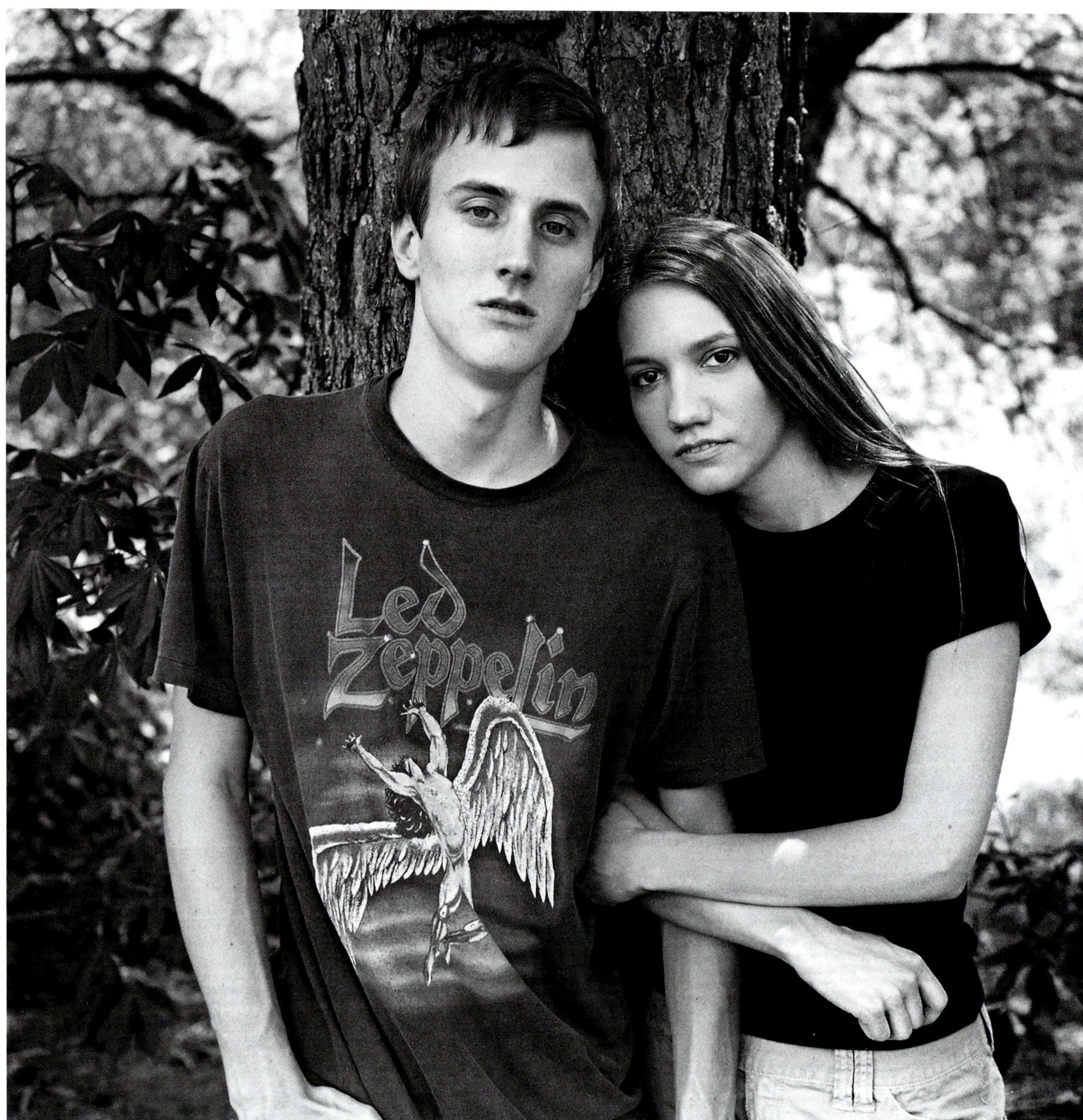

Fact file

Photographer: Ian McFarlane
Location: Botanical Gardens, Georgia, USA
Time of day: Midday, summer

Technical details

Camera: Mamiya 6
Lens: 75mm
Film: Ilford HP5
Exposure: 1/125sec at f/5.6

The concept

'This was a paid commission for an engagement portrait,' explains Ian. 'It was taken late in the shoot and the previous pictures had been very casual, with the man wearing his favourite T-shirt. For this one, I asked them to look very serious to evoke some feeling other than the typical engagement.'

The location

Ian took the couple to the Botanical Gardens near where they lived. He wanted somewhere natural-looking and private, where they would feel comfortable.

Composition

Not all couples feel at ease with public physical contact but these subjects came together in this pose of their own accord, even inclining their heads without prompting, which is always a good way of conveying a close relationship.

Lighting and technique

'It was partly cloudy with moments of very bright sun,' recalls Ian. 'I didn't want direct sun, so I placed them under a tree in a shaded area, with the sun behind them, using part of a distant tree to block my lens from flare. I metered the shaded area at head level and got a soft skin tone with bright highlights over their shoulders in the woods, which was burned down later in the print.'

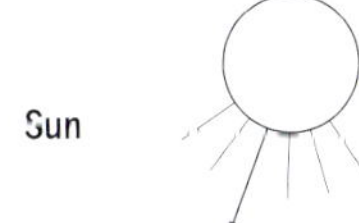

Shade of tree

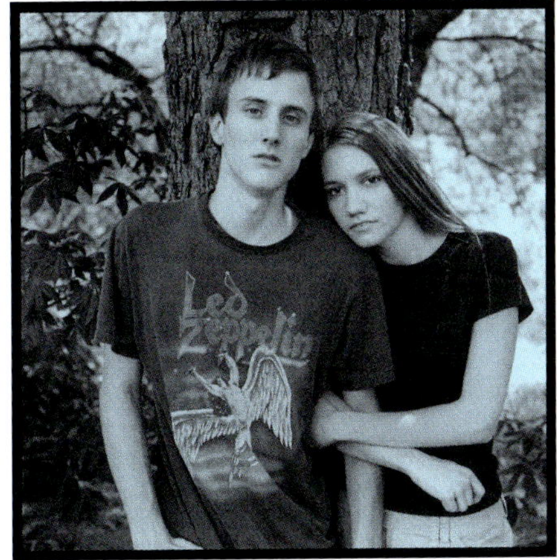

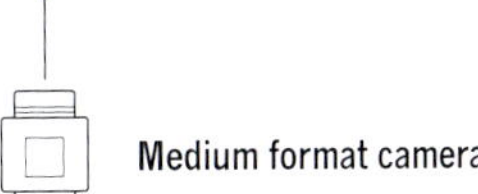

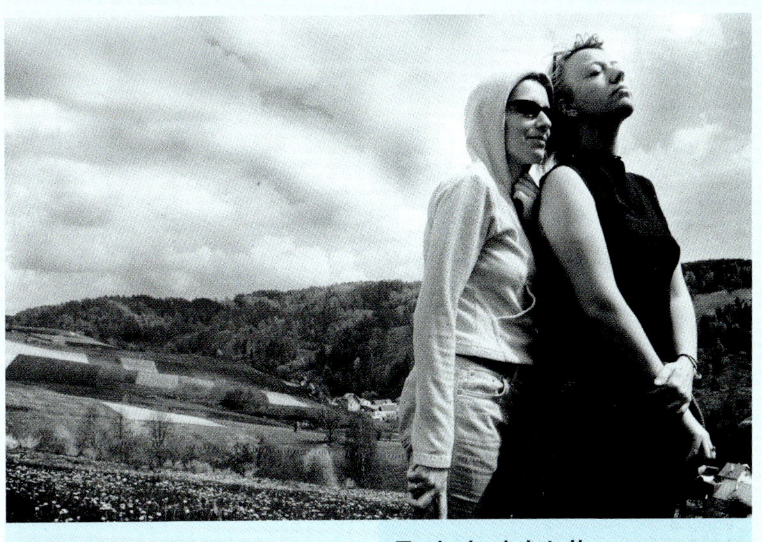

Fact file

Photographer: Tomek Paczkowski
Location: Beskidy Mountains, southern Poland
Time of day: Noon, May

Technical details

Camera: Olympus OM2n
Lens: 50mm
Film: Ilford HP5
Exposure: 1/250sec at f/11

A portrait of Tomek's wife with a friend of theirs, the pose here would work equally well for a couple as an alternative to the usual side-by-side shot. Tomek used aperture priority at f/11, providing good depth of field to keep the landscape in focus, and left plenty of room around the subjects to give a sense of the wide open space. A red filter on the lens increased contrast, especially in the clouds, for dramatic effect.

'When I saw his T-shirt, I knew that the location was almost contradictory to the subjects' look and adding the serious expressions would also make the portrait more interesting and unusual.'

Ian McFarlane

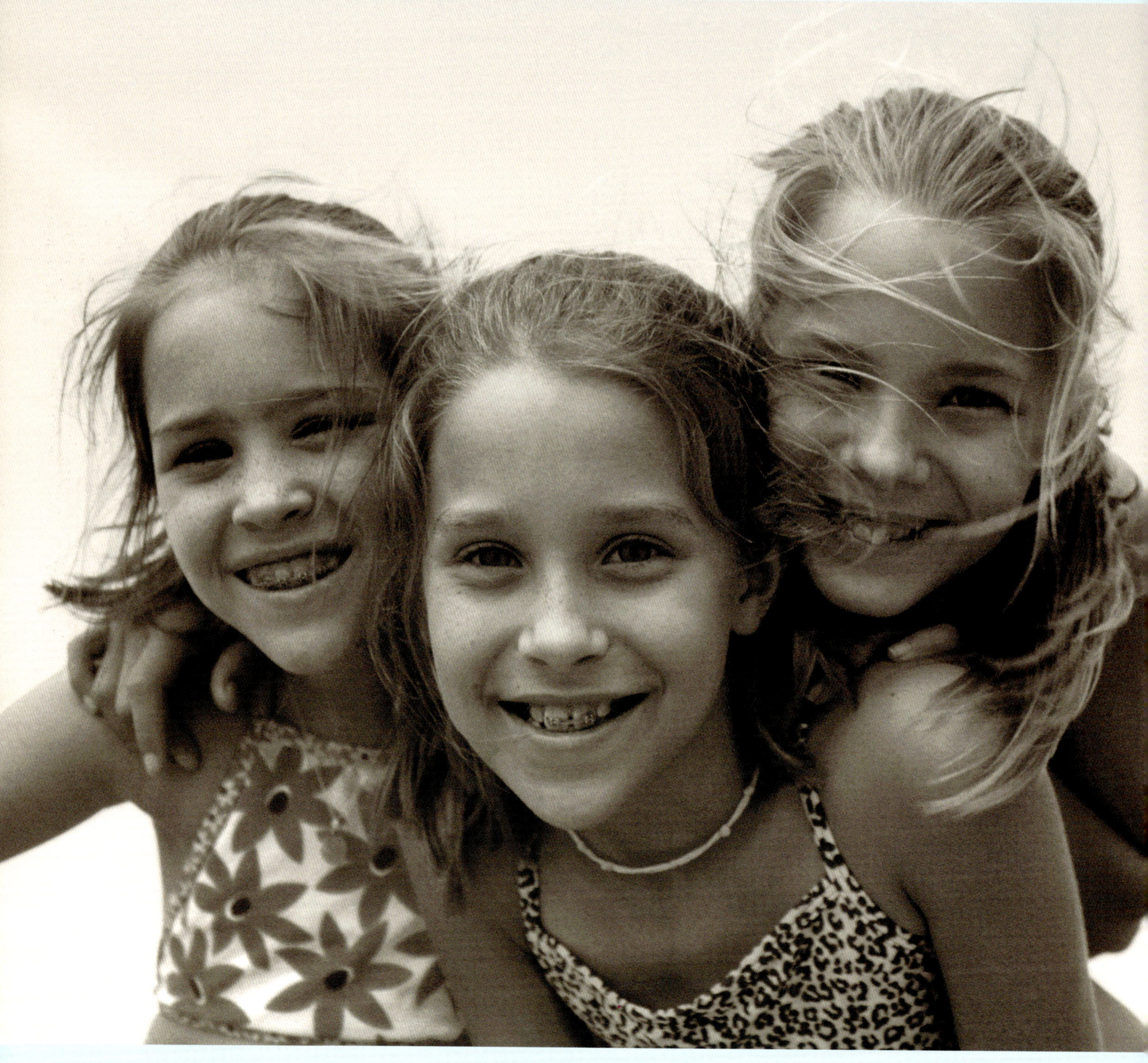

'When shooting on a nice white beach, you will often find that it serves as a giant light bounce, ideal for portraits.'

Guy Crittenden

Fact file

Photographer: Guy Crittenden
Location: British Virgin Islands
Time of day: 3pm, March

Technical details

Camera: Canon 1N RS
Lens: 28–70mm
Film: Kodak VS 100
Exposure: 1/400sec at f/11

The concept

Guy supplies pictures to a stock photography agency and this was taken for that purpose. 'Lifestyle' images are often in demand and this portrait of three sisters could be sold by the agency to many different clients.

The location

The white sands and fine weather of the British Virgin Islands are all that Guy needed here. If you're planning to shoot a number of images over a short space of time for stock, travelling to a place where the appropriate climate is virtually guaranteed can be worth the investment.

Composition

Siblings often (not always!) have a natural closeness that can be exploited to produce a tight composition, with heads touching and arms around each other. The wind gives this shot a sense of movement and naturalness, and note how the girls are leaning forward, which avoids the problem of their difference in height.

Lighting and technique

'It was a bright sunny day as most are in the BVIs,' says Guy. 'The sand reflected the light on to the subject, removing deep, hard shadow lines.' The photograph was taken in colour and colour converted to black and white in Photoshop after scanning. Guy then 'warmed' the greyscale image with minor colour adjustments in the mid-tones, to give this light and airy result.

Commissioned to take a portrait of three brothers in their garden, Ian had the challenge of creating a unified image that brought out each boy's different personality. 'I had to place the boys in a composition that allowed the viewer to see each one's expression and size difference, without the weight of the image pulling to one of the subjects more than the others,' he explains. The light was bright, but softened by cloud cover and Ian was able to use a fairly wide aperture to put the foliage behind them out of focus.

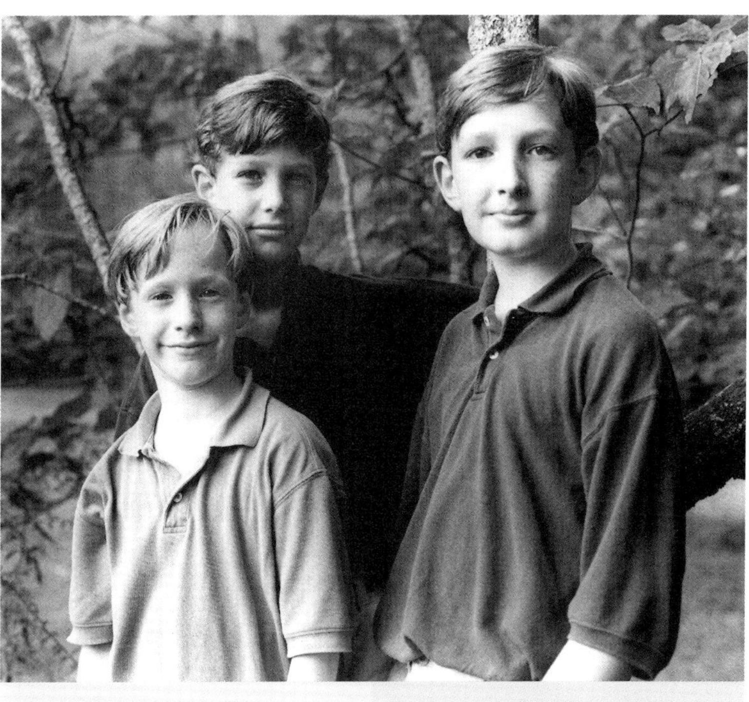

Fact file

Photographer: Ian McFarlane
Location: Athens, Georgia, USA
Time of day: Late afternoon, summer

Technical details

Camera: Mamiya RZ 67
Lens: 110mm
Film: Ilford HP5 400
Exposure: 1/125sec at f/5.6

Fact file

Photographer: Robert Ganz
Location: Vancouver Island, Canada
Time of day: 11am, August

Technical details

Camera: Canon 10D (digital)
Lens: 180mm
Film: n/a
Exposure: 1/200sec at f/3.5

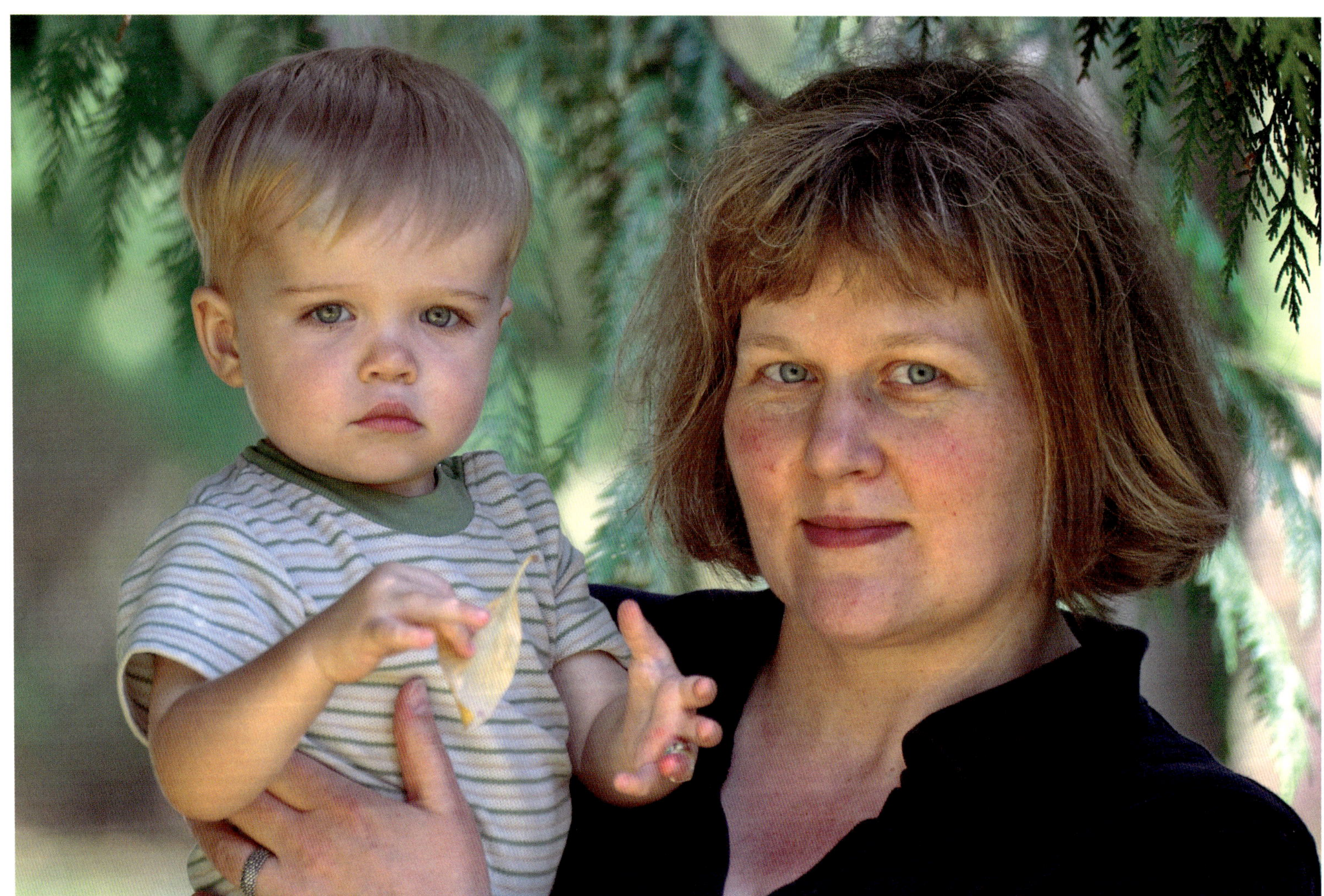

'It was really hard getting the two-year old to pose. He was always moving or looking away. I finally gave him a leaf to hold and that held his attention for long enough for me to take the shot.'

Robert Ganz

The concept

'It was the last day of a family reunion. I had already taken all the group shots and was now working on individuals and pairs. I was trying to set-up interesting pairings, and this was just one of them.'

The location

Robert had no choice about this. It was where the family had gathered and he had to make the best of whatever settings were available. The tree offered several useful functions: it provided shade from the sun, gave an interesting texture to the background and a prop to lean against.

Composition

'This was really an exercise in making the best of things and improvising,' says Robert. 'I often use a medium telephoto lens for people as it compresses the background nicely, allowing me to be very specific about how much of it I want to show.' When you're photographing babies and toddlers with an older child or adult, it helps to set the exposure and decide on the pose before introducing the baby so you can take the shot as quickly as possible. Holding the baby up to the mother's eye level gives them equal weight in the picture and makes the composition balanced.

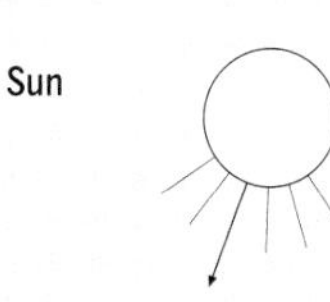

Lighting and technique

'This was an impromptu shoot so I had no equipment other than the camera with me,' he explains. 'I did have a relatively high and very bright sun to work with though, so I put my subjects under the branches of an evergreen tree. That diffused the light quite nicely. Also, I was adjacent to a parking lot with cars in it, so I had the flexibility to position the subjects so that some of the reflected light off the vehicles filled the faces a bit. I metered off the woman's hair and underexposed by 1/3 of a stop.'

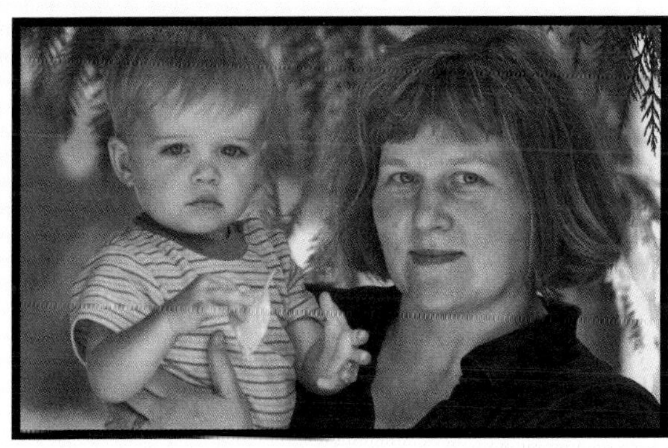

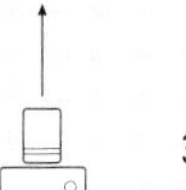

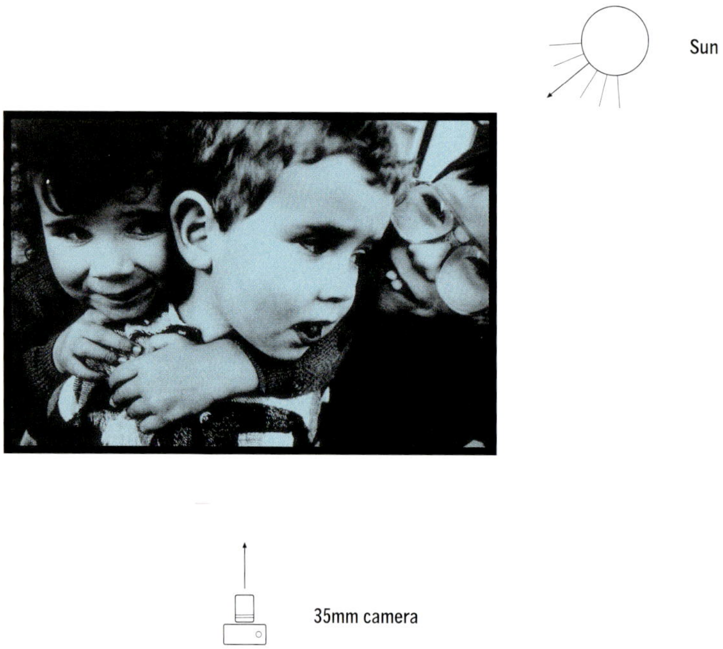

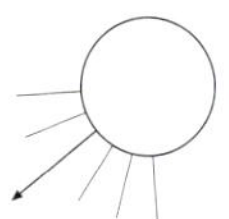

Sun

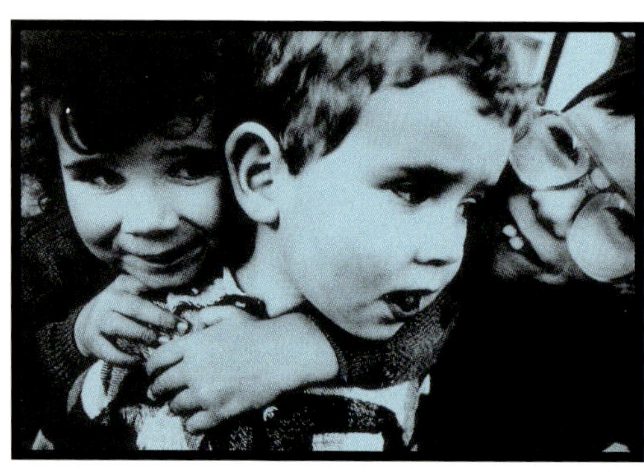

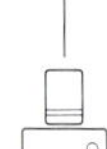

35mm camera

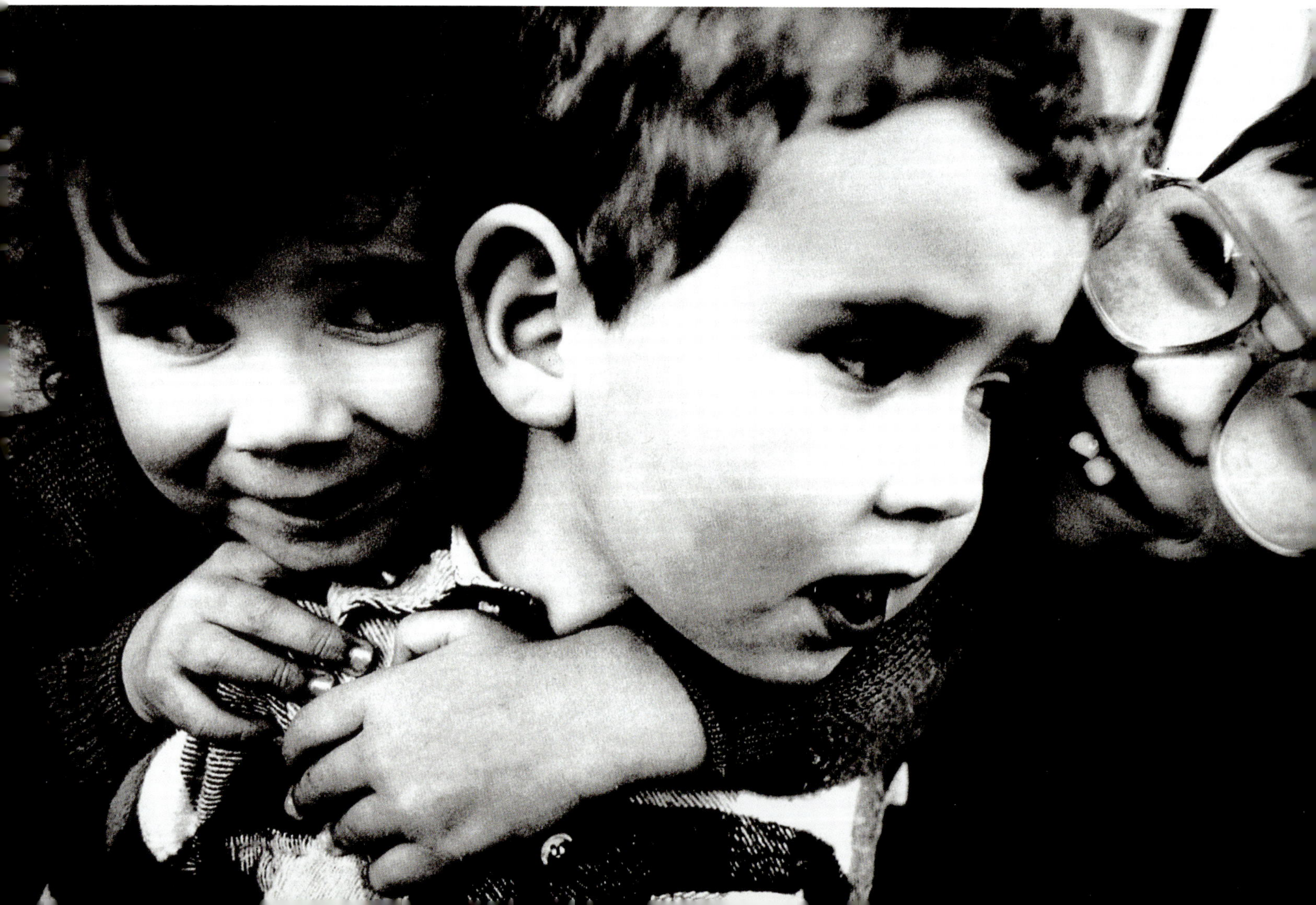

Fact file

Photographer: Paul Holmes, Trevillion Picture Library
Location: Middlesbrough, UK
Time of day: Mid-afternoon, October

Technical details

Camera: Nikon F801
Lens: 28mm
Film: Kodak Tri-X
Exposure: 1/1000sec at f/5.6

The concept

This was one of a series of images Paul took exploring the setting of inner-city Middlesbrough in the north of England. 'It's a pretty tough place to grow up and suffers from more of its fair share of society's blemishes,' says Paul. 'Although it's the antithesis of Disneyland, it provides a playground of sorts.'

The location

'Every street in Middlesbrough provides a great backdrop for this kind of photograph, but not all are as camera-friendly as this was. My main objective was not to run into a street that had too many kids with angst.'

Composition

'I didn't have to direct the children, they just moved around fearlessly,' says Paul. Spontaneous moments like this require swift reactions to catch them. He was using a wide-angle lens, intending to include the street in the background, but made this tight crop afterwards to focus on the children's great expressions.

Lighting and technique

'I used a reasonably fast film to allow a fast shutter speed and then it was a case of manoeuvring round the subjects. Black-and-white film allows for huge exposure mistakes, so there are very few moments when you are worried whether the images will turn out. The sun was quite strong and coming from the right, but I would have approached the shot the same way even if the sun was directly behind the children.'

'I think most of my favourite and most successful shots have been taken when I haven't had to carry heaps of equipment around.'

Paul Holmes

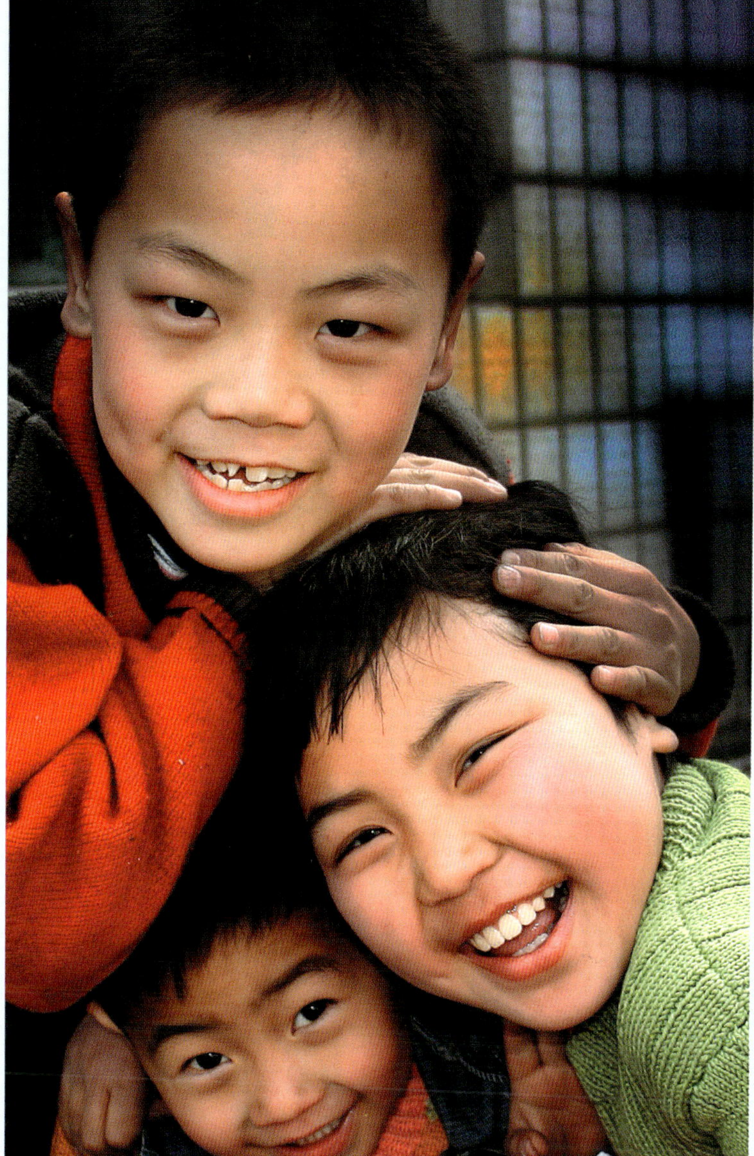

Fact file

Photographer: Jean Schweitzer
Location: Beijing, China
Time of day: 2pm, March

Technical details

Camera: Canon 300D (digital)
Lens: 18–50mm
Film: n/a
Exposure: 1/200sec at f/4.3

While travelling in China, Jean came across these boys playing in a street near a market. They were initially shy when he asked to take their picture but soon felt comfortable and played up to the camera. 'It wasn't easy to direct the children as they kept running in all directions!' Nevertheless, he succeeded by keeping the shot very tight. The pose looks fun and natural, and works much better than if the three had been standing in a line.

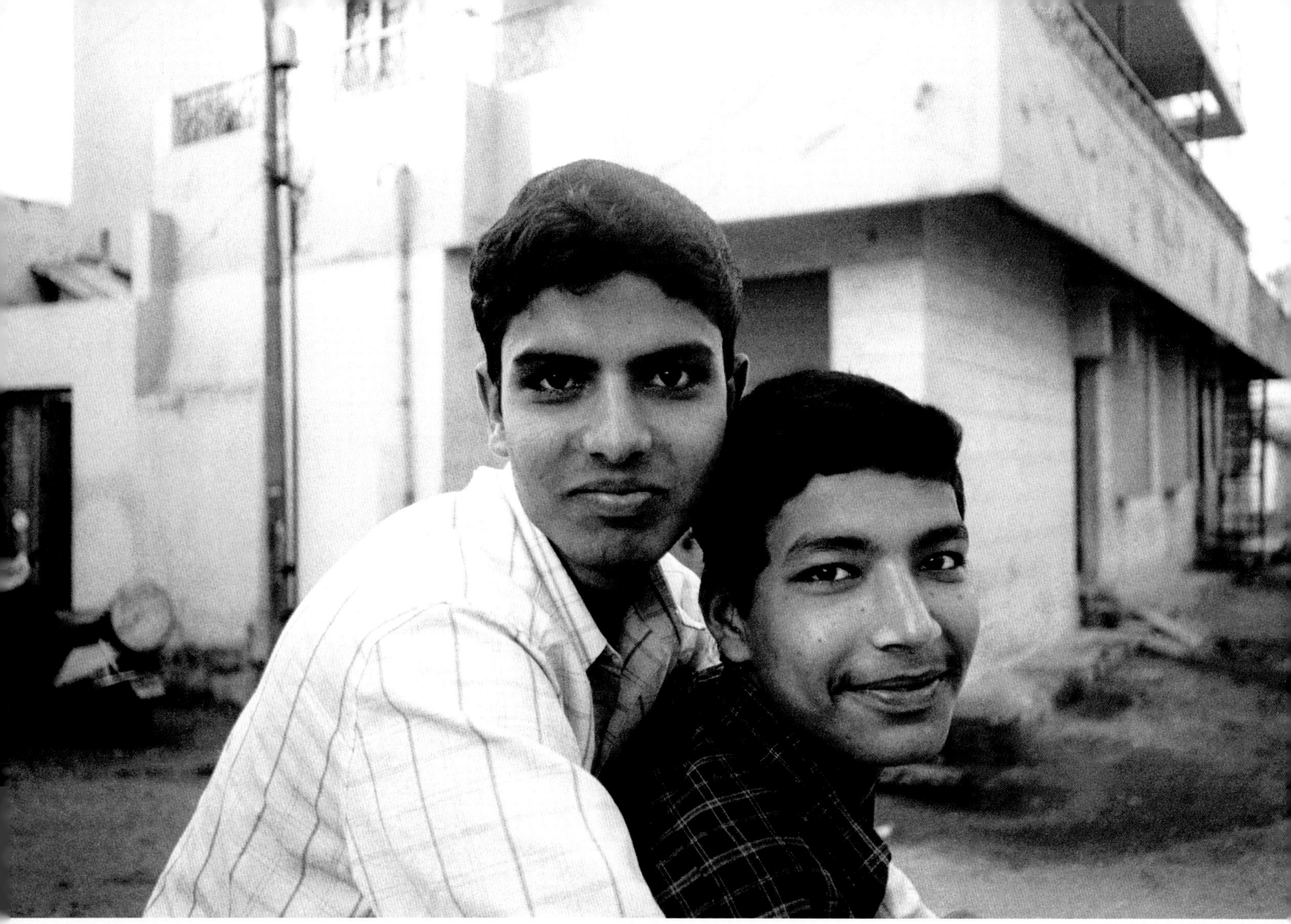

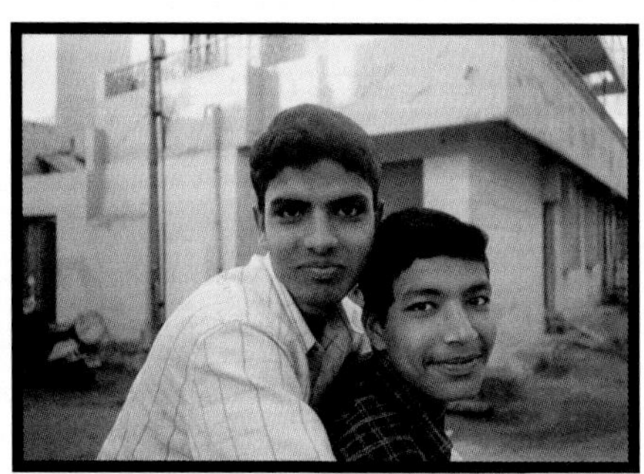

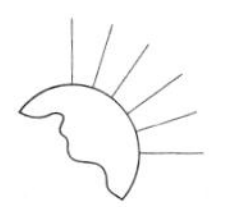

Diffused sun

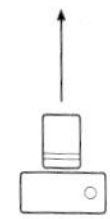

35mm camera

Fact file	
Photographer:	Aaron Schuman
Location:	Shimoga, Karnataka region, India
Time of day:	8am, January

Technical details	
Camera:	Nikon F2
Lens:	28mm
Film:	Kodak Tri-X 400
Exposure:	1/125sec at f/5.6

'The intensity of their friendship was obvious in the closeness of their bodies, and a certain sense of boyish confidence remained in their eyes as I took the shot.'

Aaron Schuman

The concept

Aaron was given a grant by a charitable organisation in England to photograph the Karnataka region of India, showing the people and character of the area. 'Early one morning I was wandering through the back streets of Shimoga's Muslim neighbourhood, which was full of people going about their daily routine,' he describes. 'At one point, two young men rode towards me, sharing a bicycle on their way to work. I took a few photographs as they approached and then stopped them as they passed, and asked to take their portrait. "Yes, yes, we are the best of friends," one told me.'

The location

Because this was a spontaneous street portrait, the location was not planned in any way, but Aaron kept the background in clear focus, rather than blur it with a wide aperture, because it helps put the subjects in the context of their environment.

Composition

This angle of the heads and shoulders works very well for photographing pairs, as it forms a pleasing triangle shape. Aaron was fortunate here as this pose happened naturally as the boys were sharing a bicycle and had no problem with physical contact. 'Their body language was intimate and playful – more like two brothers than self-conscious teenagers,' says Aaron. 'The one on the back of the bicycle leaned his cheek on his friend's head and steadied himself, without me prompting him.'

Lighting and technique

Early in the morning the sun was still relatively low in the sky and warm-toned, coming from the left of the frame. It was slightly diffused by the morning haze. 'The backstreet I was on was narrow and quite shady at that time of day, but the surrounding walls were white, providing some reflection on to the subjects. Because both the walls and one of the boys' shirts were white, I metered around the lower right of the frame and based my exposure on the neutral grey of the ground.'

Fact file	
Photographer:	Ian McFarlane
Location:	Athens, Georgia, USA
Time of day:	Late afternoon, May

Technical details	
Camera:	Mamiya RZ67
Lens:	65mm
Film:	Fujicolor NPH 400
Exposure:	1/60sec at f/8.5

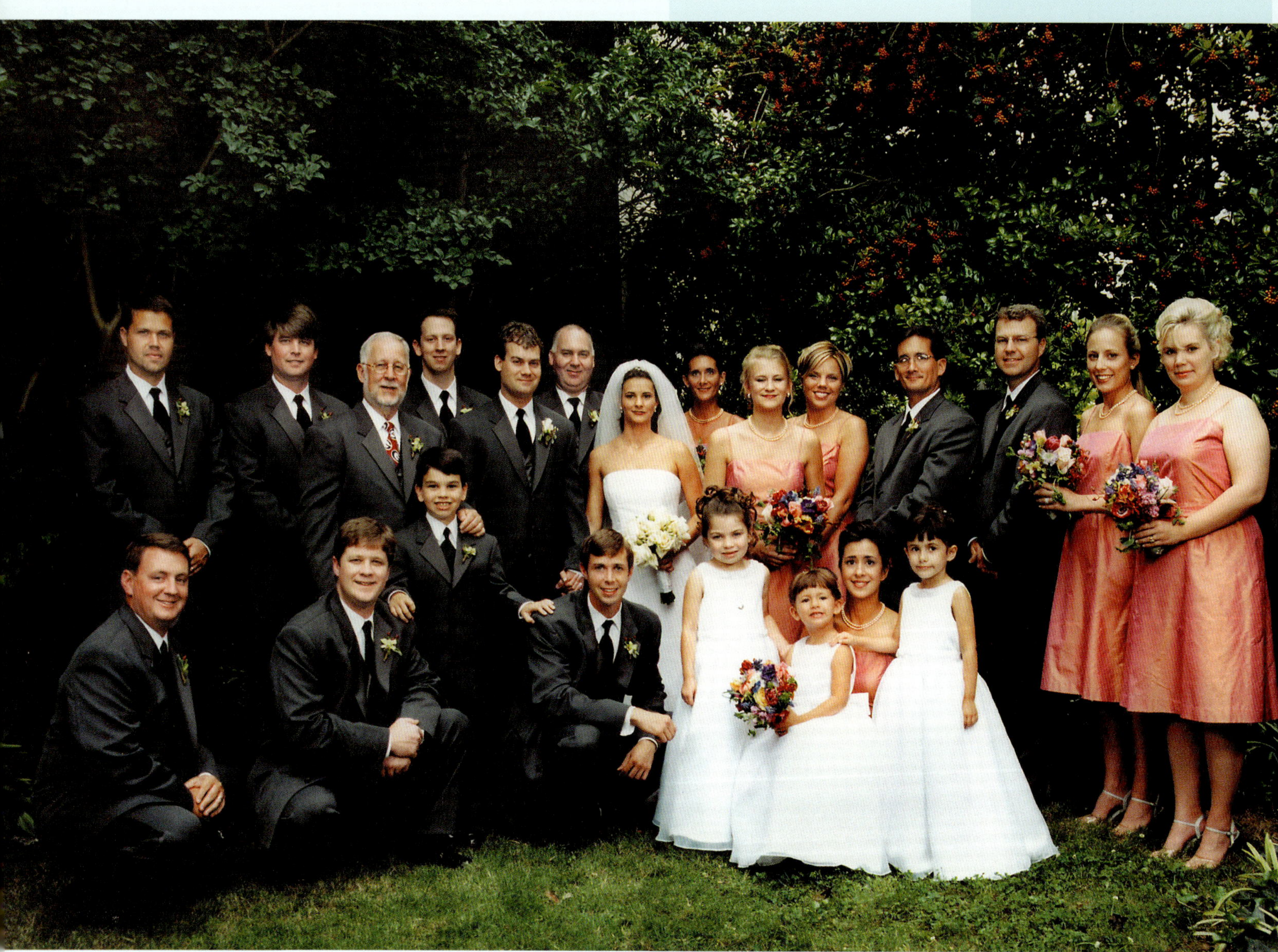

'The biggest problem was trying to arrange all the faces and heads where I could see them.'

Ian McFarlane

The concept

Ian was employed to take the photographs at a wedding party and one of the required shots was a group of 22 important members of the family and friends.

The location

'I found this tiny space beside the church, thinking I would use all the foliage around them and the large, low hanging tree above them to act as a frame, enclosing them in the green,' he explains.

Composition

'I put the bride and groom in the centre and the children up front, but apart from that, I didn't attempt to place people in any particular order other than their size,' says Ian. 'I had to line the group up in a slight arch so they could all fit in between the building, but I didn't want to include any part of this in the frame.'

Lighting and technique

'It was a bright day with the sun directly overhead, softened by cloud. I used a 300 watt strobe pack with two heads and two umbrellas. They were placed on either side of the group to fill in shadows in eye sockets created by the overhead sun. I took an ambient light reading of the natural light, and then set the strobe heads to half a stop brighter than this. It added a very slight fill on the faces without looking like a strobe shot.'

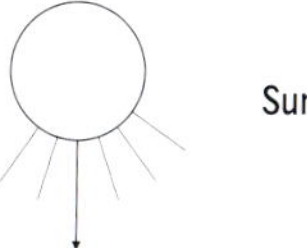

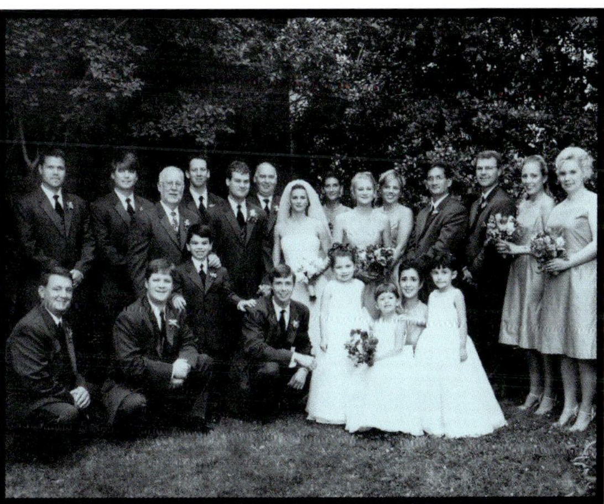

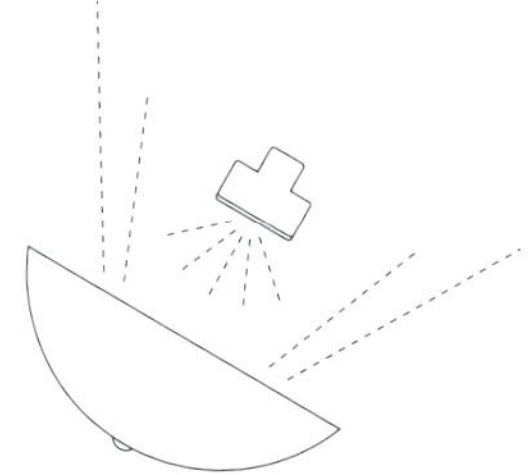

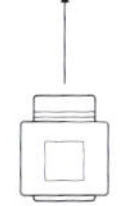

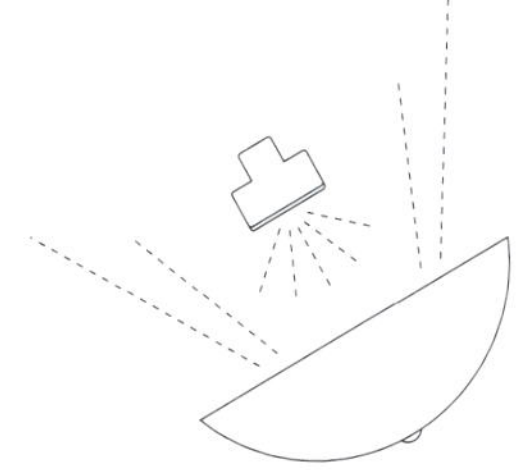

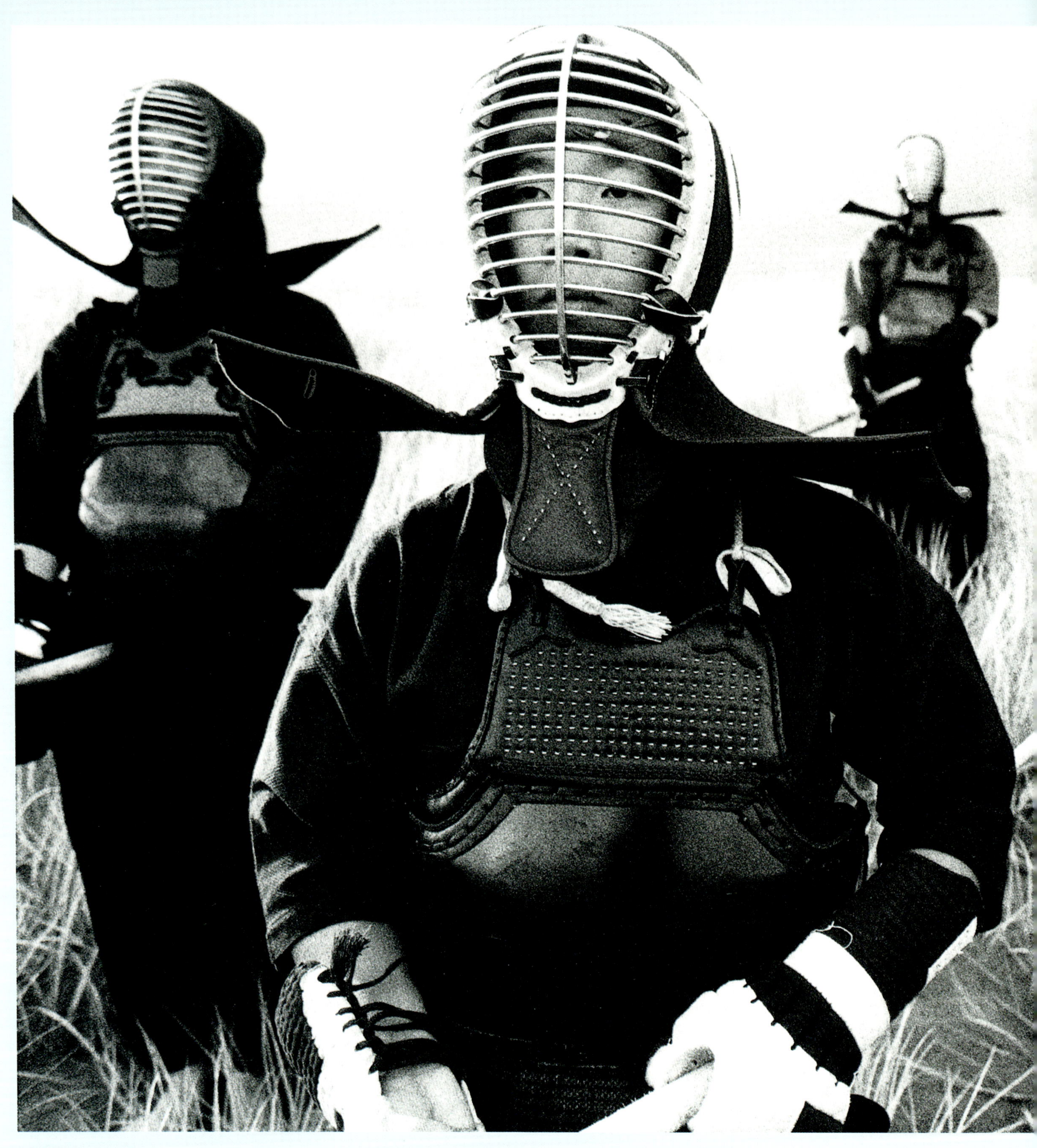

‘Although this could be a scene out of Akira Kurosawa’s “The Seven Samurai”, the only Asian warrior was the one in the foreground. The rest of the guys are Caucasian.’

Michael Hall

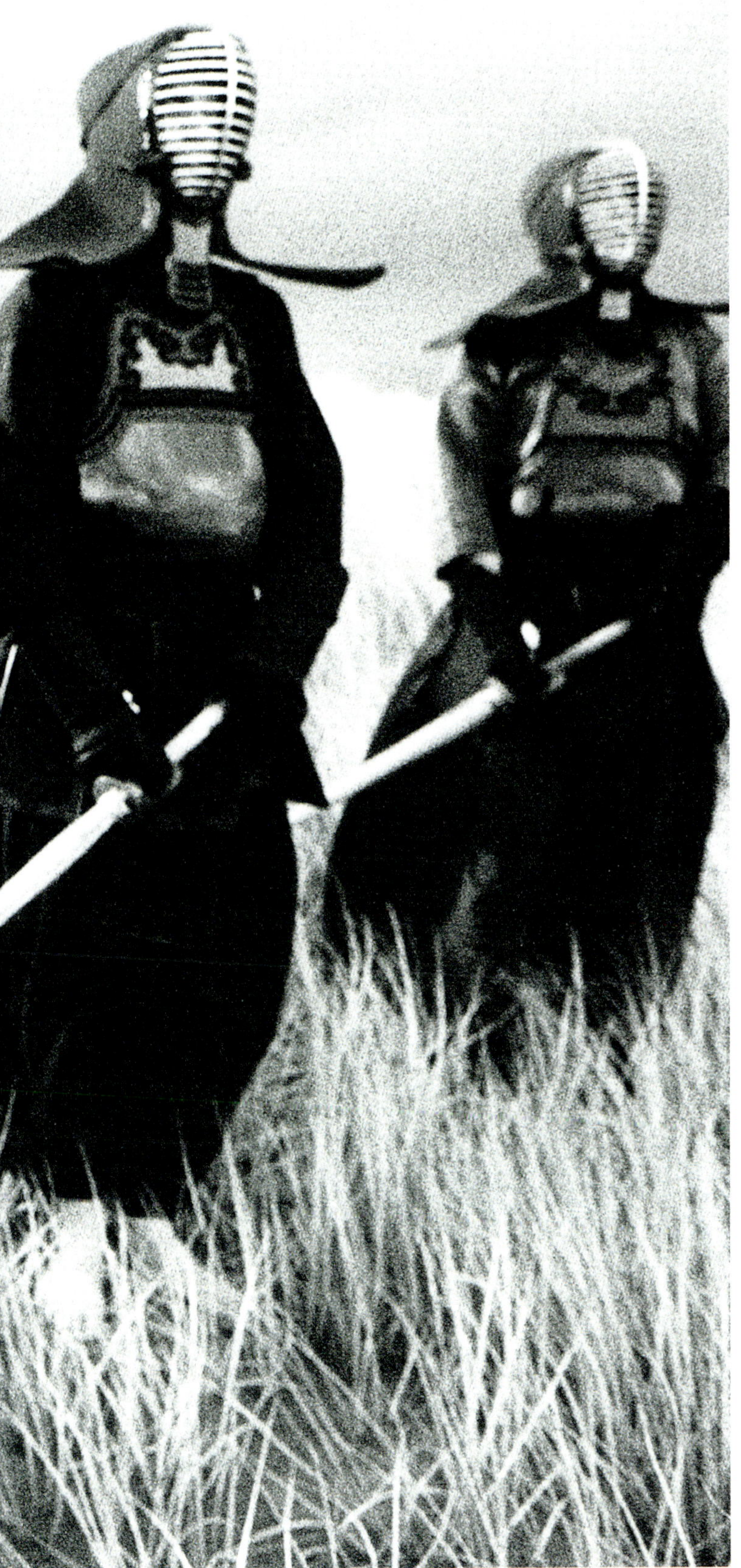

Fact file

Photographer: Michael Hall
Location: Waitarere, New Zealand
Time of day: Early morning, winter

Technical details

Camera: Nikon FM 2
Lens: 28mm
Film: Kodak T-Max 400
Exposure: 1/30sec at f/5.6

The concept

This striking shot was planned and taken by Michael for self-promotional purposes, as he explains: 'Wellington Kendo Club allowed me access to photograph them and in return I supplied them with a photograph for use on their website. I had already taken some test rolls during practice. The club used the university hall, a large space with wooden floorboards and floor-to-ceiling, south-facing windows. But after several attempts I wasn't getting what I wanted as the location didn't fit the subject matter.'

The location

Michael persuaded members of the Kendo club to take a drive an hour and a half up the coast from Wellington, to a wild outdoor location that was more in tune with how he had visualised the image. They stayed overnight at a friend's beach house, getting up early the next morning.

Composition

There's something quite surreal about this shot, with the dark-robed figures contrasting with the washed-out background resembling strange and eerie warriors. Although he had only a short time to get the shot, the positioning of the men is perfect, a tribute to their co-operation and Michael's vision. 'At the time of shooting I had Eugene Smith's image "Spanish Soldiers" firmly held in my mind,' he explains. 'This helped a great deal to be decisive and exacting when it came to situating the subjects and framing the image.'

Lighting and technique

'It took the guys forever to get their armour on and I was concerned the good early morning light was rapidly fading. By the time we got out into the sand dunes the clouds had come in and the weather was rapidly turning. Understandably the guys didn't want to get their outfits wet so we only had five minutes to get the shot before the first rain was upon us. As it turned out, the light and weather were fortuitous at the time.' Michael used a yellow filter on the lens, which helped add contrast.

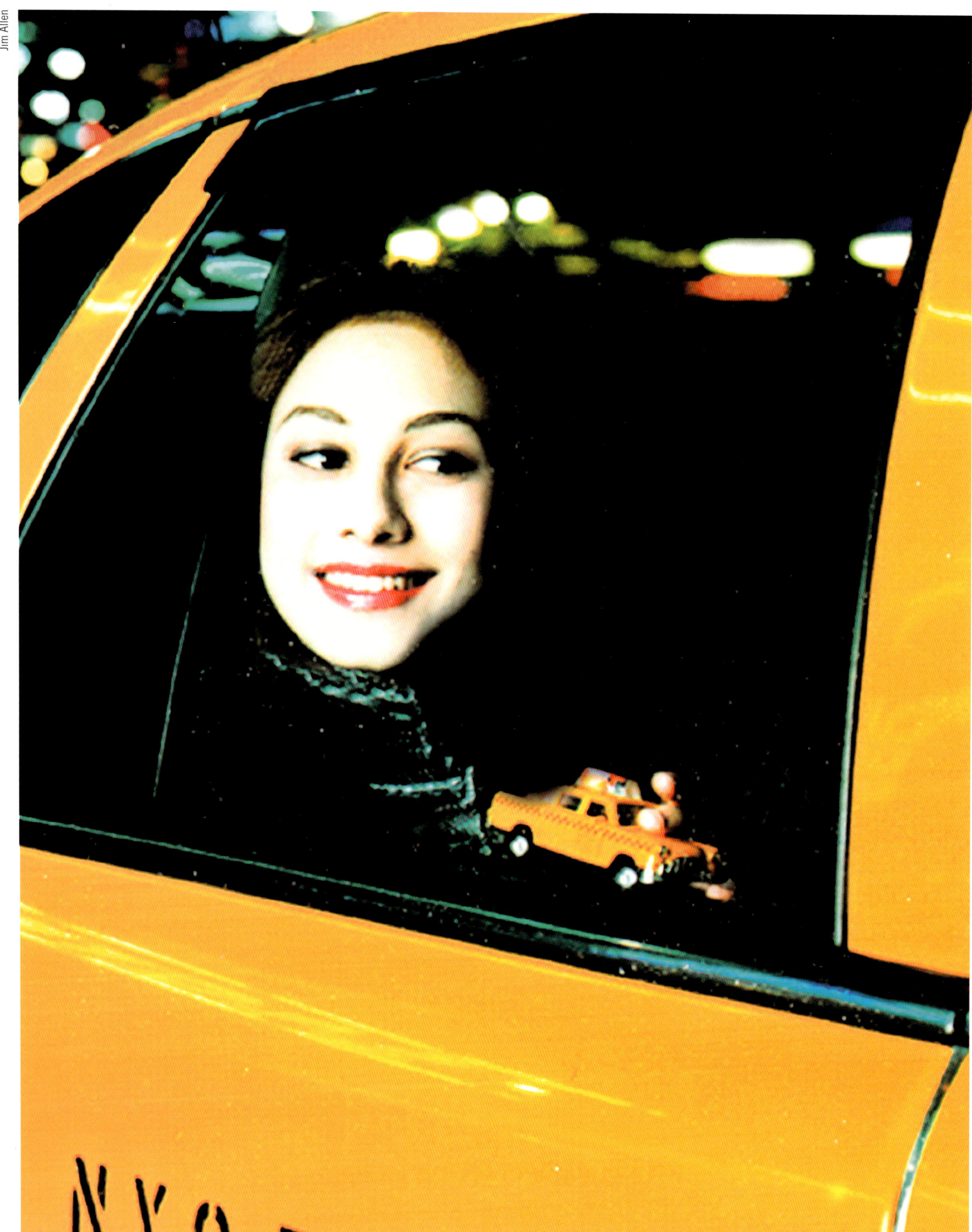

Jim Allen

Chapter 7: **Props and frames**

This chapter looks at two compositional devices – props and frames – which often work together for the same effect. Props can be virtually anything, a plant, a book, a car and so on. They can perform the simple function of giving the subject something to do with their hands, or to make a pose more comfortable by providing something to lean on. They can also be used to add interest to the picture and to reveal something about the person, perhaps to do with their work or favourite pastime.

Frames, in this context, refer to lines and shapes around the subject. They can be used to draw the viewer's eyes to the focal point, add another element of interest to the composition, or even disguise an ugly background. Doorways and windows make obvious frames, but there are many other structures, man-made and natural, that can be effective. Even the play of light and shade can be used in this way.

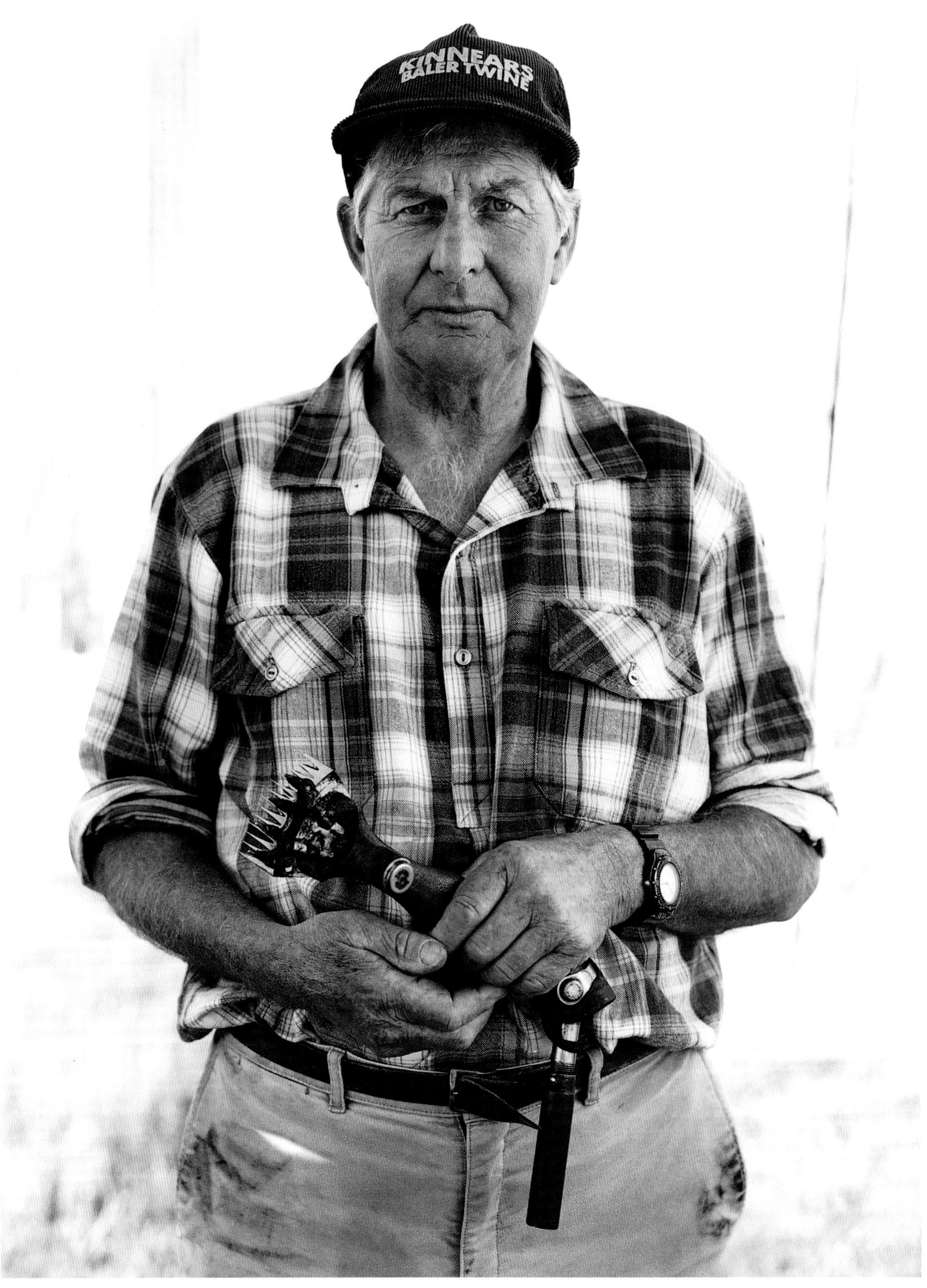
KINNEARS
BALER TWINE

Fact file

Photographer: Michael Hall
Location: North of Wellington, New Zealand
Time of day: Midday, summer

Technical details

Camera: Wista zone IV 4x5 field camera
Lens: 150mm
Film: Kodak T-Max 100
Exposure: 1/125 sec

The concept

'Mr Jenson was photographed for the Central Power Annual Report,' recalls Michael. 'My client wanted to portray the diversity of the company's customers. The portraits were to be very straightforward, even simplistic in approach and not heavily stylised. Each subject was to hold an object that would give a clue to his or her profession, and a handset seemed the most appropriate for a sheep farmer.'

The location

The subject was photographed at his own farm, but the style of the picture meant that the location was deliberately unclear.

Composition

'The brief was to almost totally blow the background out so that the images would fit in the publication as full-page bleeds, be simple and elegant in presentation, and not distract or override the presentation,' says Michael. The use of the sheep-shearing tool not only reveals the subject's line of work, but also gives him something to do with his hands, which can be a problem with three-quarter length poses.

Lighting and technique

A large, white cloth background and artificial lights could have given Michael the simplicity of style he needed, but he found an alternative plan that made such a set up unnecessary. 'I placed Mr Jenson in the shade of the shearing shed that was effectively four stops darker than the surrounding fields, which were in full mid-afternoon sun. I also employed a reflector to camera right and slightly above lens height to add a bit of lift to the face and especially the eyes. I feel it's important to have some light in the eyes in a shaded situation; otherwise, the eyes can have a tendency to look rather dull.'

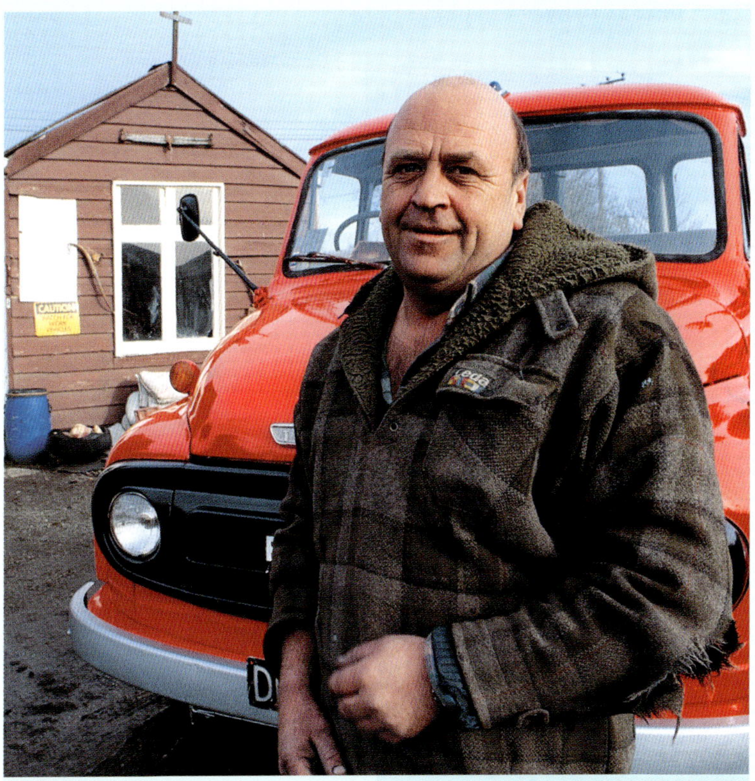

Fact file

Photographer: Michael Hall
Location: Gore, Southland, New Zealand
Time of day: Mid-morning, early winter

Technical details

Camera: Hasselblad 501C
Lens: 50mm
Film: Kodak E100s
Exposure: 1/30sec at f/5.6

This was taken for a company report with a brief to capture people in small town and rural locations. Michael came across this truck driver in his yard and he agreed to have his portrait taken. The layering of the composition works well here, with the truck in the middle distance and the building at the back providing clues about the man, without distracting attention away from him as the main subject.

'The use of 4x5-inch black-and-white film adds a special quality and clarity to the image – more than if it had been taken on 35mm, or even medium format.'

Michael Hall

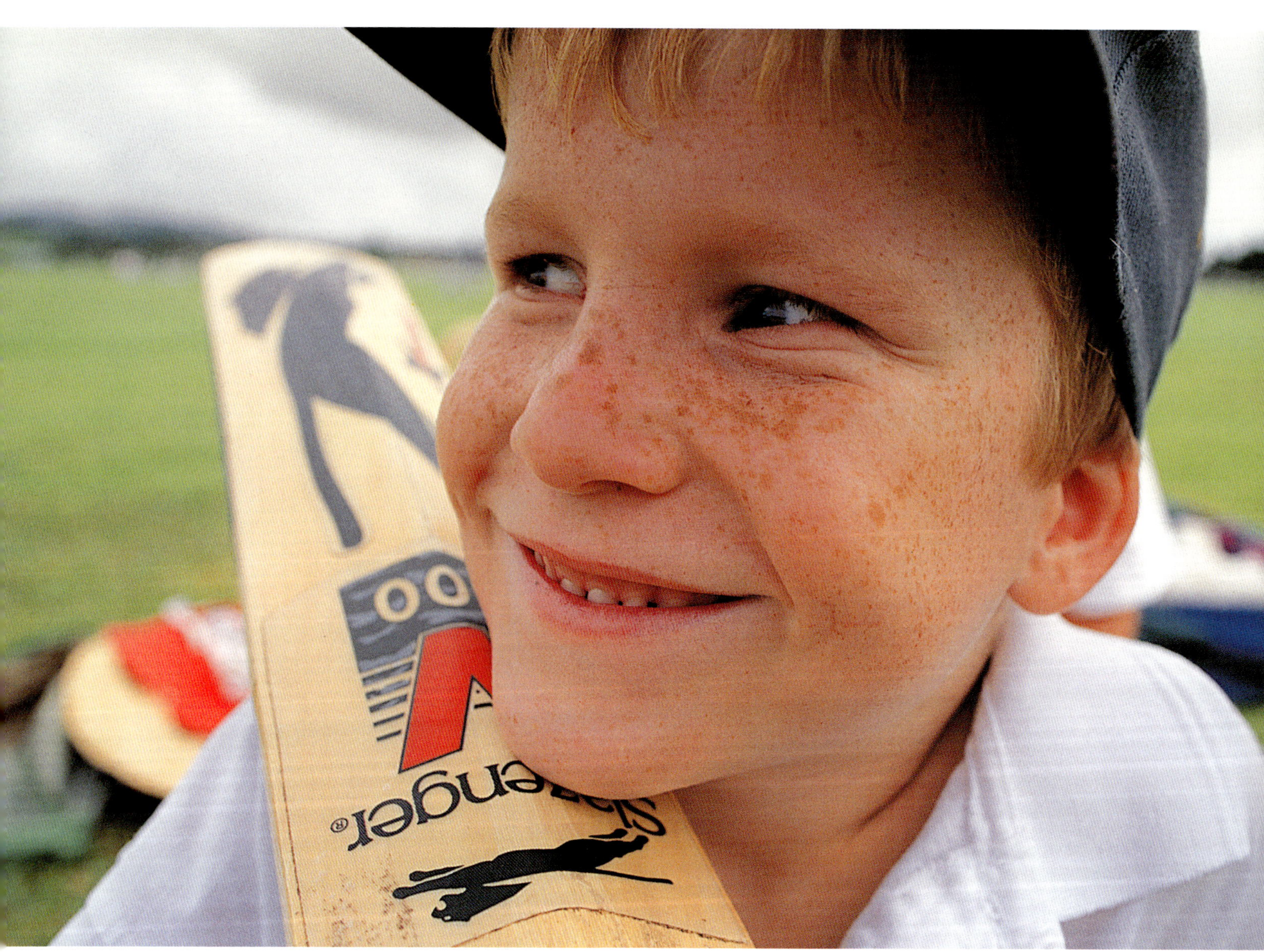

‘No matter how much planning you do for a project like this, good pictures often come as a result of stumbling upon great subjects.’

Michael Hall

Fact file

Photographer: Michael Hall
Location: Kensington Sports Ground, Whangarei, New Zealand
Time of day: Midday, summer

Technical details

Camera: Nikon FM2
Lens: 28mm
Film: Kodak E100S
Exposure: 1/250sec at f/4

The concept

This photograph was taken for a book project entitled 'New Zealand, The Millennium'. 'The idea was to commission a selection of photographers, assigning each one to a different area of the country,' explains Michael. 'It was sort of like a-day-in-the-life-of approach, except we had the luxury of shooting over several weeks instead of a single day. I was assigned the region of Northland, an area I knew well as it was where I grew up. I hadn't lived there for a decade so in a way it was rediscovery for me.'

Sun behind clouds

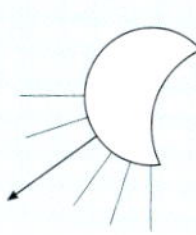

The location

Cricket is part of the culture of the area and so Michael went to a sports ground to watch a Saturday morning session for youngsters in the hope of finding some good shots for the project.

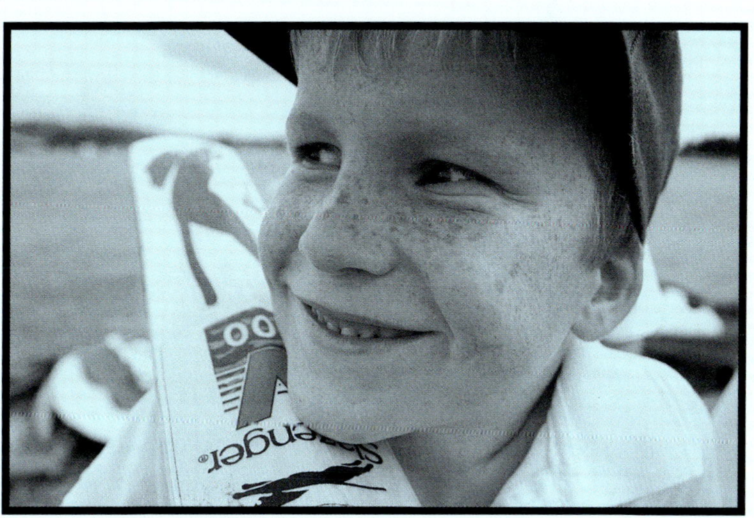

Composition

Michael spotted this young boy who was, fortunately, quite happy to be photographed as he had a great face and expression. 'I like to get close to a subject,' he says. 'It's an intuitive process. Most people are very receptive to being photographed as long as you treat them with respect. If I happen upon anyone who is even slightly uneasy about being approached I will always back away and move on. I've missed so many good portraits in the past, but if the person isn't into it, it's not something you can force.' The cricket bat is vital to the image from a compositional point of view, but more importantly here, it also helps to tell a story about the boy and his character, which was exactly what was required for the book Michael was working on.

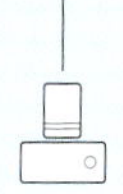

35mm camera

Lighting and technique

The sky was bright but overcast, ideal conditions for a subject like this where soft, even light is more preferable to shadows and highlights. 'It was one of those magic occasions where the cloud cover acts as a giant soft box in the sky,' says Michael.

'As a commercial photographer I feel it's imperative to do your own work. This often goes into the portfolio which in turn guides the sort of commissions you acquire.'

Michael Hall

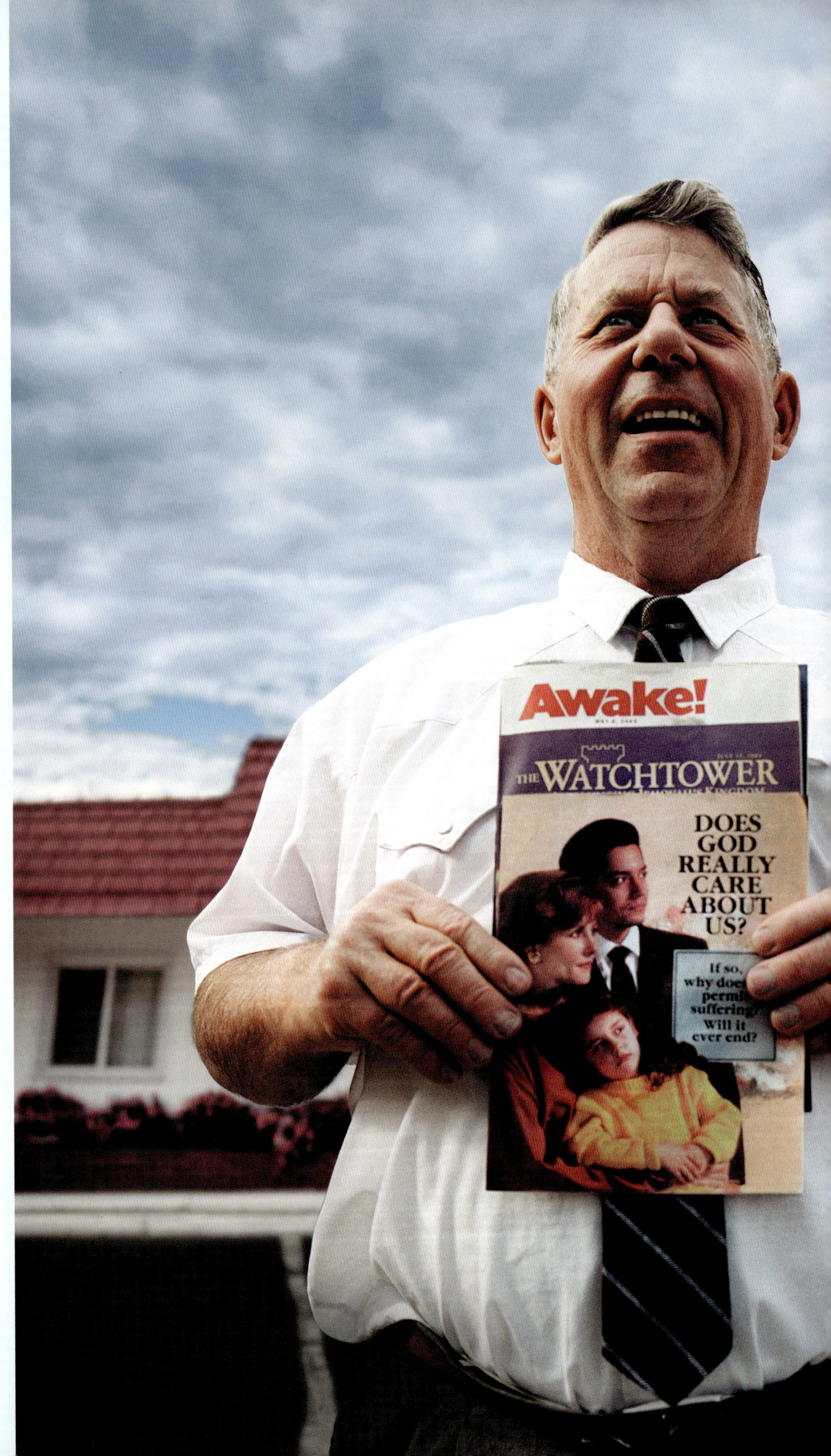

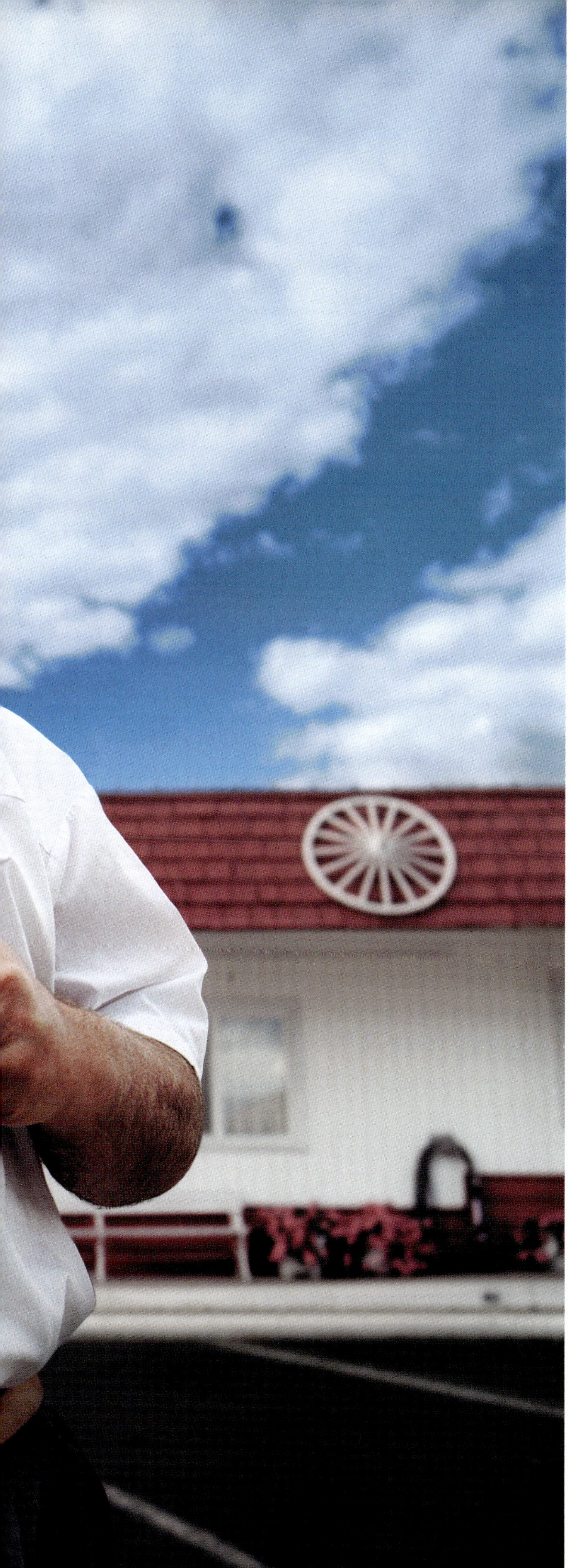

Fact file

Photographer: Michael Hall
Location: Cache Creek, Canada
Time of day: Mid-afternoon, summer

Technical details

Camera: Hasselblad 503SW
Lens: 50mm
Film: Kodak 160 VC
Exposure: 1/125sec at f/5.6

The concept

'I happened upon Lloyd in a small town five hours North of Vancouver,' Michael recalls. 'He was at the Greyhound bus station handing Awake! magazines to travellers as they disembarked from the buses. I was in the country on a commercial shoot with a few days spare before the job commenced. I had the use of a rental car so decided to take a trip into the country. I have several personal projects going on at any one time and at any opportunity I look for subject matter to photograph.'

The location

Michael is always on the lookout for interesting characters to photograph wherever he finds them and in this case the location of a bus station car park was incidental.

Composition

The clouds are a vital part of this composition and, if they had not been there, Michael might not have been so inspired to take this shot from this angle. He used a low camera angle to emphasise them, and the 50mm lens also included the motel, which adds interest to the background and places the subject in context. The magazine does this, too. It's a valuable prop, used prominently to leave the viewer in no doubt as to Lloyd's role.

Lighting and technique

This was a simple portrait, taken with no other equipment than the camera and lens Michael was carrying at the time in light that happened to be favourable. It shows that great portrait subjects can be found in the most unlikely places, if you keep your eyes open to the possibilities.

'Sometimes you get a better picture if you don't think too much, just click.'

Tomek Paczkowski

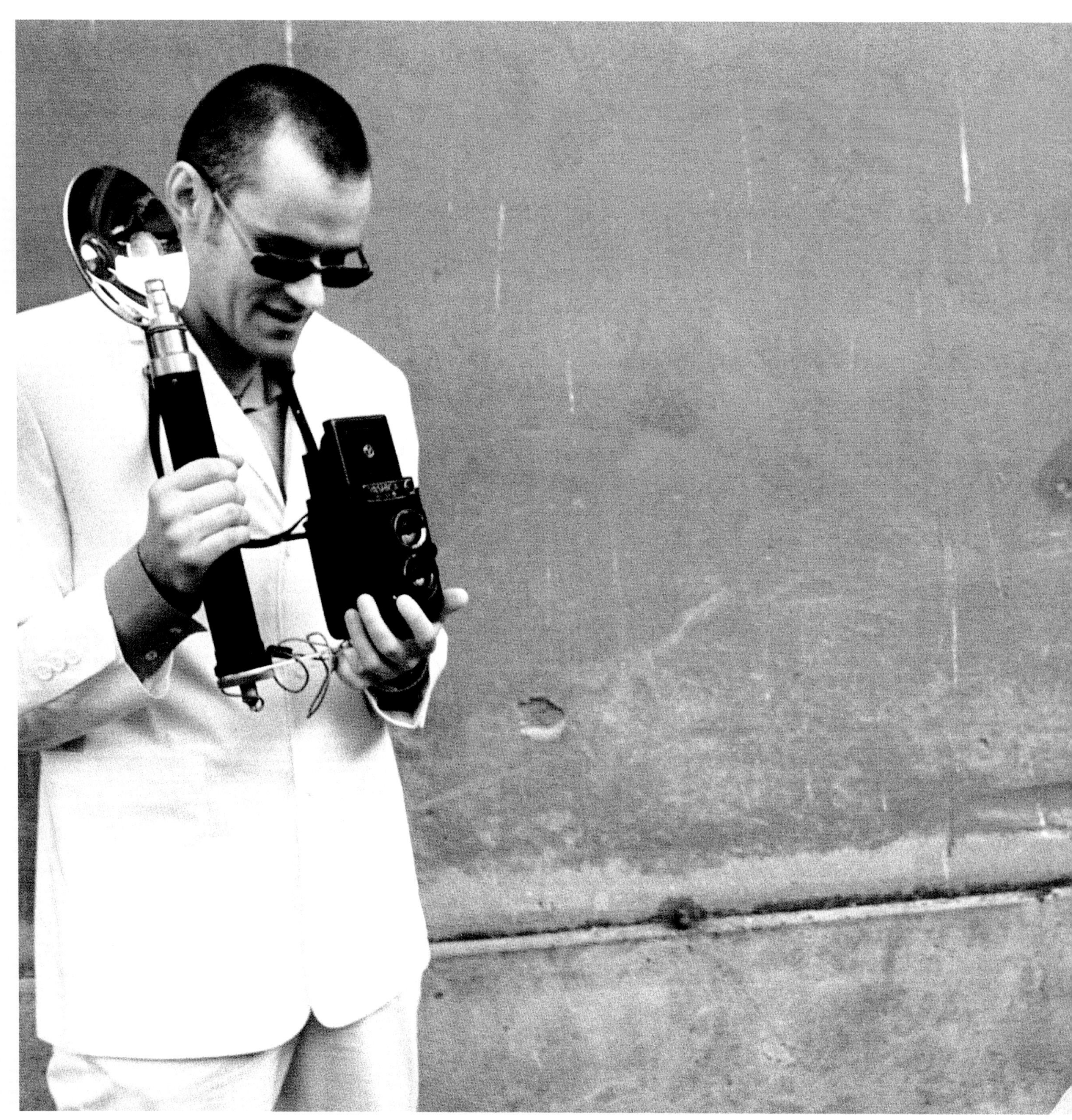

Fact file

Photographer: Tomek Paczkowski
Location: Warsaw, Poland
Time of day: 6pm, summer

Technical details

Camera: Olympus OM2n
Lens: 50mm
Film: Kodak Tri-X 400
Exposure: 1/125sec at f/8

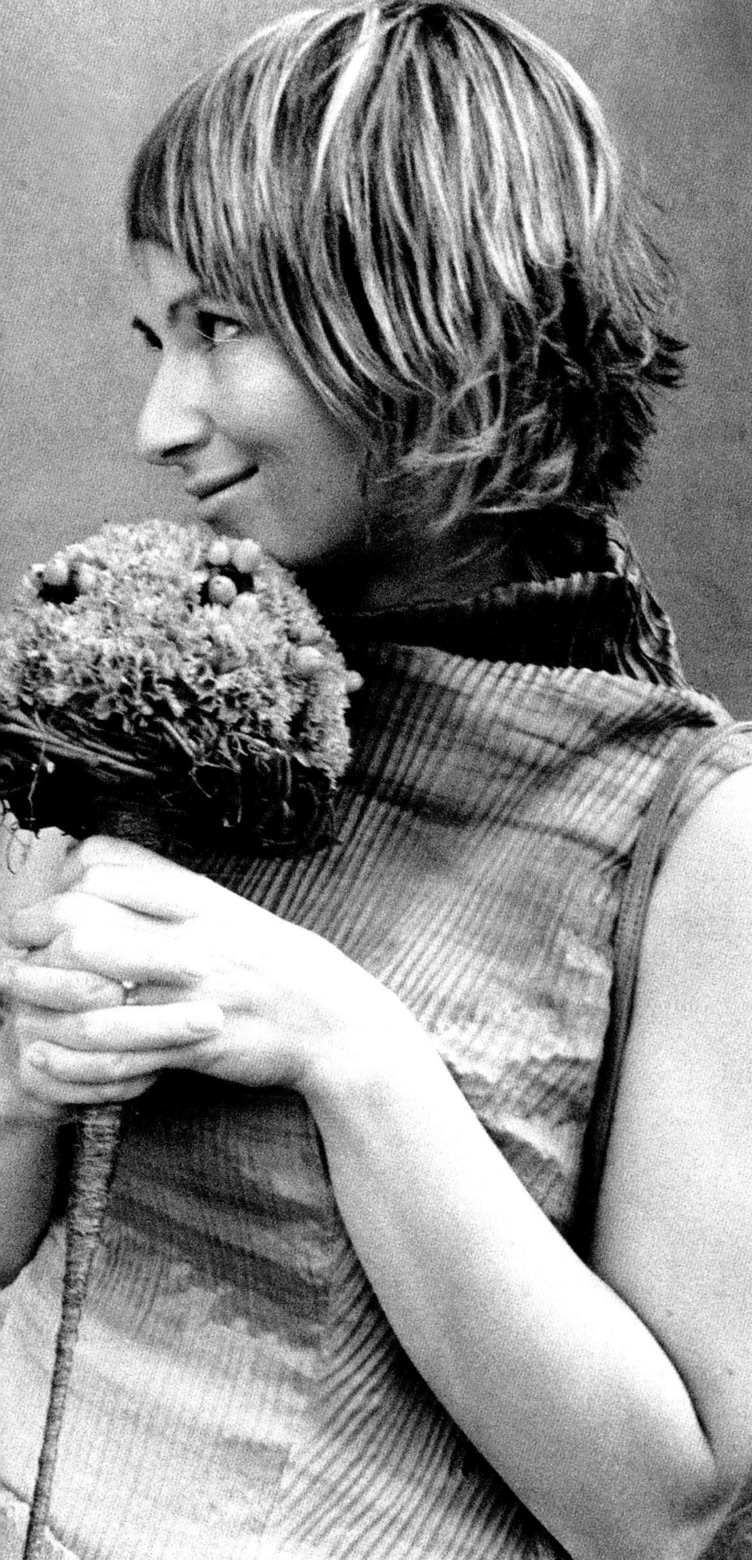

The concept

Tomek was asked to take some informal shots at his friends' wedding and this was one of those that stood out.

The location

The couple had just come out of the church after the wedding service in the old part of the city of Warsaw.

Composition

Tomek's role wasn't as the official photographer on the day – he's in the picture here – but it was his job to look for the kind of candid, informal moments that capture the atmosphere and fun of the occasion. This shot wasn't planned or set up, but it's an amusing glimpse of the bride posing for a picture. Instead of trying to shoot over the other photographer's shoulder, Tomek included him in the frame and, while this isn't a conventional composition, with each subject at either end of the frame, the space between them makes sense in this instance. The 'props' of the flowers and 'camera' describe the roles of each subject.

Lighting and technique

Tomek had no influence over the timing of the occasion and so had to make the best of whatever the light happened to be. He was lucky that, in early evening on a bright but overcast day, it was soft and diffused – just how he likes it for portraits and perfect for this shot, giving an even, rounded light on both subjects.

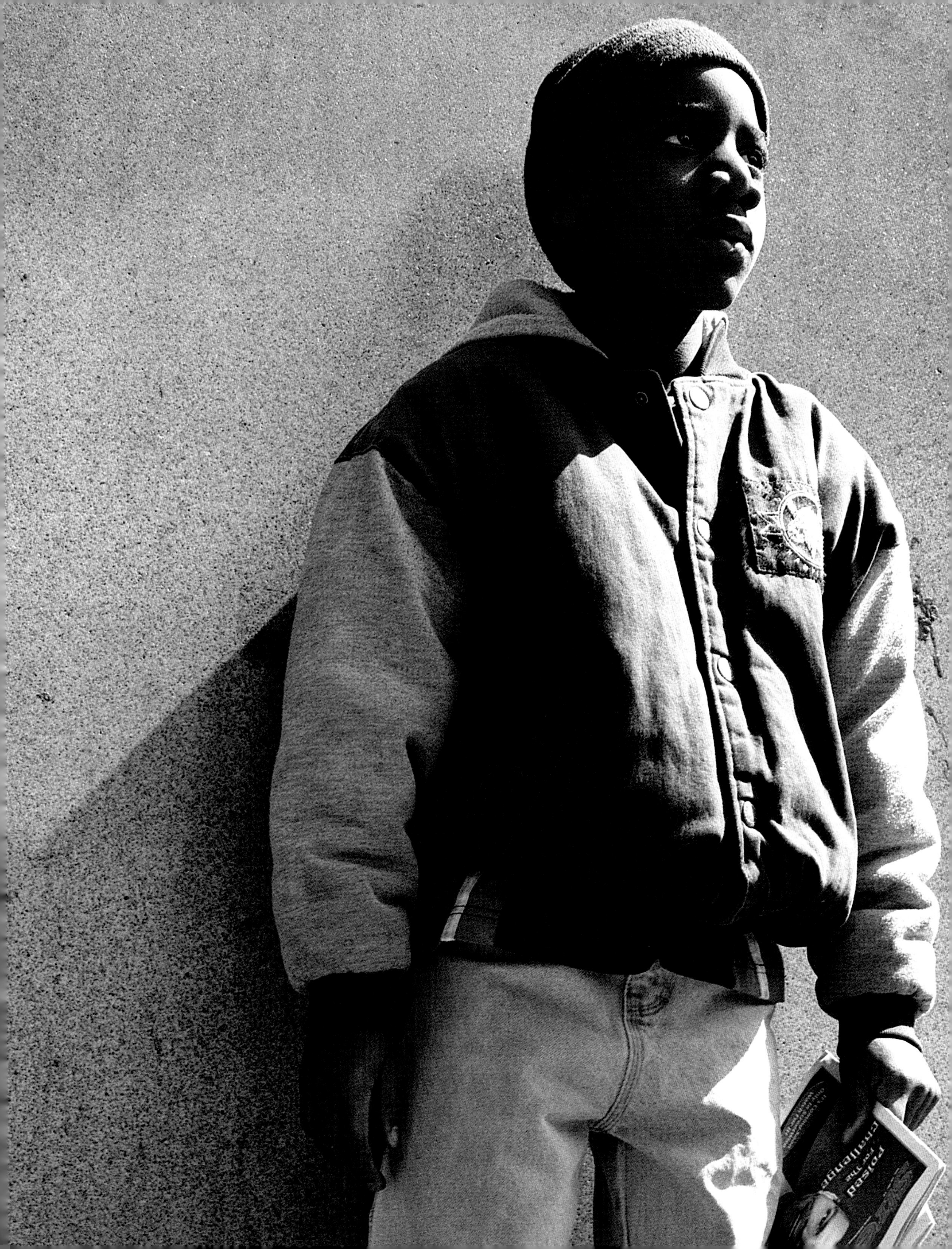
Poised
for the
Challenge

Fact file

Photographer: Jacek Pomykalski
Location: Chicago, USA
Time of day: 2pm, March

Technical details

Camera: Mamiya RB 67
Lens: 90mm
Film: Agfa APX 100
Exposure: Not recorded

The concept

'I just wanted a portrait of this young newspaper seller, and to portray him as I saw him, anonymous and lost on the main street of a huge city, among crowds of people passing by without paying any attention to him,' Jacek explains.

The location

Jacek was out on the streets of Chicago, deliberately looking for candid shots of people. He photographed this boy where he stood, not wanting to spoil the moment by making his presence known.

Composition

'By breaking the classical canons of composition, I wanted to introduce into the picture an element of chaos and anxiety – make an impression that it is showing only a small fraction of reality, which in fact is happening outside the frame,' says Jacek. The newspaper in the boy's hand explains the reason for him being there and somehow makes the shot even more poignant – he is out of place in an adult's world.

Lighting and technique

'The sun was high and the light sharp and strong,' recalls Jacek. 'Although that would not normally be an ideal situation, the strong side light and the shadow falling on the wall bring out the drama in the picture. To gauge the exposure, I measured the incident light a couple of meters in front of the subject to give me a general idea of the lighting conditions.'

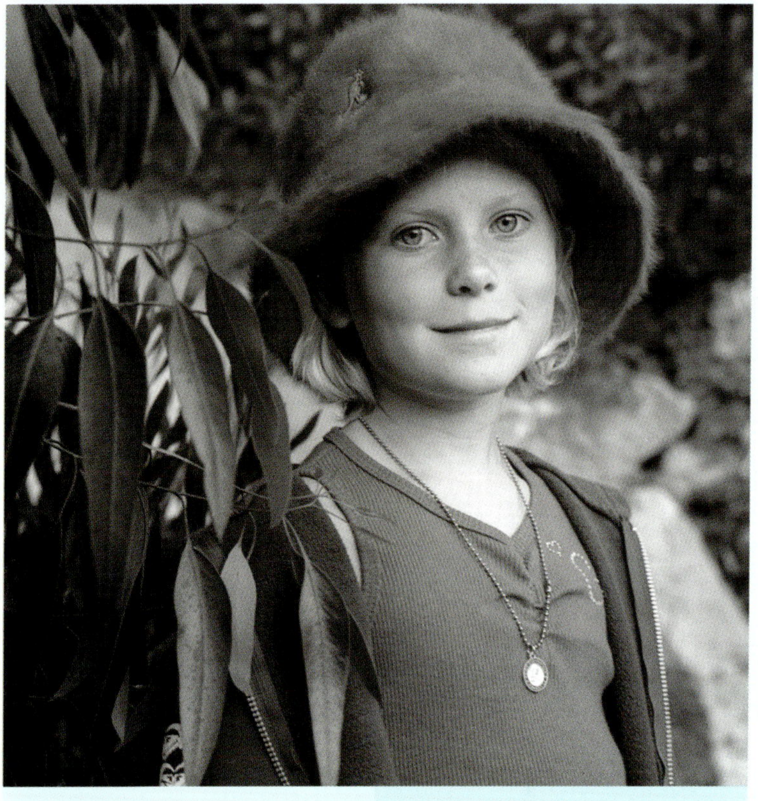

Fact file

Photographer: Ed Krebs
Location: Baseball park, Laguna Beach, California
Time of day: Early evening, June

Technical details

Camera: Rolleiflex
Lens: 75mm
Film: Kodak Tri-X 400
Exposure: 1/60sec at f/5.6

Using a prop doesn't have to mean giving the subject something to hold; often you can find something in the existing environment, like a wall, or a tree, that will suffice. In this case, the foliage on the left of the picture serves as a prop, adding interest, helping to frame the subject and adding to the naturalness of the pose.

'A busy street is the best place to capture faces in a crowd, to sketch out the tension and relations between them. People on the street do not pose, do not pretend; they are authentic.'

Jacek Pomykalski

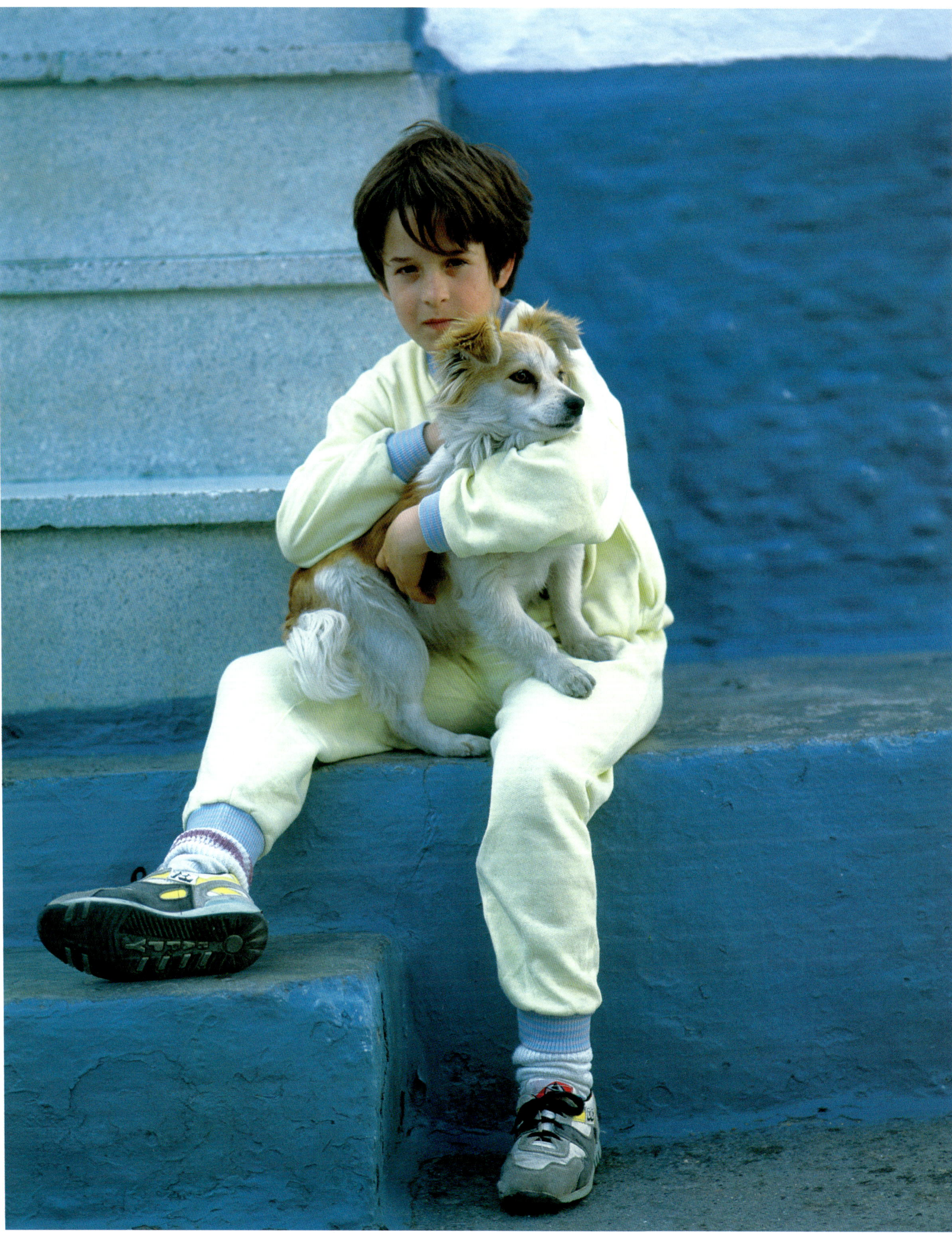

Fact file

Photographer: Jim Zuckerman
Location: Mojacar, Spain
Time of day: Noon, April

Technical details

Camera: Mamiya RZ 67 II
Lens: 110mm
Film: Fujichrome Provia 100F
Exposure: 1/60 at f/4.5

The concept

This picture was taken while Jim was leading a photo tour to southern Spain, using the opportunity to take personal pictures of the people and the area as they arose.

The location

Mojacar is a picturesque Moorish town in the region of Almeria in southern Spain, popular with tourists for its winding, cobbled streets and mountain views. This boy was sitting outside his own home and Jim took his portrait just where he was.

Composition

Pets and children make a winning combination, providing they are not imposed on each other so that one or other looks uncomfortable. There was no such danger here as the boy was already holding his dog. The picture was just waiting to be taken with no need to adjust the pose. 'I was struck by the remarkable colour of the environment, as well as the sweet relationship between the child and his dog,' says Jim. 'He had an intense expression, and when I asked if I could photograph him he simply nodded his head without a smile.'

Lighting and technique

Although taken at noon, often a time best avoided for portraits, the boy was sitting in the shade so harsh sunlight was not a problem. Jim used a hand-held incident meter to read the diffused light on him.

> 'Many photographers would use a warming filter to mitigate the colour cast caused by the blue environment. I prefer to capture what I see.'
>
> Jim Zuckerman

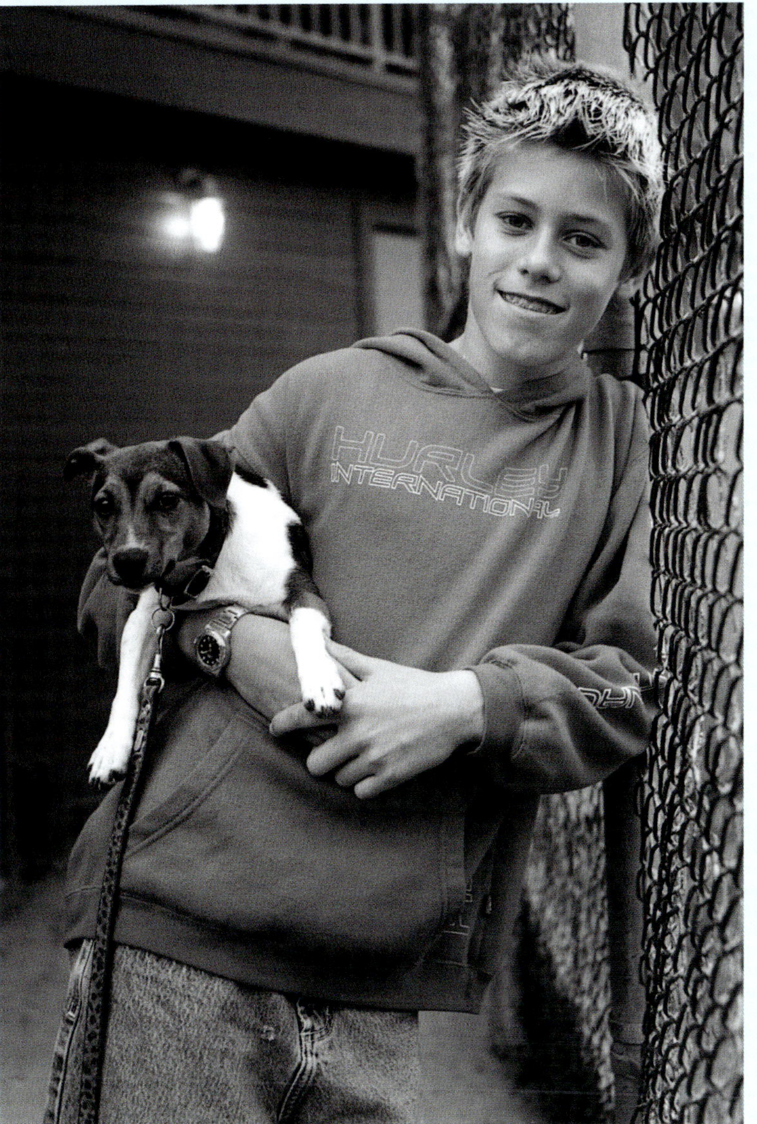

This was an opportunist shot, taken at a Little League baseball park where Ed has been taking portraits for the past 15 years. The boy was watching the game through the fence and, spotting the potential for a picture, Ed focused on him and waited until he turned round. This was the only frame he took before the boy disappeared with his friends.

Fact file

Photographer: Ed Krebs
Location: Laguna Beach, California, USA
Time of day: Just before sunset, June

Technical details

Camera: Rolleiflex
Lens: 75mm
Film: Fuji Neopan 400
Exposure: 1/50sec at f/5.6

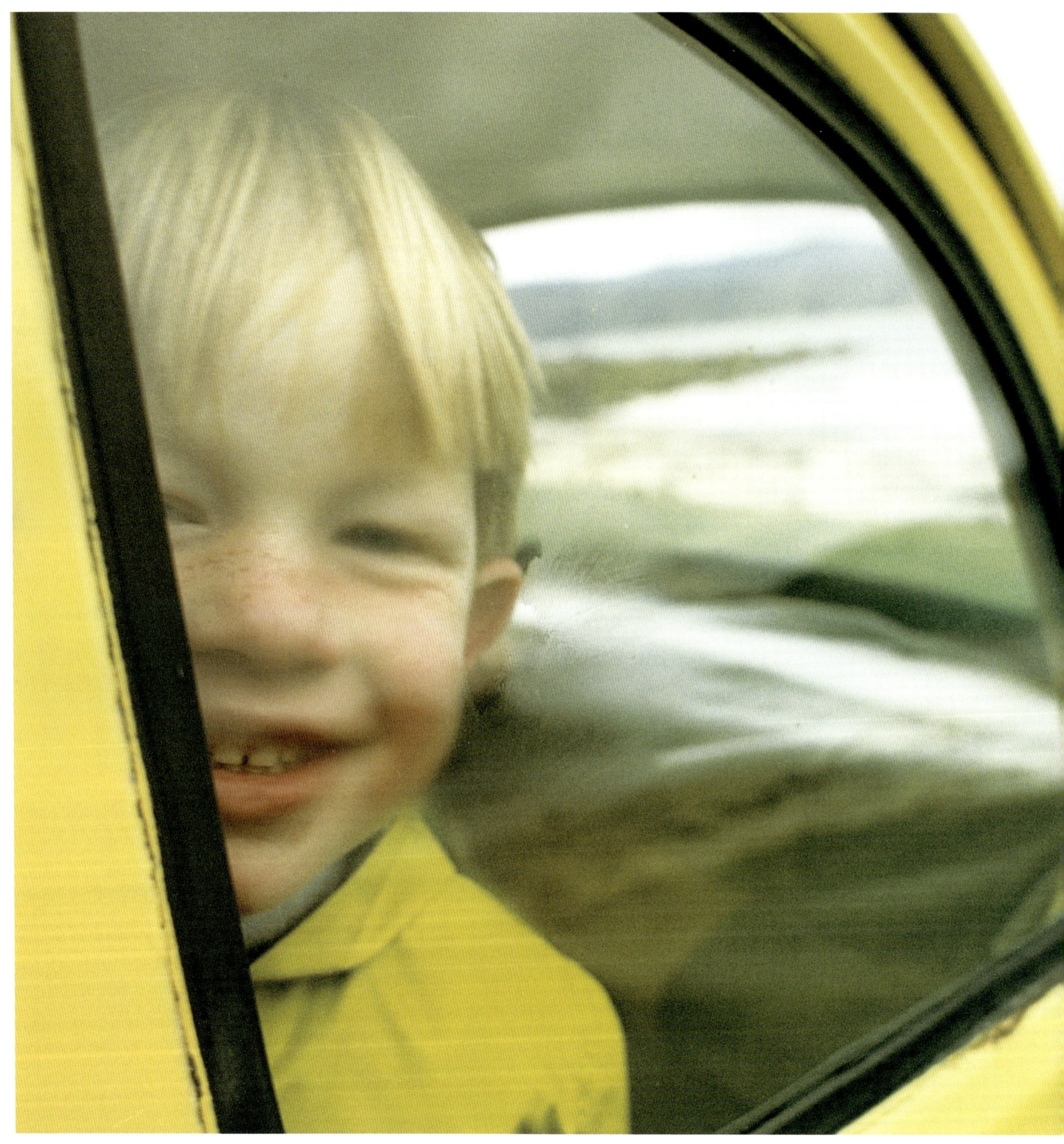

‘Negative film is kinder and gentler than transparency, especially to skin tones.’

Michael Hall

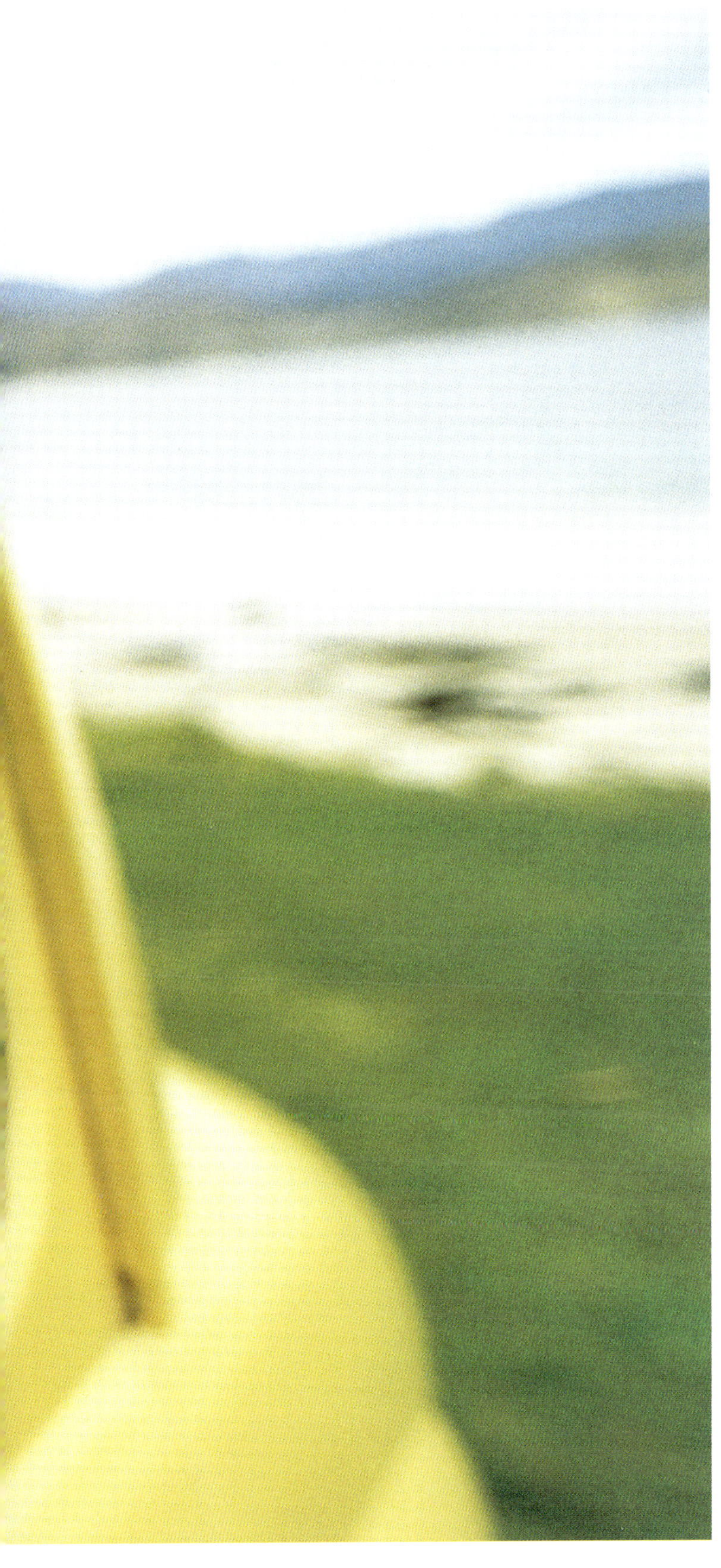

The concept

'This photograph of Finley was taken as part of a re-brand for Westpactrust Bank in New Zealand,' Michael explains. 'It was a large shoot – we had to pull together 50 shots, all showing some aspect of New Zealand life. Eventually a lot of the photographs were used as four-meter-long banners in all of the branches throughout the country. The images had to be iconic and emotive in content. Finley and his older brother, Sebastian, were booked for the afternoon and I had managed to wangle the use of an old Austin A30.'

The location

This particular shot was planned to fit the title 'Day at the beach', and so a beach location was chosen that offered sea, sand and grassy landscape to allow plenty of options.

Composition

Windows of all sorts offer great possibilities as frames for a subject and this one particularly so because of its vintage lines and bright colour that ties in with the boy's shirt. The angle that Michael chose is important for this shot because it shows the seaside seen through the back window, as well as to the side of the car, which explains the boy's excitement. Michael wanted more of an impression of this scene rather than the pin-sharp reality and so used his wide-angle lens wide open at f/2.8.

Lighting and technique

'I had actually hoped and planned for fine weather and blue skies but as the afternoon approached so did the cloud,' recalls Michael. 'I shot it anyway as I was booking up three shoots a day in order to get through the heavy workload. I like the fact it is a bit overcast and gloomy, it gives the perception of a time long gone with the de-saturation and flat light. Colour negative film also helps as it's far softer and doesn't have the punchy colour that transparency has. I shot this wide open at f/2.8 on a 28mm lens.'

Fact file

Photographer: Michael Hall
Location: Scorching Bay, Wellington, New Zealand
Time of day: Midday, late summer

Technical details

Camera: Nikon F4
Lens: 28mm
Film: Kodak 160 VC
Exposure: 1/60sec at f/4

‘I wanted to capture the innocence of my daughter’s face surrounded by the rough wood.’

Nina Andersen

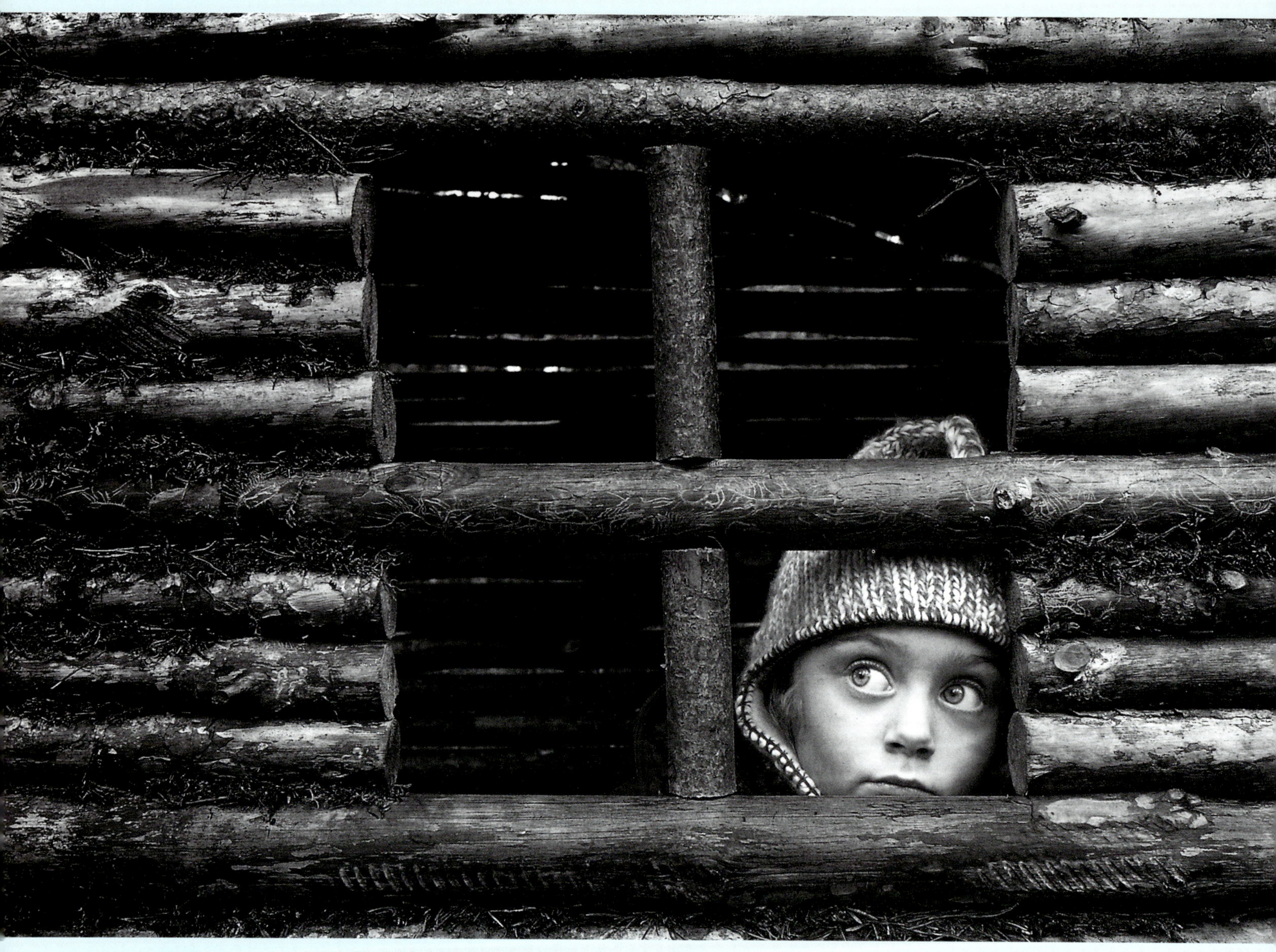

The concept

Taken while Nina was walking with her family in the woods near her home, this wasn't planned in advance, but she took her camera with her ready for just such an opportunity.

The location

'I hadn't known this little wooden house was there before. We just came across it on our walk and I took the picture as my daughter looked out of the window.'

Composition

Windows and doorways provide tailor-made frames for a subject, helping to add impact and, often disguising a dull background. Here it was the contrast that appealed to Nina. 'I liked the light soft skin against all the wood,' she says. 'The hat she had on that day also made a nice frame around her face, and the texture of it fitted well with the wood house.' Nina wanted more of the wood wall than face and she placed the face to the right in the frame according to the rule of thirds. This left the most space in the direction that her daughter was looking in, which helps to open up the picture. If she was looking the other way, the viewer's eyes would follow hers out of the frame.

Lighting and technique

The sun was to the right of the picture but behind clouds so the light was very soft and fairly low as they were in the woods. Nina used the ISO 1600 setting on her digital camera to give her a higher shutter speed. 'Just as with film, the higher the ISO, the more visible grain there is to the image (described as "noise" in digital terms), but in this case that fits with the texture of the wood.'

Fact file

Photographer:	Nina Andersen
Location:	Oslo, Norway
Time of day:	2.45pm, November

Technical details

Camera:	Canon EOS 10D (digital)
Lens:	17–40mm
Film:	n/a
Exposure:	1/90sec at f/6.7

Sun behind clouds

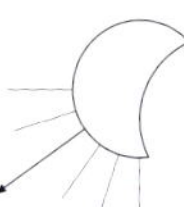

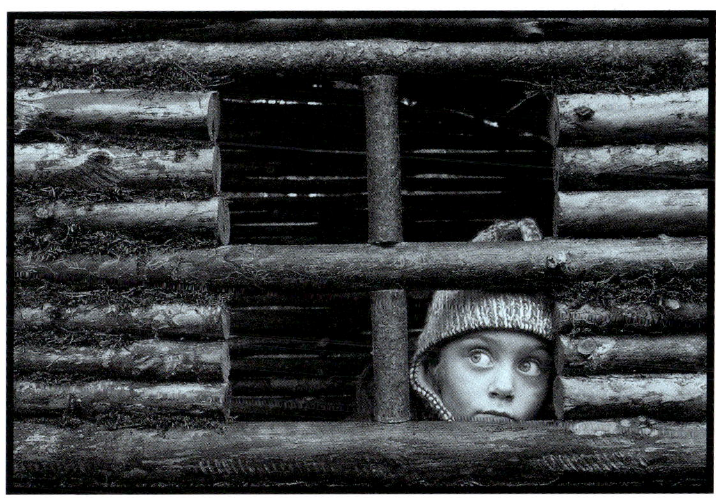

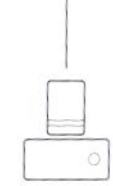

35mm camera

Glossary

Ambient light
The existing light on the scene without any added by the photographer.

Aperture
The opening to a camera's lens which controls the amount of light reaching the film or CCD.

Aperture priority
The photographer selects the aperture and the shutter speed is determined automatically.

B setting
Keeps the shutter open for as long as the release remains pressed.

Bracket
To make a series of exposures of the same subject, often at one half or one third stop intervals.

Burning in
Giving part of a print extra exposure.

Cable release
Flexible cable that screws into the camera shutter release. Allows the shutter to be fired, or held open on 'B', to reduce camera shake.

Depth of field
The area surrounding the true point of focus where the image still appears acceptably sharp.

Differential focus
Using a shallow depth of field to emphasise one part of the picture by showing it sharply focused while other areas are out of focus. Also called selective focus.

Diffuser
Translucent material used to diffuse light.

F-stops
A series of numbers used to describe the size of the lens aperture.

Fill light
A large light source used to fill in the shadows. The light intensity is less than the main, or key, light.

Fill-in flash
A burst of flash to illuminate any areas of shadow and reduce lighting contrast.

Film speed
Refers to the film's sensitivity to light, expressed as an ISO number.

Filter
A piece of glass or plastic fitted over the lens to modify the light passing through it.

High key
High key pictures concentrate on white or pale tones, often with flat, overall lighting to avoid shadows.

Incident light metering
Using an exposure meter from the subject position, pointing back towards the camera.

Lighting contrast
The difference between the amount of light falling on the shadow areas and the brightly-lit areas of a subject, usually measured in stops.

Macro lens
Lens designed for close focusing.

Medium format
Cameras that use 120 roll film, taking pictures larger than 35mm. Usually 645 (6x4.5cm picture size), 6x6 or 6x7.

Neutral density filter
Grey filter that dims the image by a known amount.

Open flash
Firing the flash manually while the camera shutter is open.

Panning
Moving the camera to follow a subject moving across the picture. Produces a relatively sharp subject against a blurred background.

Reflector
A rectangular or round sheet of white, silver or gold material or card, used to bounce light on to the subject. Also refers to a dish-shaped surround to a flash head.

Ring flash
A circular flash unit that fits around the lens to provide shadow-free lighting.

Scrim
Metal mesh attachment to lighting unit to reduce intensity.

Slow-sync flash
Combining a blurred effect from a long exposure with the freezing of motion with flash.

Softbox
A box diffuser of varying size placed over the light source to produce a large area of soft, even lighting.

Strobe
An alternative term for electronic flash.

Tungsten-balanced film
Colour film balanced to suite light sources of 3200K.

Umbrella
A special umbrella covered with highly reflective, semi-transparent material and attached to the flash unit. The flash is fired through the umbrella to soften or diffuse it and into the umbrella for reflected light.

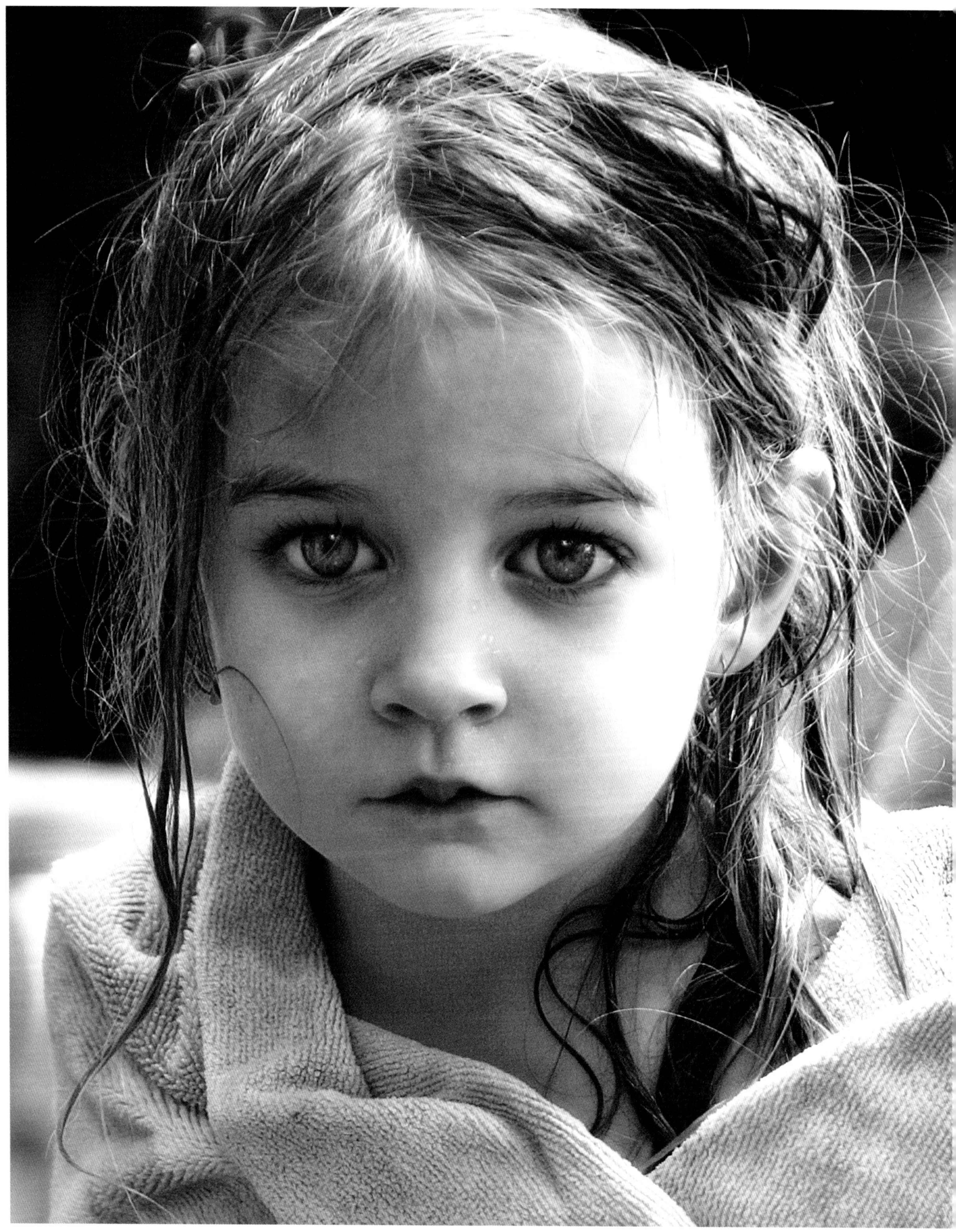

Misty Morris

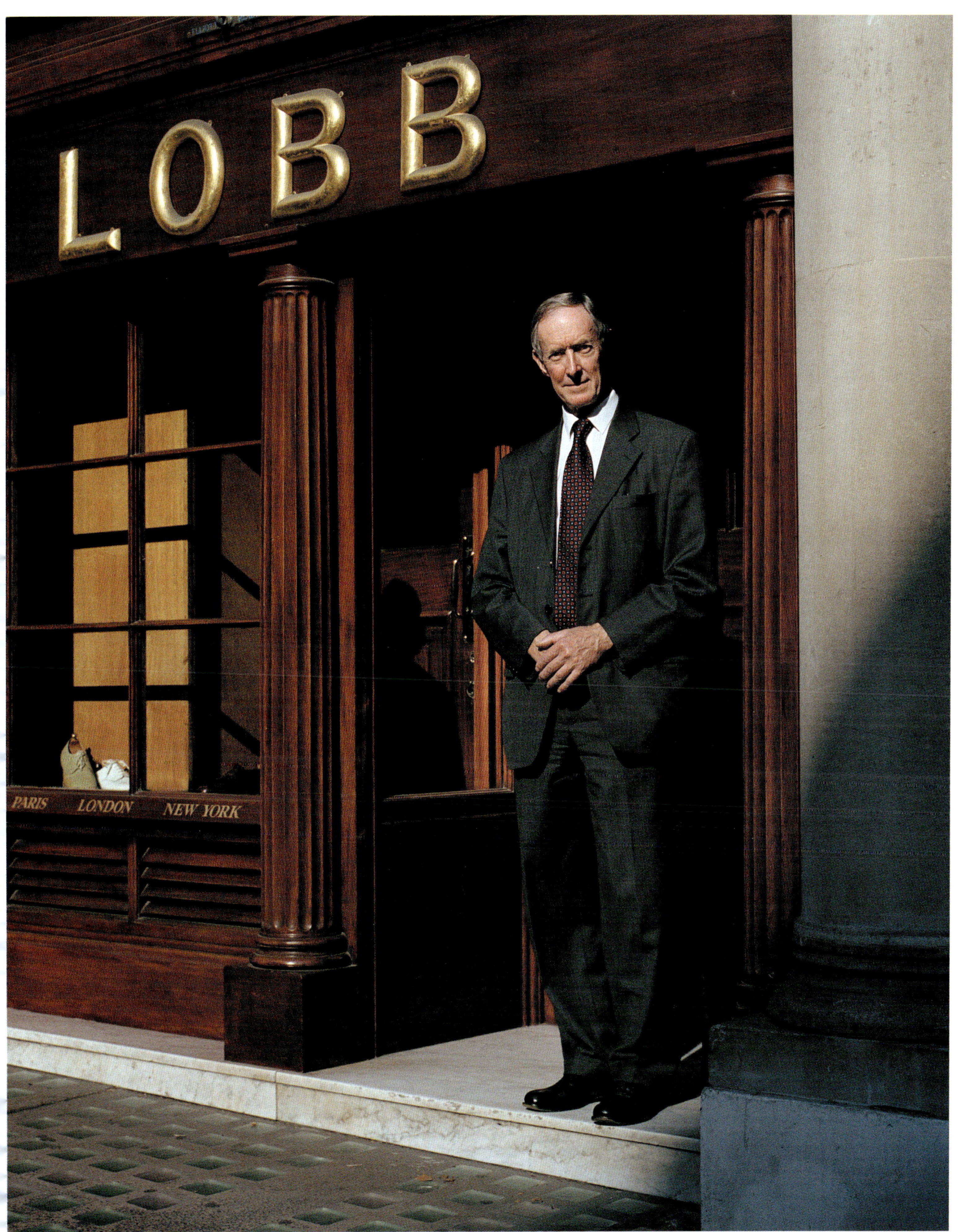
LOBB
PARIS
LONDON
NEW YORK

Contacts

Lin Alder
Springdale, Utah, USA
email: lin@alderphoto.com
web: www.alderphoto.com
p. 7, 44–45

Jim Allen
Ontario, Canada
email: j.foto@sympatico.ca
web: www.differenthats.com
www.jimallenphotographer.com
p. 6, 30–31, 54–55, 136

Nina Indset Andersen
Oslo, Norway
email: webmaster@eyesondesign.net
web: www.eyesondesign.net
p. 9, 70–71, 152–153

Craig Biertempfel
Pittsburgh, Pennsylvania, USA
email: btezra@gmail.com
web: www.whatthehellhappenedlast-night.com/photos
p. 75

Stéphane Bourson
Paris, France
email: steph@sbourson.com
web: www.sbourson.com
p. 6, 82

Trevor Brady
Vancouver, Canada
email: stoprev@gmail.com
web: www.trevorbrady.com
p. 86

Fredrik Clement
Copenhagen, Denmark
email: fc@fredrikclement.dk
web: www.fredrikclement.dk
p. 96–97, 157

Manuel Luís Cochofel
Lisbon, Portugal
email: mlcochofel@netcabo.pt
web: www.cochofel.net
p. 36, 62–63

Guy Crittenden
Richmond, Virginia, USA
email: guy@crittendenstudio.com
web: www.crittendenstudio.com
p. 6, 90–91, 118, 124–125

Steffen Ebert
Frankfurt, Germany
email: mail@steffen-ebert.com
web: www.steffen-ebert.com
p. 60–61

Roderick Field/ Trevillion Picture Library
London, UK
email: roderickfield@btinternet.com
web: www.roderickfield.com
p. 92–93

Robert Ganz
Montreal, Canada
email: accidentalphotos@hotmail.com
web: www.robertganzphotography.com
p. 126–127

Nour Eddine El Ghoumari
Worthing, UK and Taza, Morocco
email: nour@photonour.com
web: www.photonour.com
p. cover, 52, 76–77

Nikki Gibbs/ Trevillion Picture Library
London, UK
email: nikki@nikkigibbs.com
web: www.nikkigibbs.com
p. 58–59

Rene de Haan
Amsterdam, the Netherlands
email: mail@renedehaan.com
web: www.renedehaan.com
p. 9, 48–49, 98–99

Michael Hall
Sydney, Australia
email: contact@michaelhall.net
web: www.michaelhall.net
p. 6, 7, 8, 18–19, 42–43, 46–47, 56, 88–89, 94–95, 100–101, 134–135, 138–143, 150–151

Paul Holmes/ Trevillion Picture Library
Edinburgh, Scotland
email: info@sketco.org
web: www.sketco.org
p. 128

Matt Hoyle
Sydney, Australia
email: matt@matthoyle.com
web: www.matthoyle.com
p. 2, 7, 50–51, 104, 112–117

Brad Kim
Los Angeles, USA
email: bradkim@photo.net
Byonghokim@yahoo.com
web: www.photo.net/photodb/member-photos?include=all&photo_id=1769037
p. 6, 34

Paul Knight/ Trevillion Picture Library
St Albans, UK
email: paul@paulknight.org
web: www.paulknight.org
p. 6, 40–41, 160

Piotr Kowalik
London, UK
email: kpiotr@btinternet.com
web: www.piotrkowalik.co.uk
p. 24

Roumen Koynov
Manaus, Brazil
email: koynov@bol.com.br
web: www.photo.net/photodb/member-photos?include=all&user_id=324733
p. 7, 74

Ed Krebs
South Laguna, California, USA
email: ed@edkrebs.com
web: www.edkrebs.com
p. 147, 149

Ian McFarlane
Athens, Georgia, USA
email: ian@ismphotography.com
web: www.ianmcfarlane.com
p. 6, 122, 125, 132–133

Alberto Monteiro
Lisbon, Portugal
email: fotex2001@hotmail.com
web: www.albertomonteiro.com
p. 106–111

Misty Morris
Aiken, South Carolina, USA
email: misticole22@hotmail.com
web: www.mistymorrisphotography.com
p. 6, 17, 25, 156

Tomek Paczkowski
Warsaw, Poland
email: tomek@dania.com.pl
web: www.graaf.art.pl
p. 78–81, 120–121, 123, 144–145

Frédéric Pascual
Barcelona, Spain
email: info@fredericpascual.com
web: www.fredericpascual.com
p. 6, 64–67

Jacek Pomykalski
Krakow, Poland
email: kot74@go2.pl
web: www.pomykalski.com
p. 6, 146

Igor Sarzynski
Warsaw, Poland
email: igoryl@o2.pl
website: www.fotoplaster.prv.pl
p. 20–21

Jean Schweitzer
Birkeroed, Denmark
email: jean@cliclac.dk
web: www.cliclac.dk
p. 7, 9, 29, 53, 129

Aaron Schuman
Bathford, UK
email: aaron@aaronschuman.com
web: www.aaronschuman.com
p. 7, 28–29, 130–131

Arthur Sevestre
Leiden, the Netherlands
email: arthur@artsevestre-photography.com
web: www.artsevestre-photography.com
p. 16, 22–23

Trine Sirnes Thorne
Fredrikstad, Norway
email: trine@sirnesphotography.com
web: www.sirnesphotography.com
p. 6, 14–15, 26–27, 72

Alan Smilie
Orlando, Florida, USA
email: alan@alansmiliephoto.com
web: www.alansmiliephoto.com
p. 6, 32, 68–69

Frantisek Staud
Czech Republic
email: fstaud@phototravels.net
web: www.phototravels.net
p. 73

Christel Sundebäck
Gothenburg, Sweden
email: christel_gbg@hotmail.com
web: www.christelsundeback.com
p. 33, 84–85

Marco Tenaglia
Rome, Italy
email: marco.tenaglia@marcotenaglia.com
web: www.marcotenaglia.com
p. 6, 87

Sam Devine Tischler
Santa Fe, New Mexico, USA
email: sam@samdevinetischler.com
web: www.samdevinetischler.com
p. 102–103

Michael Trevillion/ Trevillion Picture Library
London, UK
email: michael@trevillion.com
web: www.trevillion.com
p. 12, 38–39

Jim Zuckerman
Nashville, Tennessee, USA
email: photos@jimzuckerman.com
web: www.jimzuckerman.com
p. 35, 148–149

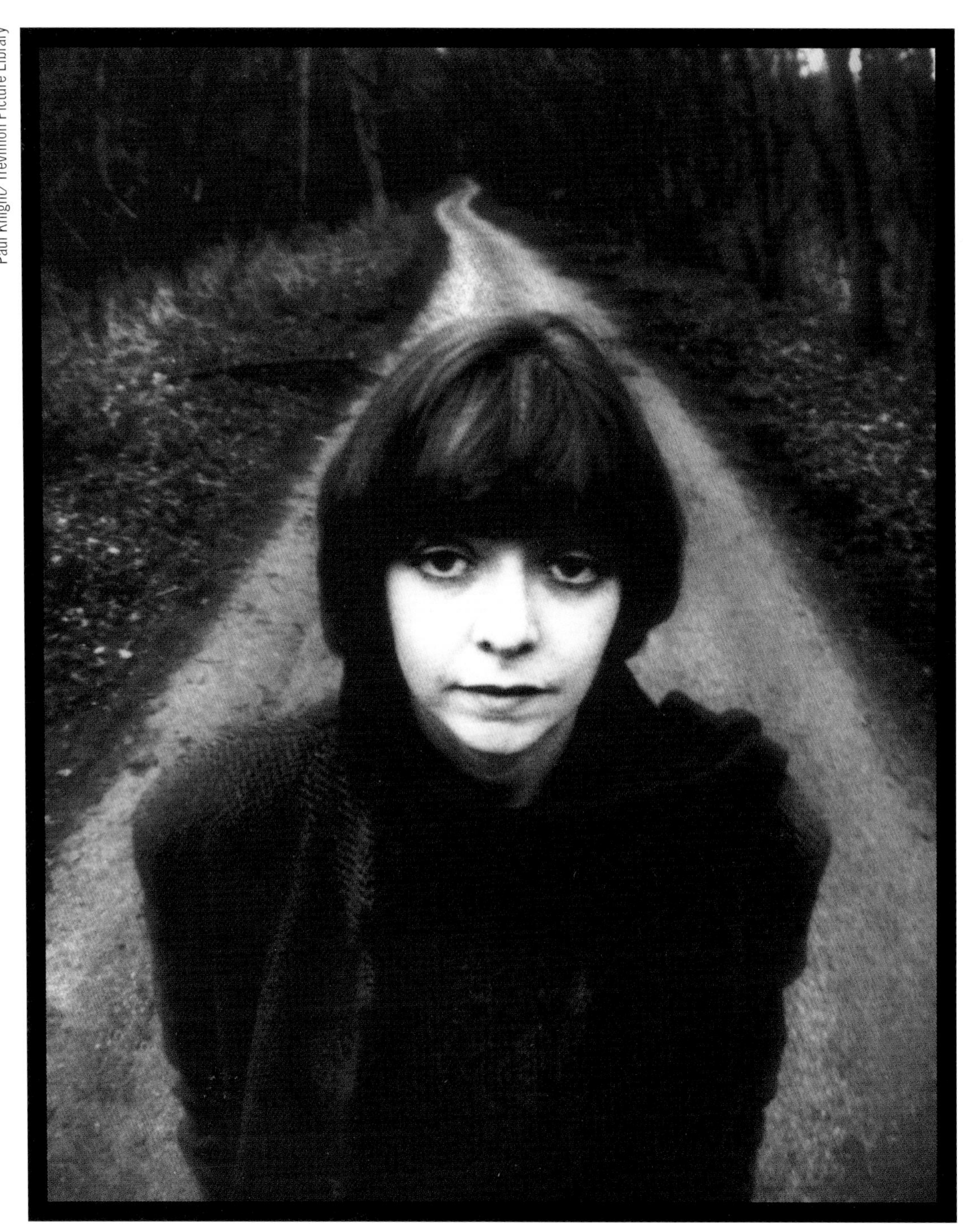

Paul Knight/Trevillion Picture Library